# Excel® 2007 Just the Steps™

## FOR

# DUMMIES®

by Diane Koers

BICENTENNIAL

1807

WILEY

2007

BICENTENNIAL

Wiley Publishing, Inc.

**Excel® 2007 Just the Steps™ For Dummies®**

Published by
**Wiley Publishing, Inc.**
111 River Street
Hoboken, NJ 07030-5774
www.wiley.com

WILEY

# About the Author

**Diane Koers** owns and operates All Business Service, a software training and consulting business formed in 1988 that services the central Indiana area. Her area of expertise has long been in the word-processing, spreadsheet, and graphics areas of computing. She also provides training and support for Peachtree Accounting Software. Diane's authoring experience includes over thirty five books on topics such as PC Security, Microsoft Windows, Microsoft Office, Microsoft Works, WordPerfect, Paint Shop Pro, Lotus SmartSuite, Quicken, Microsoft Money and Peachtree Accounting. Many of these titles have been translated into other languages such as French, Dutch, Bulgarian, Spanish and Greek. She has also developed and written numerous training manuals for her clients.

Diane and her husband enjoy spending their free time fishing, traveling and playing with their four grandsons and Little Joe, their Yorkshire Terrier.

# Dedication

To my little buddy Joe. We're attached at the heart. You may be small in size but you are huge in love. Thanks for being what you are.

# Author's Acknowledgments

I am deeply thankful to the many people at Wiley Publishing who worked on this book. Thank you for all the time and assistance you have given me.

To Bob Woerner: Thanks for the opportunity to write this book and for your confidence in me. A very special thank you to Chris Morris for his assistance (and patience) in the book development; to Mary Lagu for keeping me grammatically correct, and to Bill Morehead for checking all the technical angles. And, last but certainly not least, a BIG thank you to all those behind the scenes who helped to make this book a reality. It's been an interesting experience.

## Publisher's Acknowledgments

We're proud of this book; please send us your comments through our online registration form located at www.dummies.com/register/.

Some of the people who helped bring this book to market include the following:

*Acquisitions, Editorial, and Media Development*

**Senior Project Editor:** Christopher Morris

**Senior Acquisitions Editor:** Bob Woerner

**Copy Editor:** Mary Lagu

**Technical Editor:** Bill Moorehead

**Editorial Manager:** Kevin Kirschner

**Editorial Assistant:** Amanda Foxworth

**Cartoons:** Rich Tennant (www.the5thwave.com)

*Composition Services*

**Project Coordinator:** Erin Smith

**Layout and Graphics:** Denny Hager, Melanee Prendergast, Heather Ryan, Amanda Spagnuolo, Erin Zeltner

**Anniversary Logo Design:** Richard J. Pacifico

**Proofreaders:** Melissa D. Buddendeck, Jessica Kramer, Brian Walls

**Indexer:** Rebecca R. Plunkett

---

*Publishing and Editorial for Technology Dummies*

    **Richard Swadley,** Vice President and Executive Group Publisher

    **Andy Cummings,** Vice President and Publisher

 **Mary Bednarek,** Executive Acquisitions Director

    **Mary C. Corder,** Editorial Director

*Publishing for Consumer Dummies*

    **Diane Graves Steele,** Vice President and Publisher

    **Joyce Pepple,** Acquisitions Director

*Composition Services*

    **Gerry Fahey,** Vice President of Production Services

    **Debbie Stailey,** Director of Composition Services

# Contents at a Glance

*W*elcome to the world of Microsoft Excel, the most popular and powerful spreadsheet program in the world. You may ask: "What is a spreadsheet program?" A spreadsheet program is a computer program that features a huge grid designed to display data in rows and columns. You can use it to perform mathematical, logical, and other types of operations on the data you enter. You can sort the data, enhance it, and manipulate it in a plethora of ways — including creating powerful charts and graphs from it. Whether you need a list of names and addresses or a document to calculate next year's sales revenue based on prior year's performance, Excel is the application you want to use.

## About This Book

This book provides the tools you need to successfully tackle the potentially overwhelming challenge of learning to use Microsoft Excel. In this book, you learn how to create spreadsheets; however, what you do with them is totally up to you. Your imagination is the only limit!

## Why You Need This Book

Time is of the essence, and most of us don't have the time to do a lot of reading. We just need to get a task done effectively and efficiently. This book is full of concise, easy-to-understand steps designed to get you quickly up and running with Excel. It takes you directly to the steps for a desired task without all the jibber-jabber that is often included in other books.

Even if you've used Excel in the past, Excel 2007 brings many new features and major changes to existing features. This book helps ease the transition from the previous Excel version.

# Introduction

## Conventions used in this book

➥ When you should type something, I put it in **bold** typeface.

➥ For menu commands, I use the ⇨ symbol to separate menu options. For example, the directions "Choose Insert⇨Illustrations⇨ Picture" is saying, "Click the Insert tab and then from the Illustrations group, click the Picture option."

➥ In some figures, you see circled items. This is done to help you locate items mentioned or referred to in the text.

 This icon points out tips and helpful suggestions related to the current task.

# How This Book Is Organized

This book is divided into 25 different chapters broken into 6 convenient parts:

## Part I: Putting Excel to Work

In Chapter 1, you uncover the basics of working with Excel files, such as opening, closing, and saving files. In Chapter 2, you work with entering the different types of data into Excel worksheets, and in Chapter 3, you create various types of formulas and functions to perform worksheet calculations. Chapter 4 shows you how to protect your work with Excel's security features.

## Part II: Sprucing Up Your Spreadsheets

Chapters 5 and 6 both show you how to dress up the data you enter into a worksheet using data alignment, formatting values, fonts, colors, and cell borders. In Chapter 7, you work with graphics such as arrows and clip art. Then, in Chapter 8, you begin to use workbooks consisting of multiple worksheets, hyperlinks, and cross references.

## Part III: Viewing Data in Different Ways

This part, in four different chapters, shows how you can modify the way Excel displays certain workbook options on your screen. Chapter 9 illustrates changing the worksheet views. In Chapter 10, you sort your data to make it easier to locate particular pieces of information. Chapter 11 enables you to create charts to display your data in a superb graphic manner.

Finally, in Chapter 12, you work with the different output methods, including printing and e-mailing your worksheets.

## Part IV: Analyzing Data with Excel

Use these chapters to effectively analyze all the data you input into a worksheet. In Chapters 13, 14, and 15, you work with Excel Outlines, Filters, and Pivot Tables. Chapters 16 and 17 show some of the time-saving data-entry tools included with Excel.

## Part V: Utilizing Excel with Other People and Applications

Chapters 18 through 21 are all about sharing: sharing Excel with others by using Excel's collaboration features, or sharing Excel with Microsoft Office applications such as Word, PowerPoint, and Access.

## Part VI: Practical Applications for Excel

Go to these chapters to save yourself time with a gorgeous organization chart (Chapter 22), a commission calculation worksheet (Chapter 23), or a medical-expense-tracking worksheet (Chapter 24). Chapter 25 helps you plan for your future. You can use Excel to chart the path to purchase a house, pay off your debts, and save for college or retirement.

## Back cover: Using Excel Shortcut Keys

This helpful appendix shows you many shortcut keys that make access to Excel functions faster and easier.

# Part I

# Putting Excel to Work

"No, that's not the icon for Excel, it's the icon for Excuse, the database of reasons why you haven't learned the other programs in Office."

# Working with Excel Files

*I*n this book, you discover the new Excel interface that provides you with the right tools at the right time. In most Windows programs, you see menus and toolbars from which you select your options. Now you discover the new Excel interface that provides you with the right tools at the right time. Instead of the traditional look, Excel now provides tabs with icon-and-button-laden tabs on the Ribbon containing your favorite Excel features. Galleries and themes are also a new addition to Excel, helping you maintain consistency and style in workbook appearance. The Office Quick Access toolbar, which is now the only toolbar, provides fast and easy access to basic file functions. You discover later in this chapter how you can customize the Quick Access toolbar.

Throughout the course of this book, you discover methods to use Excel as a spreadsheet, of course; but you also discover how to use it as a database, a calculator, a planner, and even a graphic illustrator. You start with the basics and work into the more advanced Excel actions.

In this chapter you:

➡ Open and close the Excel program

➡ Open, close, and save Excel workbooks

➡ Explore the Excel screen including customizing it to make it even faster and easier to use.

➡ Use workbook properties to better manage your files.

➡ Set Excel default file locations, which saves you time and frustration when you open and save your workbooks.

## Chapter 1

### Get ready to . . .

# Open and Explore Excel

1. Choose Start➪All Programs➪Microsoft Office➪ Microsoft Office Excel. The Microsoft Excel program begins with a new, blank workbook displayed like the one shown in Figure 1-1, ready for you to enter data.

2. The icon at the top-left of the screen is called the Office Button. As you hover your mouse over it, a description of the Office Button functions appears.

 When you click the Office Button, Excel displays a list of options. Click the Office Button to close the menu if you don't want to make a selection at this time.

3. Pause your mouse over any of the three icons next to the Office Button. By default, the Quick Access toolbar functions include Save, Undo, and Redo.

4. Hover your mouse over the *tabs*, or task-oriented portions, of the Ribbon and a description of a tab's feature appears. The tabs are broken down into subsections called *groups*. The Home tab includes the Clipboard, Font, Alignment, Number, Styles, Cells, and Editing groups.

5. Click the Insert tab. The Ribbon changes to reflect options pertaining to Insert. Groups include Shapes, Tables, Illustrations, Charts, Links, and Text.

6. On the Home tab, click the down arrow under Format As Table. A Gallery of table styles appears. (Click the arrow again to close the Gallery.)

7. On the Home tab, clicking the Dialog Box Launcher on the bottom-right of the Font group opens a related dialog box. (See Figure 1-2.) In this example, the Format Cells dialog box opens.

 Click the Cancel button to close a dialog box without making any changes.

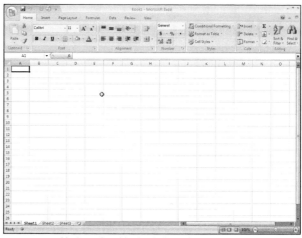

**Figure 1-1:** A blank Excel workbook, which Excel calls Book1.

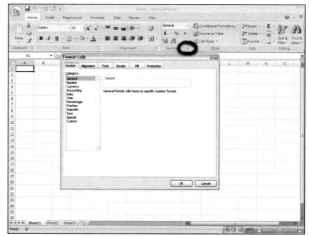

**Figure 1-2:** Click a Dialog Box Launch icon to display a relevant dialog box.

## Select Commands with the Keyboard

1. If appropriate for the command you intend to use, place the insertion point in the proper word or paragraph.

2. Press Alt on the keyboard. Shortcut letters and numbers appear on the Ribbon. See Figure 1-3.

 Numbers control commands on the Quick Access toolbar.

3. Press a letter to select a tab on the Ribbon; for this example, press P. Excel displays the appropriate tab and letters for each command on that tab.

4. Press a letter or letters to select a command. Excel displays options for the command you selected.

5. Press a letter or use the arrow keys on the keyboard to select an option. Excel performs the command you selected, applying the option you choose.

 Press the Esc key to step the key controls back one step.

Press F6 to change the focus of the program, switching between the document, the status bar, and the Ribbon.

## Close Excel

1. Choose Office Button⇨Exit Excel, as you see in Figure 1-4.

 Optionally, Click the Close button (x).

2. Click Yes or No if prompted to save your workbook. (See "Save a Workbook" later in this chapter.)

 Optionally, choose Office ⇨Close. The current workbook closes, but the Excel program remains open.

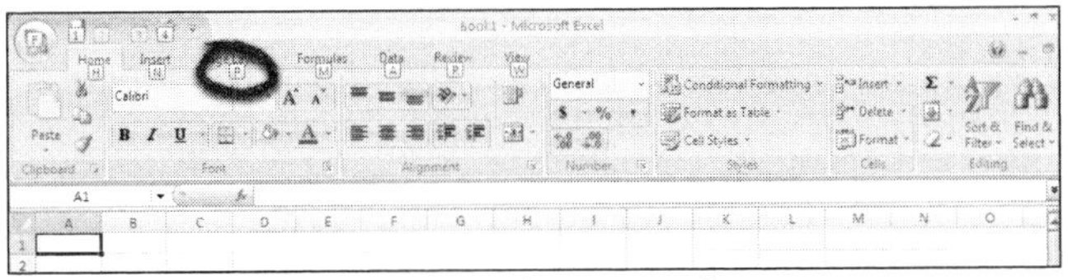

**Figure 1-3:** Use the keyboard to select Ribbon commands.

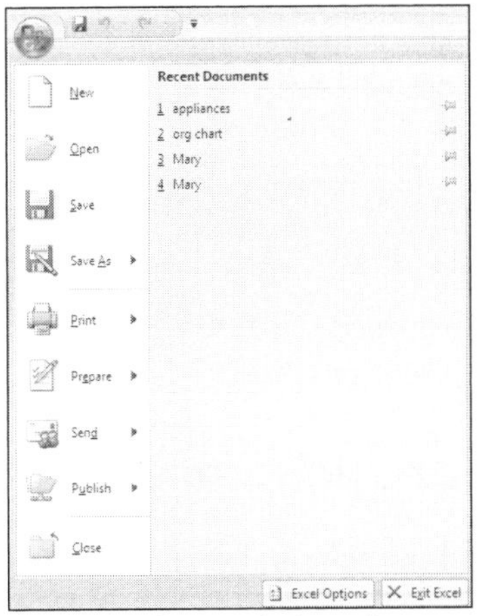

**Figure 1-4:** Closing Excel releases the program from your computer memory.

# Customize the Quick Access Toolbar

1. Right-click any tool or group title you want to add to the Quick Access toolbar. A menu appears.

2. Choose Add to Quick Access Toolbar. The tool or group icon appears on the Quick Access bar.

3. Right-click an icon on the Quick Access toolbar. A menu appears.

4. Choose Remove from Quick Access Toolbar. The selected item disappears from the Quick Access toolbar.

5. Right-click the Quick Access toolbar and select Customize the Quick Access Toolbar. The Excel Options dialog box, seen in Figure 1-5, appears.

6. Open the Choose Commands From drop-down menu and select a tab name. Excel displays a list of available features.

7. Select a feature and click the Add button. The selected feature appears on the right panel. Click OK.

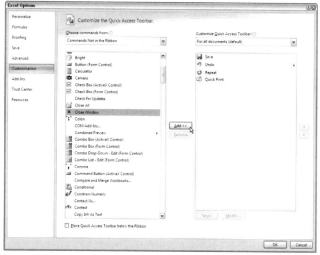

**Figure 1-5:** You can select any Excel options to add to the Quick Access toolbar.

# Change Status Bar Indicators

1. Right-click anywhere along the status bar at the bottom of the window. Excel opens the Status Bar Configuration menu.

2. To activate an inactive feature, click it. This automatically adds a check mark and displays the feature's status. In Figure 1-6, the Caps Lock feature is on, and now the status bar shows the Caps Lock status.

3. To deactivate any active feature, click it.

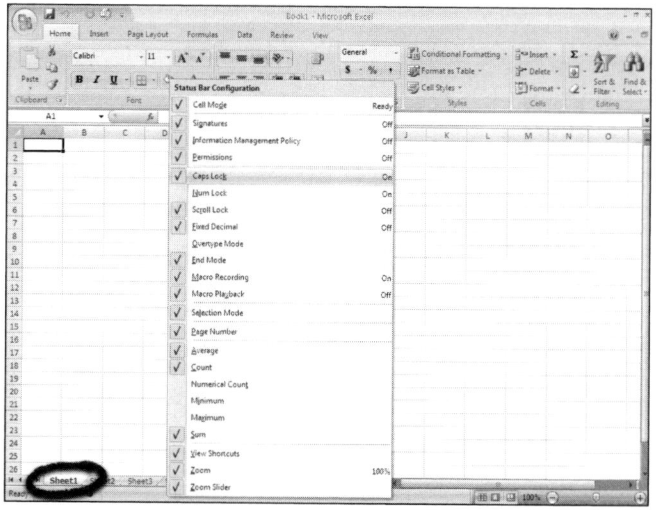

**Figure 1-6:** Customize what you see along the Excel status bar.

# Create a New Excel File

1. Click the Office Button.

2. Choose New. The New Workbook dialog box opens. (See Figure 1-7.)

3. Click Blank Workbook.

4. Click the Create button. Excel creates a blank workbook based on the default template.

See Chapter 8, "Changing Worksheet Views," for more information about Excel templates.

Optionally, press Ctrl+N to create a new workbook without opening the New Workbook dialog box.

# Save a Workbook

1. Choose Office Button⇨Save or click the Save button on the Quick Access toolbar. The Save As dialog box appears, as shown in Figure 1-8.

The Save As dialog box only appears the first time you save a file.

2. By default, Excel saves your files in the My Documents folder. If you want to save your file in a different folder, select that folder from the Save In drop-down list.

3. In the File Name text box, type a descriptive name for the file.

4. Click the Save button. Excel saves the workbook in the location with the name you specified.

Filenames cannot contain asterisk, slash, blackslash, or question mark characters.

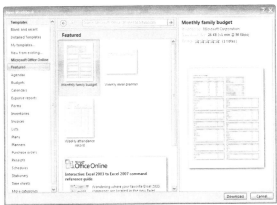

**Figure 1-7:** Excel names each new workbook incrementally such as Workbook 2 or Workbook 3.

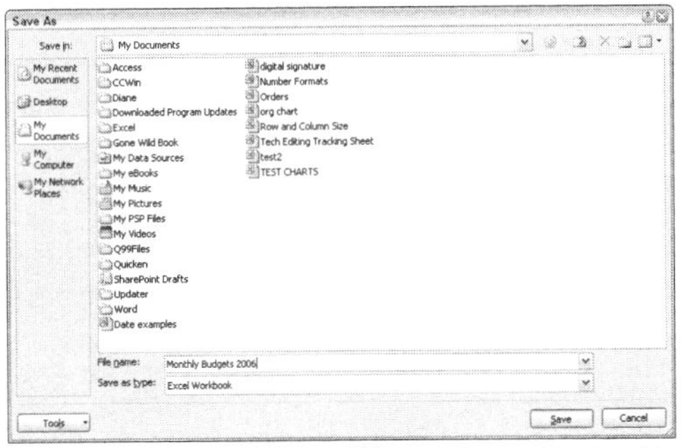

**Figure 1-8:** Choose a folder and filename for your Excel workbook.

# Save a Workbook in a Different Format

1. Choose Office Button➪Save As. The Save As dialog box appears.

2. Select the folder where you want to save the file from the Save In drop-down list.

3. In the File Name text box, type a descriptive name for the file.

4. Open the Save As Type drop-down menu. A list of file formats appears.

5. Choose one of the 26 different file formats. Files saved in the Excel 2007 format have a .xlsx extension, whereas files created in earlier versions of Excel have a .xls extension.

6. Click Save. Depending on the format you choose, Excel may prompt you for additional information.

# Open an Existing Excel File

1. Choose Office Button➪Open. The Open dialog box, seen in Figure 1-10, appears.

2. If necessary, select the appropriate folder from the Look In drop-down list. Then select the file you want to open.

 Open the Files of Type drop-down menu to display files saved in other formats.

3. Click the Open button. The workbook appears in the Excel workspace, ready for you to edit.

 If the file you open was created in a previous version of Excel, the words Compatibility Mode appear on the title bar next to the document name.

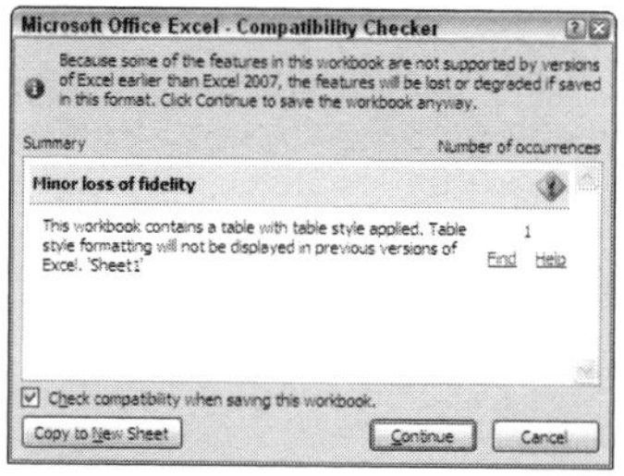

**Figure 1-9:** Excel warns you of compatibility conflicts.

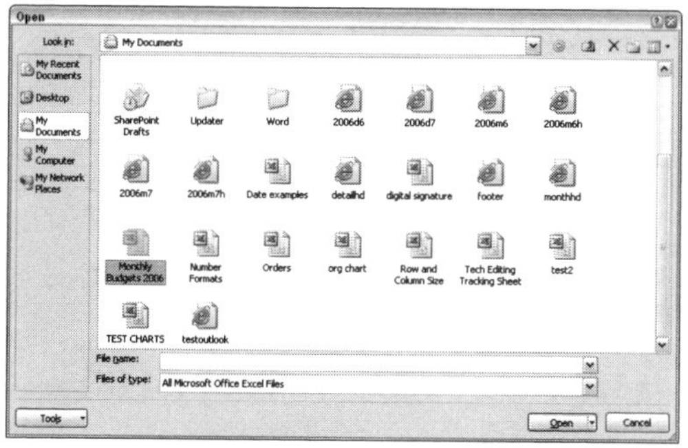

**Figure 1-10:** Open a previously created Excel file.

 Excel displays recently used files on the right side of the Office Button menu. Click any listed filename to quickly open it.

# Rename a File

1. Open Excel, but not the file you want to rename. Choose Office Button⇨Open. The Open or Save As dialog box appears.

    Optionally, choose Office Button⇨Save As and continue as described.

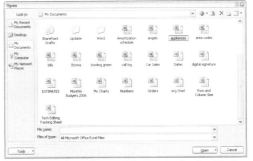

**Figure 1-11:** Change the name of an existing Excel workbook.

2. If necessary, click the Look In list and navigate to the folder containing the file you want to delete.

3. Right-click the file. Do not double-click the file because double-clicking the file opens it.

4. Choose Rename from the shortcut menu. (See Figure 1-11.) The original filename becomes highlighted.

5. Type the new file name. Filenames cannot contain asterisk, slash, blackslash, or question mark characters.

6. Press Enter when you are finished typing.

7. Click the Cancel button to close the Open dialog box.

# Delete a File

1. Open Excel, but not the file you want to delete. Choose Office Button⇨Open or Office⇨Save As. Either the Open or Save As dialog box appears.

2. If necessary, click the Look In list and navigate to the folder containing the file you want to delete.

3. Right-click on the unwanted file. Do not double-click the file.

4. Choose Delete from the shortcut menu. (See Figure 1-12.) A confirmation message appears.

5. Click Yes. Excel deletes the file.

6. Click the Cancel button to close the Open or Save As dialog box.

# Set the Default File Locations

1. Click the Office Button and click Excel Options. (It's located at the bottom of the Office list.) The Excel Options dialog box opens.

2. From the options on the left side of the dialog box, click the Save category. You see the options shown in Figure 1-13.

3. In the Default file location, enter the data path to the place where you want to save most of your files. Click OK.

 By default, Excel saves your files in the My Documents folder stored on your local hard drive, but your company may have another location where it wants you to keep most of your Excel files. An example might be **G:\COMPANY DOCUMENTS\DIANE**

 To override the default file location, you can click the Look In list when saving or opening a file and choose a location different from the default location.

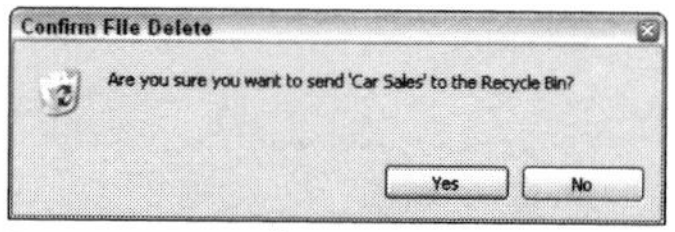

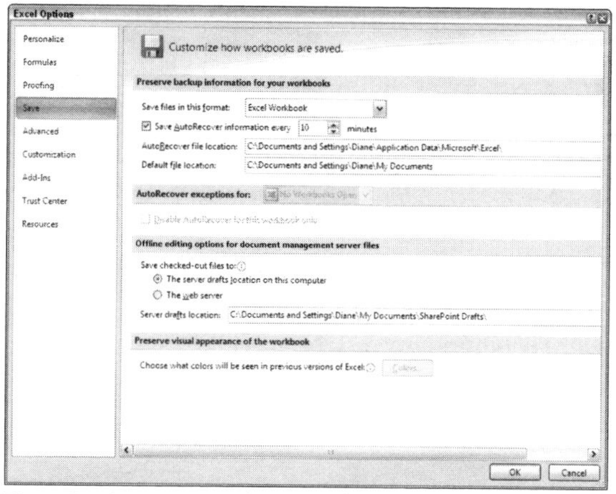

**Figure 1-12:** Delete unwanted files through the Open or Save As dialog box.

**Figure 1-13:** Customize to determine where Excel stores your workbooks.

# Specify Workbook Properties

1. Click the Office Button and click Prepare. A list of options appears.

2. Click Properties. The Document Information Panel appears.

3. Enter identifying information such as the author's name, subject, or a list of keywords. See Figure 1-14.

 Excel automatically adds statistical information such as the workbook's original creation date, the last time it was printed or modified, and the workbook size.

4. Click the Close box to close the Document Information Panel.

# View Workbook Properties

1. Choose Office Button⇨Open. The Open dialog box appears.

2. If necessary, click the Look In list and navigate to the folder containing the file you want to delete.

3. Click the Views button drop-down arrow to display a Views shortcut menu or click the Views button itself to cycle through the available views.

4. Choose Properties. The Open window splits into two panels like the ones you see in Figure 1-15.

5. Click a file name. Excel displays the workbook properties in the right panel.

6. Click OK to open the file or Cancel to close the Open dialog box.

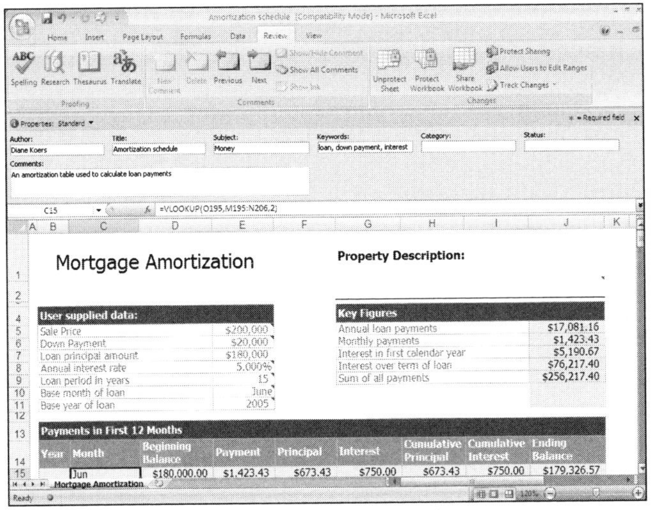

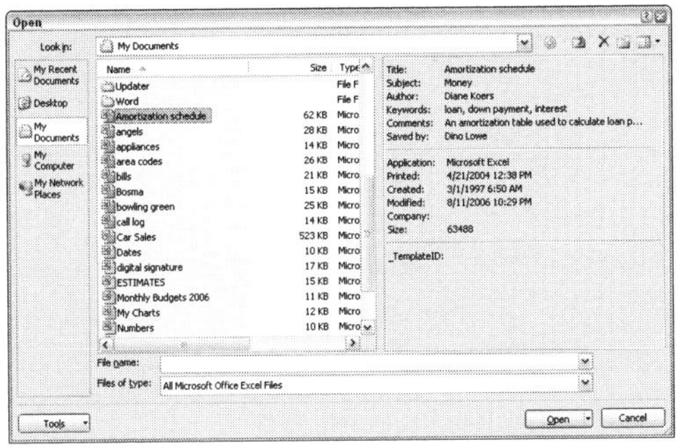

**Figure 1-14:** Enter information to identify your workbook.

**Figure 1-15:** View the workbook's properties and file statistics.

# Entering Spreadsheet Data

**Chapter**

**2**

*E*xcel is a huge grid made up of columns and rows. If you've used previous versions of Microsoft Excel, you know the new spreadsheet is larger than ever. A single worksheet now contains 16,384 columns (stretching from column A to column XFD) and 1,048,576 rows.

You enter three types of data in the cells:

➡ **Labels** are traditionally descriptive pieces of information such as names, months, or other identifying statistics, and they usually include alphabetic characters.

➡ **Values** are generally raw numbers or dates.

➡ **Formulas** are instructions for Excel to perform calculations.

In the first part of this chapter, I show you how to easily enter labels and values into your worksheet. But, alas, human beings sometimes make mistakes or change their minds. So I also show you how to delete incorrect entries, duplicate data, or move it to another area of the worksheet. You even discover an Excel feature that prevents worksheet cells from accepting incorrect data.

## Get ready to . . .

# *Change the Active Cell*

1. Open a spreadsheet in Excel. The formula bar displays the active cell location. Columns display the letters from A to XFD and rows display numbers from 1 to 1048576. A cell address is the intersection of a column and a row such as D23 or AB205.

2. Move the focus to an adjacent cell with one the following techniques:

   • **Down:** Press the Enter key or the down arrow key.

   • **Up:** Press the up arrow key.

   • **Right:** Press the right arrow key.

   • **Left:** Press the left arrow key.

3. To move to a cell farther away, use one of these techniques:

   • Click the mouse pointer on any cell to move the active cell location to that cell. You can use the scroll bars to see more of the worksheet. In Figure 2-1, the cell focus is in cell E10.

   • Choose Home ⇨Editing⇨Find & Select⇨Go To. The Go To dialog box displays, as shown in Figure 2-2. In the Reference box, enter the address of the cell you want to make active and then click OK.

    Press the F5 key to display the Go To dialog box.

   • Press Ctrl + Home. Excel jumps to cell A1.

   • Press Ctrl + End. Excel jumps to the lower-right cell of the worksheet.

   • Press Ctrl + PageDown or Ctrl + PageUp. Excel moves to the next or previous worksheet in the workbook.

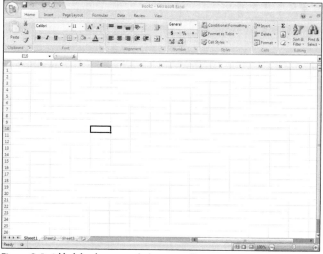

**Figure 2-1:** A black border surrounds the active cell.

**Figure 2-2:** Specify a cell address in the Go To box.

# Enter Cell Data

1. Type the label or value in the desired cell.

2. Press Enter. The data is entered into the current cell and Excel makes the next cell down active. (See Figure 2-3.) How Excel aligns the data depends on what it is:

> To enter a value as a label, type an apostrophe before the value.

- **Label:** Excel aligns the data to the left side of the cell. If the descriptive information is too wide to fit, Excel extends that data past the cell width if the next cell is blank. If the next cell is not blank, Excel displays only enough text to fit the display width. Widening the column displays additional text.

- **Whole value:** If the data is a whole value such as 34 or 5763, Excel aligns the data to the right side of the cell.

- **Value with a decimal:** If the data is a decimal value, Excel aligns the data to the right side of the cell, including the decimal point, with the exception of a trailing 0. For example, in Figure 2-4, if you enter **246.75**, then **246.75** displays; if you enter **246.70**, however, **246.7** displays. (See Chapter 5 to change the display appearance, column width, and alignment of your data.)

> If a value displays as scientific notation or number sign, it means the value is too long to fit into the cell. You need to widen the column width.

- **Date**: If you enter a date, such 12/3, Dec 3, or 3 Dec, Excel automatically returns 03-Dec in the cell, but the formula bar displays 12/03/2006. Figure 2-4 also illustrates an example of date entry. See Chapter 5 to change the date format.

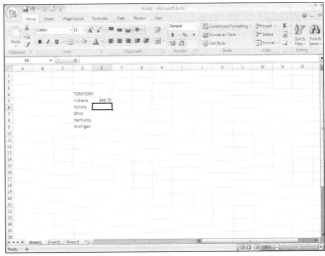

**Figure 2-3:** Enter labels or values into a cell.

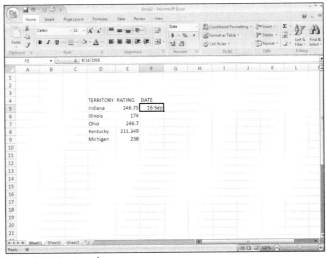

**Figure 2-4:** Entering values.

## Undo Data Entry

1. Enter text into a spreadsheet.

2. To undo any actions or correct any mistakes you make when entering data, perform one of the following:

    • Choose Undo from the Quick Access toolbar.

    • Press Ctrl+Z.

3. Keep repeating your favorite undo method until you're back where you want to be.

4. To undo several steps at once, click the arrow on the Undo icon and select the step from which you want to begin the Undo action. (See Figure 2-5.)

## Edit or Delete Cell Data

1. To delete the entire contents of a cell, use one of the following methods:

    • Choose Home⇨Editing⇨Clear.

    • Press the Delete key.

2. To edit the cell contents, use one of these methods:

    • Delete the contents and retype new cell information.

    • Press F2 and edit the cell contents from the formula bar.

    • Double-click the cell contents and edit the cell contents from the cell. (See Figure 2-6.)

**Figure 2-5:** Select the steps you want to reverse.

**Figure 2-6:** Edit cell contents without having to start over.

To repeat your last action, click the Redo icon on the Quick Access toolbar or press Ctrl+Y. You can't repeat some actions, however.

If you clear the wrong cell, use the Undo command.

# Select Multiple Cells

*1.* Click the first cell in the group you want to select.

*2.* Depending on the cells you want to select, perform one of the following actions.

- To select sequential cells, hold down the Shift key and select the last cell you want. All cells in the selected area are highlighted, with the exception of the first cell. (Don't worry; it's selected, too.) Figure 2-7 shows a sequential area selected from cell **B4** to cell **F15**. Notice the black border surrounding the selected area.

- To select nonsequential cells, hold down the Ctrl key and click each additional cell you want to select. Figure 2-8 shows the nonsequential cells **A4**, **C7**, and **E4** through **E9** selected.

- To select a single entire column, click a column heading.

- To select multiple columns, drag across multiple column headings.

- To select a single entire row, click the row number.

- To select multiple rows, drag across multiple row numbers.

- To select the entire worksheet, click the small gray box located to the left of column A and above row 1. Optionally, you can select all cells in a worksheet by pressing Ctrl + A

When making nonsequential cell selections, you can include entire rows and entire columns along with individual cells or groups of cells.

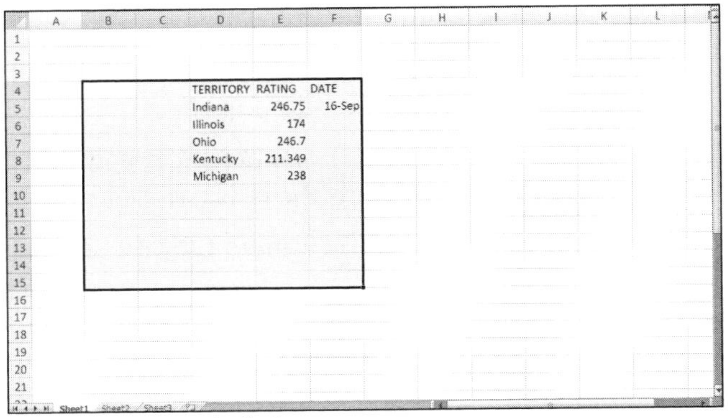

**Figure 2-7:** A sequential cell selection.

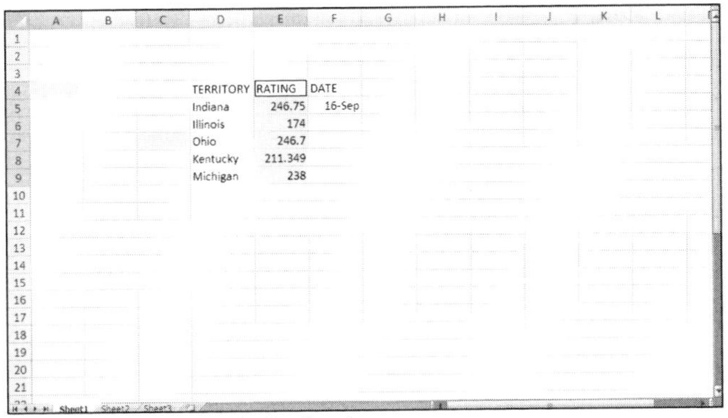

**Figure 2-8:** Non-sequential cells selected.

Click any nonselected cell to clear the selection.

Optionally, click and drag the mouse over a group of cells to select a sequential area.

# Copy and Paste Data

1. Select the area of data you want to copy.

2. Choose Home⇨Copy. A *marquee* (which looks like marching ants) surrounds the cells (see Figure 2-9).

3. Click the cell to which you want to copy the selected area.

4. Choose Home⇨Paste. The selected cells are pasted into the new location.

5. Paste the cells into another location or press Esc to cancel the marquee.

 Choose Home⇨Cut and then Home⇨Paste to move (instead of duplicate) the selected cells to a different location.

 Optionally, press Ctrl+C to copy the selected cells; Ctrl+X to cut the selected cells, or Ctrl+V to paste the selected cells.

# Transpose Data

1. Select the cells you want to transpose.

2. Choose Home⇨Copy.

The Transpose feature will not work if you choose Cut instead of Copy.

3. Click the cell where you want the transposed cells to begin.

4. On the Home tab of the Ribbon, click the down arrow below Paste. A menu of options appears.

5. Choose Transpose. As you see in Figure 2-10, Excel copies the selected cells into the new area, transposing rows into columns or columns into rows.

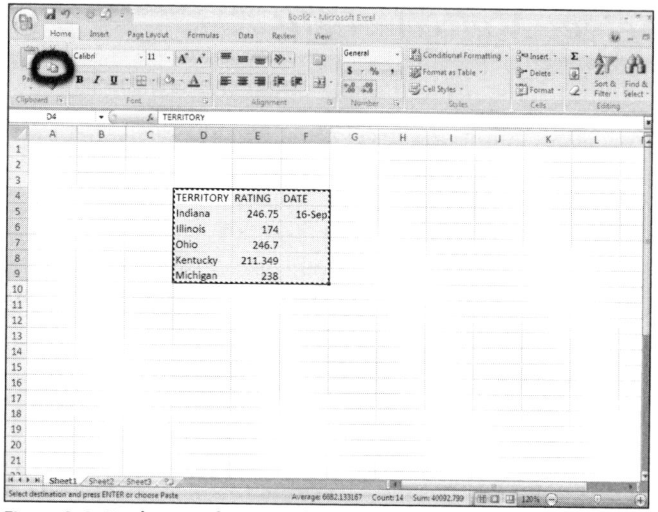

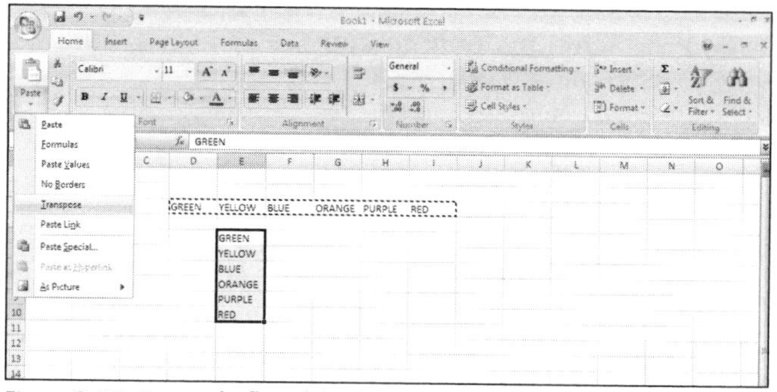

**Figure 2-9:** Marching ants form around a copied area.

**Figure 2-10:** Reverse the flow of data by transposing cells.

# *Extend a Series with AutoFill*

1. Type the first cell of data with data such as a day or month, such as Wednesday or September. AutoFill works with days of the week, months of the year, or yearly quarters such as 2nd Qtr. You can enter the entire word or you can enter the abbreviated form (Wed or Sep).

2. Press Enter.

3. Position the mouse pointer on the small black box at the lower-right corner of the data cell. Your mouse pointer turns into a small black cross. (See Figure 2-11.)

 To AutoFill a series of numbers, enter two values in two adjacent cells, such as 1 and 2 or 5 and 10. Select both cells, and then use the AutoFill box to highlight cells. Excel continues the series as 3, 4, 5, or 5, 10, 15, and so forth.

4. Drag the small black box across the cells you want to fill. You can drag the cells up, down, left, or right.

5. Release the mouse. Excel fills in the selected cells with a continuation of your data. Figure 2-12 shows how Excel fills in the cells with the rest of the days of the week.

 If you use AutoFill on a single value or a text word, Excel duplicates it. For example, if you use AutoFill on a cell with the word **Apple**, all filled cells contain **Apple**.

 To quickly use the AutoFill, highlight the cell that has the data and the cells you want to fill and then double-click the fill-handle.

Chapter 10 includes instructions for creating your own customized list. Autofill can enter lists you often use, such as sales rep names or product types.

**Figure 2-11:** The AutoFill handle.

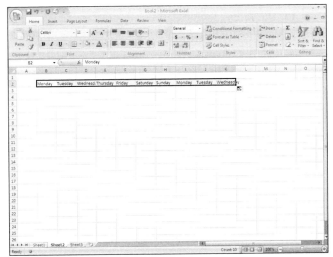

**Figure 2-12:** Using AutoFill for days of the week.

# Name a Range of Cells

1. After selecting the cells you want to name, click Formulas➪Named Cells➪Name a Range. The New Name dialog box appears. (See Figure 2-13.)

2. In the Name text box, type up to a 255-character name for the range. Range names are not case-sensitive; however, range names must follow these conventions:

   • The first character must be a letter, an underscore, or a backslash.

   • No spaces are allowed in a range name.

   • Do not use a name that is the same as a cell address. For example, you can't name a range AB32.

3. Click OK.

 Optionally, enter a range name into the Name box located at the left end of the Formula bar. You can jump quickly to a named range by clicking the down arrow in the Name box and selecting the range name.

**Figure 2-13:** For faster formula entry, use range names.

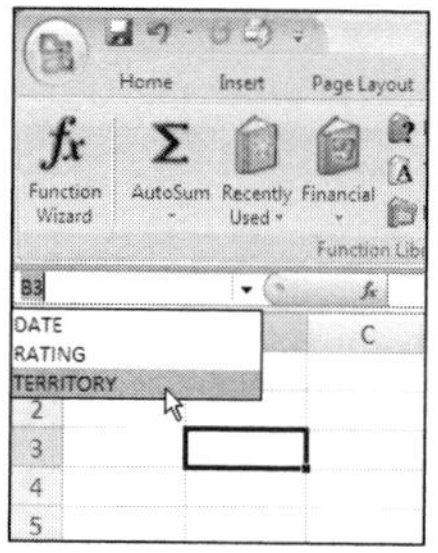

**Figure 2-14:** Quickly locate an area by using a range name.

# Use Named Ranges

1. Click the down arrow in the Name box. A list of named ranges appears. (See Figure 2-14.)

2. Select the range name you want to access. Excel highlights the named cells.

 Optionally, choose Home➪Editing➪Find & Select➪Go To. Double-click on the range name you want to access.

# Manage Range Names

1. Choose Formulas⇨Named Cells⇨Name Manager. The Name Manager dialog box, shown in Figure 2-15, appears.

     Excel automatically adds tables to the Name Manager. See Chapters 6 and 10 for more on working with tables.

2. Select one of the following options.

    - Click the New button, which displays the New Name dialog box in which you can enter a range name and enter the cell location it refers to.

     Instead of typing the range cell locations, click the Collapse button, which moves aside the New Name dialog box. You can then use your mouse to select the desired cells. Press Enter or click the Collapse button again to return to the New Name dialog box.

    - Click an existing range name and then click the Edit button, which displays the Edit Name dialog box shown in Figure 2-16. Use this dialog box to change the range name or the range cell location reference.

    - Click an existing range name and then click the Delete button. A confirmation message appears, making sure you want to delete the range name.

     If you have a lot of range names, you can click the Filter button and elect to display only the items meeting selected criteria.

3. Click the Close button to close the Name Manager dialog box.

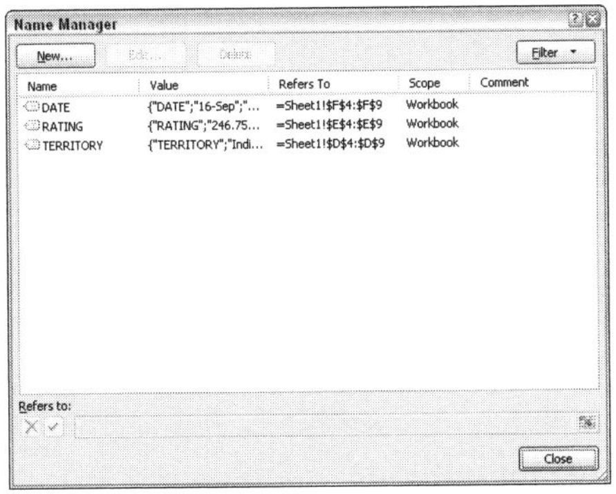

**Figure 2-15:** Use the Name Manager to add, edit, or delete range names.

**Figure 2-16:** Edit a range name and cell location.

# Validate Data Entry

1. Select the cell or cells you want Excel to validate. Next, choose Data⇨Data Tools⇨Validation. The Data Validation dialog box displays.

2. In the Settings tab, open the Allow drop-down list and choose the type of validation, such as:

   • Values such as Whole Number or Decimal, where you specify the upper and lower limits of allowable data values.

   • Lists such as a list you define, a range of cells in the existing worksheet, or a named range. (See Figure 2-17.)

   • Dates or Times, where you specify ranges or limitations such as greater than or less than or even a specific date.

   • Text Length, where the number of characters in the data must be within the limits that you specify.

3. If necessary, display the Data drop-down list and select criteria such as Between, Greater Than, and so on.

4. Select criteria such as maximum and minimum values, or specify a data location. Enter values or cell addresses. Precede a value with an equal sign (=) to specify a range name.

5. From the Input Message tab, optionally enter a comment to display whenever someone clicks the validated cell.

6. On the Error Alert tab, choose from the Style drop-down list whether Excel warns you or completely stops you from entering an invalid entry. (See Figure 2-18.)

7. Click OK.

**Figure 2-17:** Create a list of acceptable options or select one from the worksheet.

**Figure 2-18:** Determine the action to take when an invalid data entry occurs.

 When creating a list, if you want the available choices to appear when the cell is selected, make sure to select the In-Cell drop-down check box.

On the Error Alert tab of the Data Validation dialog box, you can customize the error message Excel displays if an invalid entry is entered.

# Enter Data in Validated Cells

1. Click a cell that has a validation requirement.

2. Type data into the cell.

3. Press Enter. One of two things happens:

   - If the data meets the validation rules, Excel accepts the entry and moves to the next cell down.

   - If the data does not meet the validation rules, Excel displays an error message similar to the one you see in Figure 2-19.

4. Depending on the setting you selected on the Error Alert tab in the Data Evaluation dialog box, choose an option:

   - Stop: Choose Retry or Cancel

   - Warning: Choose Yes or No or Cancel

   - Information: Choose OK or Cancel

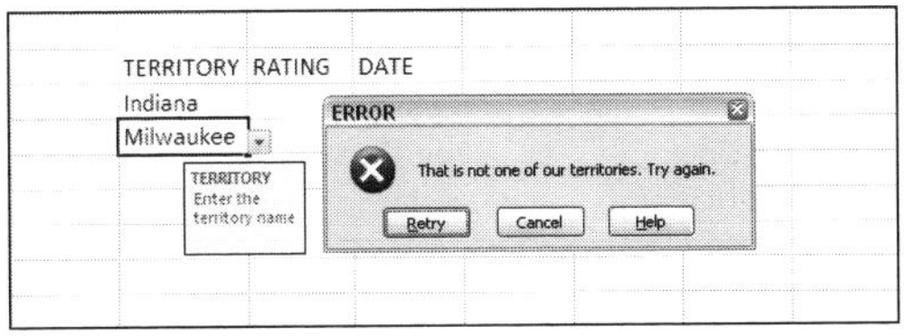

# Locate Cells with Data Validation

1. To have Excel highlight all cells that have data validation, select one of the following methods (see Figure 2-20):

   - Choose Home⇨Editing⇨Find & Select⇨Data Validation.

   - Choose Home⇨Editing⇨Find & Select⇨Go To Special. Select the Data Validation option, choose All, and then click OK.

2. Click any cell to deselect the highlighted cells.

To remove data validation, choose Data⇨Data Tools⇨Data Validation. From the Data Validation dialog box, click the Clear All button and then click the OK button.

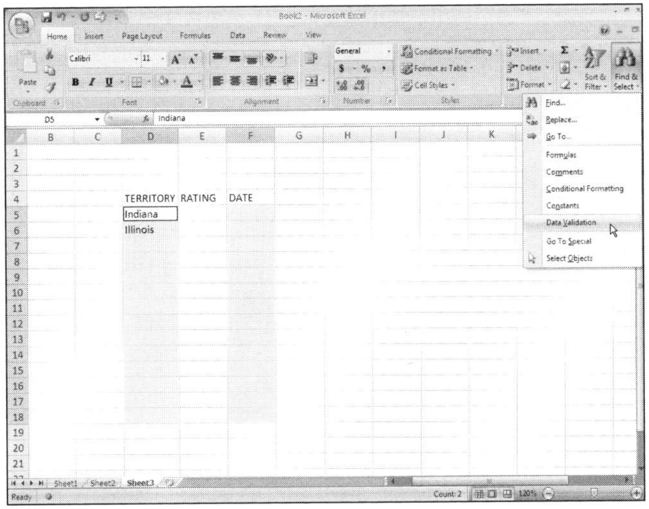

**Figure 2-19:** Entering data into validated cells.

**Figure 2-20:** Locating cells with data-validation restrictions.

# Building Formulas

*T*his chapter is all about the math. With Excel, you can create formulas to perform calculations. The calculations can be simple, such as adding 2 plus 3, or they can be extremely complex, such as those used to calculate depreciation. But don't despair; you don't have to do most of the work. Excel includes more than 335 built-in calculations, which are called *functions*, in 11 different categories. Functions contain *arguments*, which appear in parentheses following the function's name. The arguments are the details you provide to Excel to indicate which numbers to calculate in the function. Some functions require several arguments to function correctly, but again I say, don't worry; Excel contains a Function Wizard to walk you through the entire process.

The primary tasks in this chapter include:

➡ Creating simple and complex formulas by typing them into a cell.

➡ Analyzing data with Excel's time-saving functions.

➡ Creating cell ranges separated by colons for a sequential cell selection or by commas to list specific cell locations.

➡ Evaluating formula errors and locating a cell's precedents and dependents.

# Chapter

# 3

## Get ready to . . .

# Create Simple Formulas with Operators

1. Enter values in two different cells; remember, however, formulas do not need to reference cell addresses. They can contain actual numbers.

2. In the cell where you want to perform the calculation for the two values, type an equal sign (=). All Excel formulas begin with an equal sign.

3. Click or type the first cell address or type the first value you want to include in the formula. In the example in Figure 3-1, I'm adding two cell references (B5 and B6) together.

Excel displays a color border that surrounds the cell reference you enter.

4. Type an operator. Operators can include:
   - The plus sign (+)
   - The minus sign (–)
   - The asterisk (*) to multiply
   - The slash (/) to divide
   - The percentage symbol (%)
   - The exponentiation symbol (^)

5. Type the second cell address or the second value you want to include in the formula.

6. Press Enter and Excel displays the results of the calculation in the selected cell. (See Figure 3-2.)

The formula bar at the top displays the actual formula.

Formulas can have multiple references. For example, =B5+B6+B6+B8 is a legitimate formula. Formulas with multiple operators are called *compound formulas.*

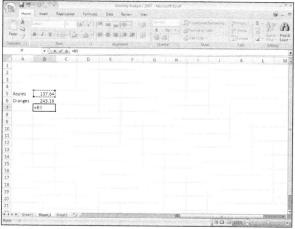

**Figure 3-1:** All formulas begin with an equal sign.

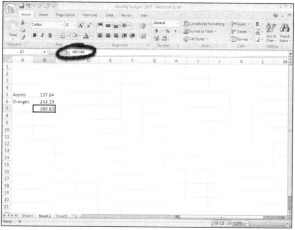

**Figure 3-2:** A simple formula.

# Create Compound Formulas

1. Type values in three or more different cells.

2. Select the cell where you want the formula.

3. Type the equal sign and then the first cell reference.

4. Type the first operator and then the second cell reference.

5. Type the second operator and then the third cell reference.

 Compound formulas are not limited to three references, and you can use cell references multiple times in a compound formula.

6. Press Enter. Excel displays the results of the calculation in the selected cell. The actual formula appears in the formula bar. (See Figure 3-3.)

 If you were paying attention in your high school algebra class, you might remember the Rule of Priorities. In a compound formula, Excel calculates multiplication and division before it calculates addition and subtraction. This means that you must include parentheses for any portion of a formula you want calculated first. As an example, in Figure 3-4, you see that the formula $3+5*2$ gives a result of $13$, but $(3+5)*2$ gives a result of $16$.

 You can include range names in formulas such as $=D23*$ CommissionRate where a specific cell is named CommissionRate. See Chapter 2 about using range names.

 Compound formulas can have multiple combinations in parentheses and can contain any combination of operators and references. A formula might read ((B5+C5)/2)*SalesTax. This formula adds B5 and C5, divides that result by 2, and then multiplies that result times the value in the cell named SalesTax.

 A great tool to review formulas is the capability to display the actual formula in the worksheet rather than the formula result. Choose Formulas⟹ Formula Auditing⟹Show Formulas. Click the Show Formulas button again to return to the formula result.

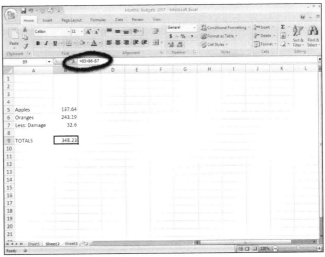

**Figure 3-3:** A compound formula.

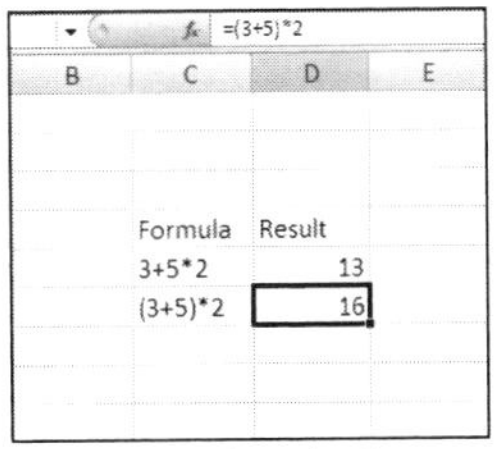

**Figure 3-4:** The Rule of Priorities in action.

# Add Numbers with AutoSum

1.  Click the cell beneath a sequential list of values.

2.  Click Formulas⇨Function Library⇨AutoSum. Excel places a marquee (marching ants) around the cells directly above the current cell. (See Figure 3-5.)

3.  Press the Enter key to display the sum total of the selected cells.

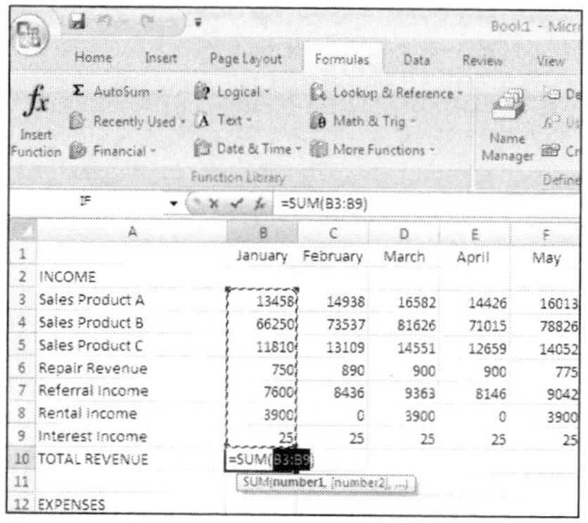

# Find an Average Value

1.  After selecting the cell beneath a sequential list of values, click the arrow beneath the AutoSum button. Excel displays a list of calculation options, including (see Figure 3-6):

    - **Average**. Calculated by adding a group of numbers and then dividing by the count of those numbers.

    - **Count Numbers**. Counts the number of cells in a specified range that contain numbers.

    - **Max**. Determines the highest value in a specified range.

    - **Min**. Determines the lowest value in a specified range.

2.  Choose Average. A marquee appears around the group of cells. Highlight a different group of cells if necessary.

3.  Press Enter. The selected cell displays the average value of the cell group.

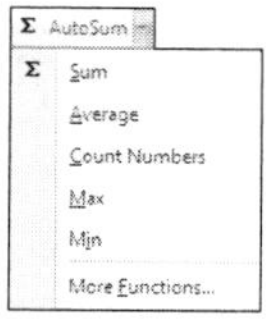

**Figure 3-5:** Using the AutoSum function.

**Figure 3-6:** Selecting the Average function.

If the cells directly above the current cell have no values, Excel selects the cells directly to the left of the current cell. If you want to add a group of different cells, highlight them.

The formula bar displays the formula beginning with the equal sign and the word SUM. The selected cells appear in parentheses, the first and last cells separated by a colon.

## Copy Formulas with AutoFill

1. Position the mouse on the AutoFill box in the lower-right corner of a cell with a formula. Make sure the mouse pointer turns into a black cross.
2. Click and drag the AutoFill box to include the cells to which you want to copy the formula. (See Figure 3-7.) The AutoFill method of copying formulas is helpful if you're copying a formula to surrounding cells.

Copied formulas are slightly different than the originals because of the relative change in position. For example, if the formula in cell **D23** is `B23+C23` and you copy the formula to the next cell down, to cell **D24**, Excel automatically changes the formula to `B24+C24`. If you do not want the copied formula to change, you must make the originating formula an *absolute formula* (see the "Define an Absolute Formula" section later in this chapter).

## Edit a Formula

1. Double-click the cell containing the formula you want to edit. The cell expands to show the formula instead of the result. (See Figure 3-8.)

Optionally, press the F2 key to expand the formula so you can edit it.

2. Use the arrow keys to navigate to the character you want to change.
3. Using the Backspace key, delete any unwanted characters and type any additional characters.
4. Press Enter.

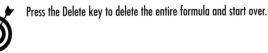

Press the Delete key to delete the entire formula and start over.

B10 =SUM(B3:B9)

| | A | B | C | D | E | F | G | H |
|---|---|---|---|---|---|---|---|---|
| 1 | | January | February | March | April | May | June | |
| 2 | INCOME | | | | | | | |
| 3 | Sales Product A | 13458 | 14938 | 16582 | 14426 | 16013 | 17774 | |
| 4 | Sales Product B | 66250 | 73537 | 81626 | 71015 | 78826 | 87497 | |
| 5 | Sales Product C | 11810 | 13109 | 14551 | 12659 | 14052 | 15597 | |
| 6 | Repair Revenue | 750 | 890 | 900 | 900 | 775 | 825 | |
| 7 | Referral Income | 7600 | 8436 | 9363 | 8146 | 9042 | 10037 | |
| 8 | Rental Income | 3900 | 0 | 3900 | 0 | 3900 | 0 | |
| 9 | Interest Income | 25 | 25 | 25 | 25 | 25 | 25 | |
| 10 | TOTAL REVENUE | 103793 | | | | | | |
| 11 | | | | | | | | |

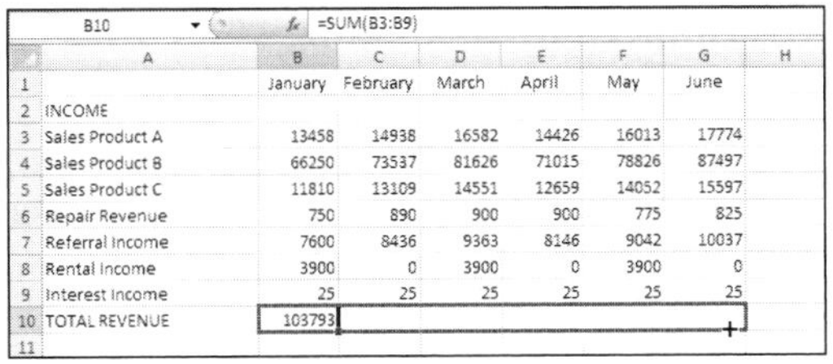

**Figure 3-7:** Using AutoFill to duplicate a formula.

IF =SUM(G3:G9)

| | A | B | C | D | E | F | G | H |
|---|---|---|---|---|---|---|---|---|
| 1 | | January | February | March | April | May | June | |
| 2 | INCOME | | | | | | | |
| 3 | Sales Product A | 13458 | 14938 | 16582 | 14426 | 16013 | 17774 | |
| 4 | Sales Product B | 66250 | 73537 | 81626 | 71015 | 78826 | 87497 | |
| 5 | Sales Product C | 11810 | 13109 | 14551 | 12659 | 14052 | 15597 | |
| 6 | Repair Revenue | 750 | 890 | 900 | 900 | 775 | 825 | |
| 7 | Referral Income | 7600 | 8436 | 9363 | 8146 | 9042 | 10037 | |
| 8 | Rental Income | 3900 | 0 | 3900 | 0 | 3900 | 0 | |
| 9 | Interest Income | 25 | 25 | 25 | 25 | 25 | 25 | |
| 10 | TOTAL REVENUE | 103793 | 110935 | 126947 | 107171 | 122633 | =SUM(G3:G9) | |
| 11 | | | | | | | | |

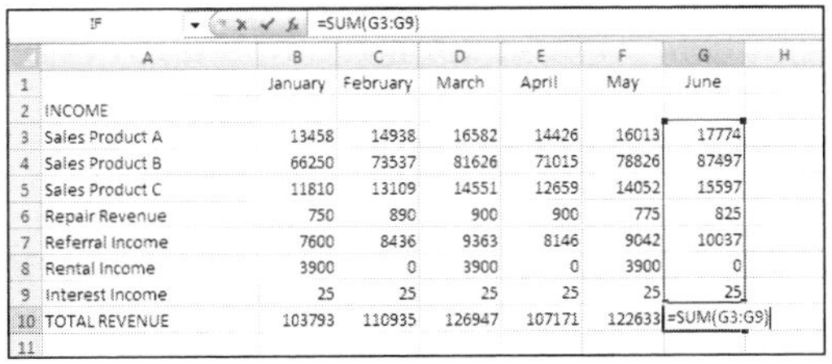

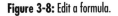

**Figure 3-8:** Edit a formula.

# Define an Absolute Formula

1. To prevent a formula from changing a cell reference as you copy it to a different location, you lock in an absolute cell reference using one of these methods:

   - **Lock in a cell location:** Type a dollar sign in front of both the column reference and the row reference (as in **$C$2**). If the original formula in cell F5 is =E5*$C$2, and you copy the formula to cell F6, the copied formula reads E6*=$C$2 instead of E6*C3, which is how it would read were it not absolute. (See Figure 3-9.)

   - **Lock in the row or column location only:** Type a dollar sign in front of the column reference (**$C2**) or in front of the row reference (**C$2**).

2. Copy the formula, as needed, to other locations. Notice that the absolute cell reference in the original formula remains unchanged in the copied formulas.

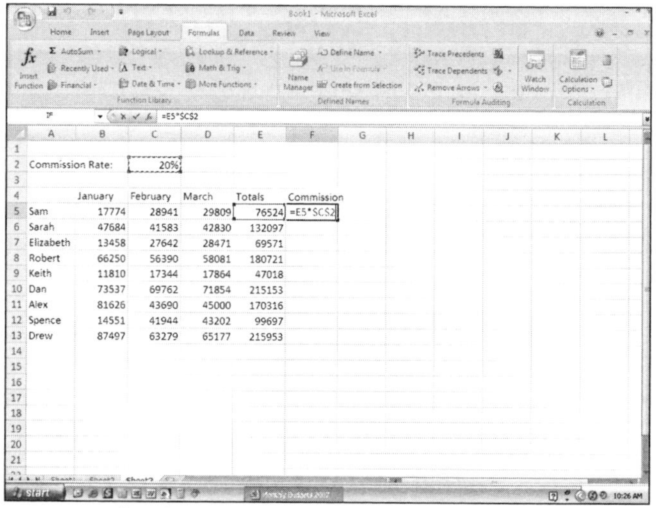

# Copy Values Using Paste Special

1. Select a cell (or group of cells) containing a formula and then choose Home⇨Clipboard⇨Copy. A marquee appears around the selected cell.

2. Select the cell where you want the answer; then click the arrow under the Paste button on the Home tab.

3. Choose Paste Special. The Paste Special dialog box, shown in Figure 3-10, appears.

4. Select the Values option.

5. Click OK.

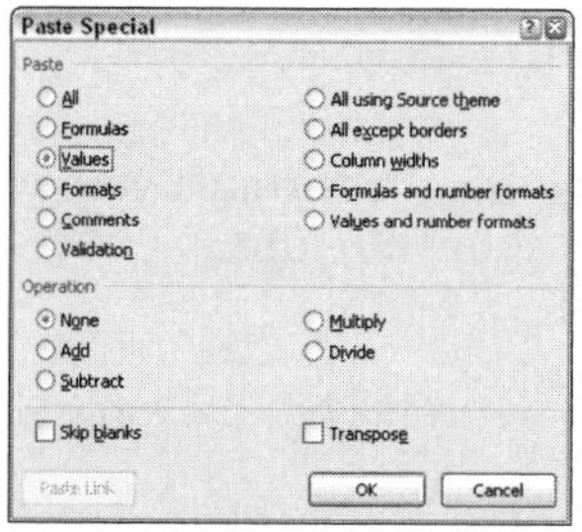

**Figure 3-9:** A formula containing an absolute reference.

**Figure 3-10:** Paste only the value, not the formula with the Paste Special feature.

# Build a Formula with the Function Wizard

1. Select the cell where you want to enter a function.

2. Click Insert Function, which is the icon located in the lower-right corner of the Function Library group on the Formulas tab. The Insert Function dialog box appears.

3. Select a function category from the Or Select a Category drop-down list. (See Figure 3-11.)

    To make the functions easier to locate, Excel separates them into categories including Financial, Date, Math & Trig, Statistical, Lookup and Ref, Database, Text, Logical, Information, and — new to Excel 2007 — the Engineering and Cube categories. For example, the Sum function is in the Math category, while the Average, Count, Max, and Min are Statistical functions. Functions that calculate a payment value are considered Financial functions.

4. Select a function name from the Select a Function list. A brief description of the function and its arguments appears under the list of function names.

5. Click OK. The Function Arguments dialog box displays. The contents of this dialog box depend on the function you've selected. Figure 3-12 shows the PMT function that calculates a loan payment based on constant payments and interest.

6. Type the first argument amount or cell reference or click the cell in the worksheet. If you click the cell, Excel places a marquee around the selected cell.

7. Press Tab to move to the next argument.

8. Type or select the second argument.

9. Repeat Steps 7 and 8 for each necessary argument.

10. Click OK. Excel calculates the result.

 Arguments in bold type are required. Those in normal type are optional.

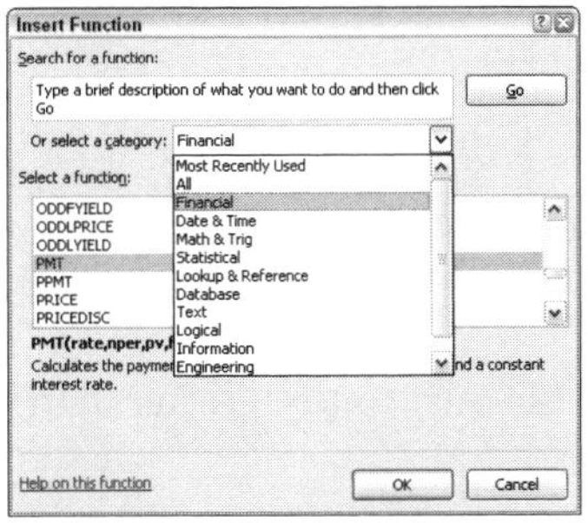

**Figure 3-11:** Select from more than 335 built-in functions.

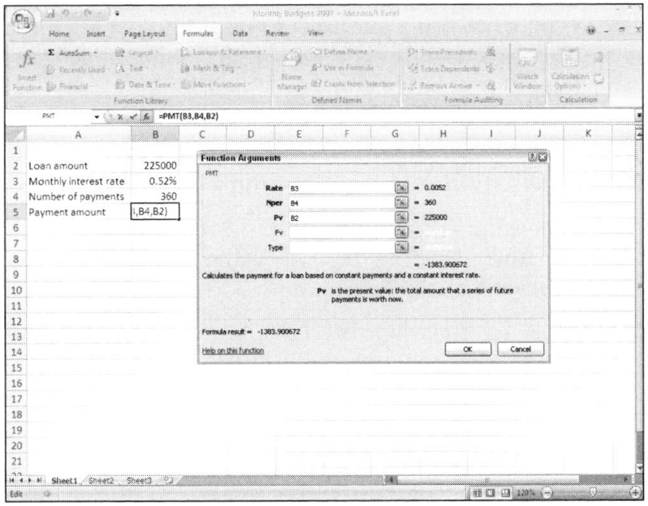

**Figure 3-12:** Specifying arguments for the PMT function.

# Generate an IF Statement Formula

1. Select a cell where you want to show the formula result.

2. Type the equal sign and then the word **IF**.

3. Type an open parenthesis (.

4. Begin the first argument by referencing the cell you want to check. For example, if you want to check whether cell B10 is greater than 100, type **B10**.

5. Type an operator such as equal to (=), greater than (>), or less than (<).

6. Type the value or cell reference you want to compare against.

7. Type a comma to begin the second argument.

8. Type what you want Excel to do if the first argument is true. If you want Excel to display a value or cell value, type the value or cell reference; but if you want Excel to display text, enclose the text in quotation marks. (See Figure 3-13.)

9. Type a comma to begin the third and final argument.

10. Type what you want Excel to do if the first argument is not true. As before, type the value, cell reference, or text you want Excel to display.

11. Press the Enter key. Excel displays the results of the analysis in the selected cell. In Figure 3-14, you see the result of NO I CAN'T in cell B8 because the payment amount was not less than the limit.

Arguments in an IF statement can also contain formulas.

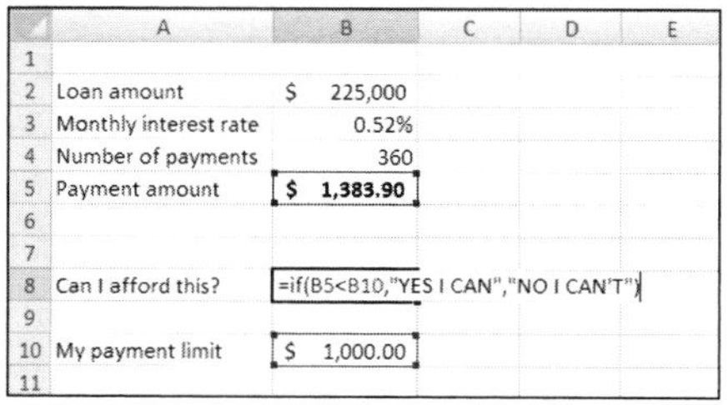

**Figure 3-13:** Entering IF statement arguments.

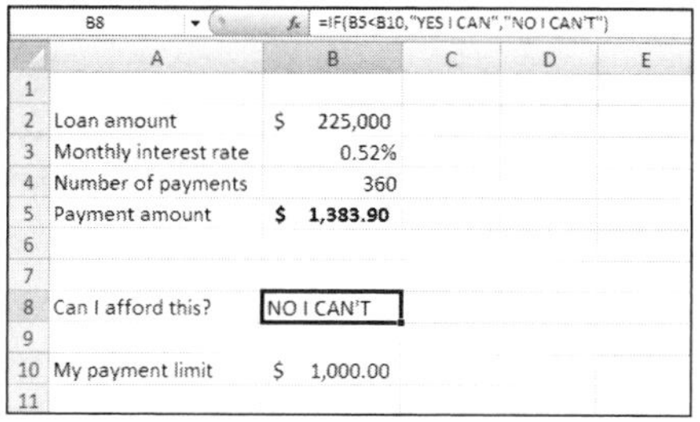

**Figure 3-14:** The results of a statement that was NOT TRUE.

# Troubleshoot Formula Errors

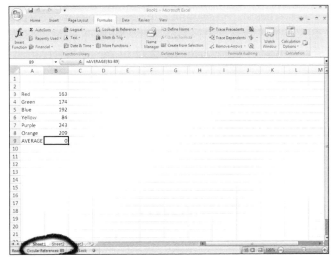

**Figure 3-15:** Let Excel find potential formula errors.

1. Choose Formulas⇨Formula Auditing⇨Error Checking. If Excel finds *potential* formula errors in your worksheet, it jumps to the cell containing the error and displays the Error Checking dialog box shown in Figure 3-15. If the worksheet contains no errors, Excel displays a message box saying the error-checking is complete. Here are just a few of the error types Excel might locate:

   - **DIV/0!:** Divide by zero error. This error means the formula is trying to divide by either an empty cell or one with a value of zero. Make sure all cells referenced in the division have a value other than zero in them.

   - **#VALUE!:** This means the formula references an invalid cell address. For example, text is in a cell where the formula is expecting to find a value. You might also see this error if you delete a value in a cell that was used in a formula. Locate and correct the invalid cell reference.

   - **NAME#:** This occurs when Excel doesn't recognize text in a formula, perhaps because of a misspelling of a range name. Make sure the name actually exists and is spelled correctly. Also verify the spelling of the function name.

   - **Circular:** This means that the formula in a cell is referring to itself. Locate the circular reference and edit the formula so it does not include itself. Figure 3-16 shows a circular reference.

   - **Number Stored as Text**: This means a cell contains what looks like a value, but the content is stored as text. Verify that you did intend to store the value as a text entry.

**Figure 3-16:** Circular References: Where a formula refers to its own cell address.

- **Formula Omits Adjacent Cells:** This means a formula refers to a group of cells that have numbers adjacent to it. Study the formula to make sure you didn't forget to include additional cell references in the formula.

2. Perform one of the following steps, depending on the error type:

    - Click in the cell and edit the formula as needed. Click Resume when you are finished.

    - Click Ignore Error to jump to the next potential problem.

    - Click an option, if available, to allow the Error Checking dialog box to assist you with repairing the problem.

3. Click Next to review the next problem area. When the error-check process is complete, Excel displays a message box.

4. Click OK.

## Identify Formula Precedents and Dependents

1. Select a cell that contains a formula or one that is referenced in one or more formulas.

2. Choose Formulas⇨Formula Auditing⇨Trace Precedents or Trace Dependents. Excel displays one or more blue arrows pointing out either precedents or, as shown in Figure 3-18, dependents.

3. Click Remove Arrows. The blue arrows disappear.

**Figure 3-17:** Show formulas instead of results.

| B | C | D | E | F | G | H | I |
|---|---|---|---|---|---|---|---|
| January | February | March | April | May | June | TOTALS | |
| 13458 | 14938 | 16582 | 14426 | 16013 | 17774 | 93191 | |
| 66250 | 73537 | 81626 | 71015 | 78826 | 87497 | 458751 | |
| 11810 | 13109 | 14551 | 12659 | 14052 | 15597 | 81778 | |
| 750 | 890 | 900 | 900 | 775 | 825 | 5040 | |
| 7600 | 8436 | 9363 | 8146 | 9042 | 10037 | 52624 | |
| 3900 | 0 | 3900 | 0 | 3900 | 0 | 11700 | |
| 25 | 25 | 25 | 25 | 25 | 25 | 150 | |
| 103793 | 110935 | 126947 | 107171 | 122633 | 131755 | 703234 | |

**Figure 3-18:** Tracer arrows indicate formula precedents or dependents.

 To help you determine the nature or origin of the problem, some error messages have a Show Calculation Steps button to display the logic behind the formula.

 Another great troubleshooting tool is the capability to display the actual formula, instead of the result, in the worksheet. Choose Formulas⇨Formula Auditing⇨Show Formulas. Click the same button again to return to the formula result. (See Figure 3-17.)

 Dependent cells are those that are referred to by a formula in another cell. Precedent cells are those that contain formulas that refer to other cells.

# Protecting Excel Data

*W*orksheets often contain numerical information that is confidential in nature, such as financial or payroll data. In today's world of electronic snooping, it's up to you to protect your work against prying eyes. Fortunately, Excel provides a large number of security tools such as password protection, hiding sensitive worksheet areas, or locking data against unwanted changes.

This chapter is about the security concerns surrounding Excel workbooks. I'll show you many distinctive protection methods including how to:

➠ Hide all or selected areas of a workbook

➠ Specify that users can view a file but not modify it

➠ Restrict the access to designated worksheet ranges

➠ Mark a file as final to protect it from changes

➠ Assign passwords to open or modify a workbook

➠ Remove private data from a workbook before sending it on to others.

# Chapter 4

## Get ready to . . .

# *Quickly Hide an Open Workbook*

1. Choose View⇨Hide. Excel hides the current workbook, leaving the Excel program open and visible. If you have another workbook open, you see that workbook, but not the hidden workbook.

2. Choose View⇨Unhide. Excel displays the Unhide dialog box listing all hidden workbooks, as you see in Figure 4-1.

3. Select the workbook you want to unhide.

4. Click OK.

# *Make a File Read-Only*

1. Choose Office Button⇨Save As. The Save As dialog box opens.

2. Optionally, select a file location from the Save-in drop-down list.

3. Enter a filename.

4. Click the Tools button. A drop-down menu appears.

5. Choose General Options. The General Options dialog box, shown in Figure 4-2, appears.

6. Click the Read-Only Recommended option.

7. Click OK.

8. Click Save.

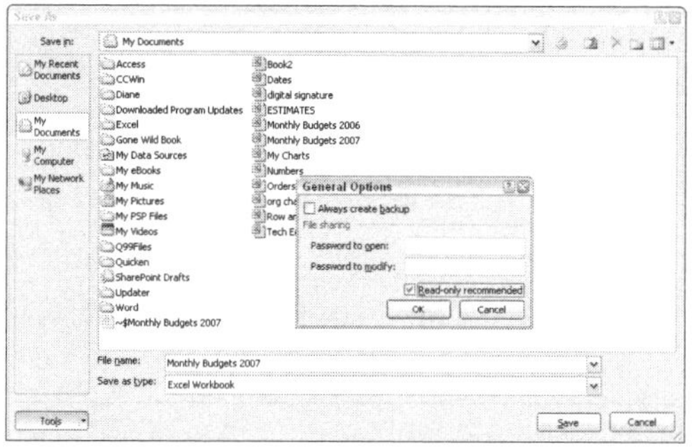

**Figure 4-1:** Hidden workbooks do not even appear on the Windows taskbar.

**Figure 4-2:** Protect against accidental changes by making a file Read-Only accessible.

The Read-Only option is only a recommendation. Users can save changes to a read-only file by giving it a different name or saving it in a different folder.

# Open a File as Read-Only or Copy

1.  Choose Office Button⇨Open. The Open File dialog box appears.

2.  Locate and select the file you want to open.

3.  Click the arrow on the Open button. A list of options appears. (Figure 4-3).

4.  Choose Open Read-Only or Open as Copy. The file opens.

5.  To save any changes to the file, you must choose Home⇨Save As and specify a different file name.

 If you open a file as a copy and do not use the Save As option, Excel uses the filename "Copy (#) *filename*" where # represents the copy number and *filename* is the current filename.

# Mark a Workbook as Final

1.  Choose Office Button⇨Finish⇨Mark as Final. The message box seen in Figure 4-4 appears.

2.  Click OK.

3.  If you have not yet saved the file, the Save As dialog box appears. Enter the filename and save the file. Otherwise, Excel saves the file and the words *Read-Only* appear next to the filename on the Title bar.

 The Mark as Final feature is designed to prevent accidental changes and is not permanent. If you find you need to make changes to the workbook, choose Office Button⇨Finish⇨Mark as Final again to turn off the Read-Only function.

**Figure 4-3:** Different approaches to opening your workbook.

**Figure 4-4:** Marking a workbook as final makes it a read-only file.

# Hide and Unhide Rows and Columns

1. Select the column or row headings you want to hide. If you want to unhide rows or columns, select the row or columns both before and after the hidden rows or columns.

2. Choose Home⇨Cells⇨Format⇨Hide and Unhide. A menu of options appears.

You cannot hide selected cells; only entire columns or rows.

3. Make a selection. In Figure 4-5, notice that columns D & E are hidden and seem to have disappeared.

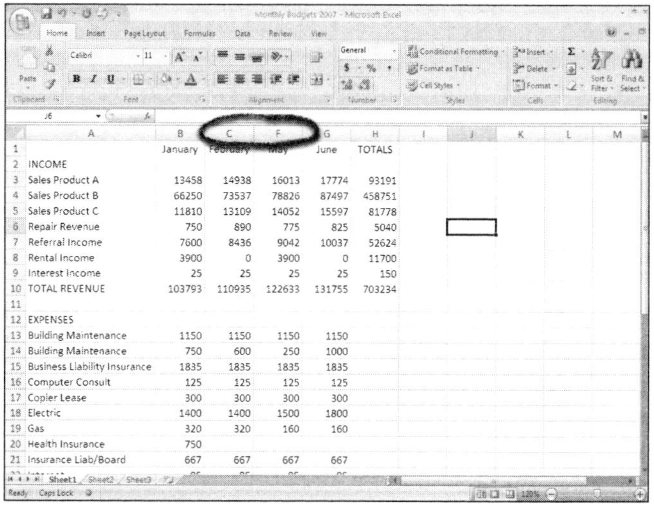

# Unlock Cells

1. Select the cells you want users to be able to modify.

2. Choose Home⇨Cells⇨Format⇨Cells, which displays the Format Cells dialog box.

3. Click the Protection tab, as shown in Figure 4-6.

4. Deselect the Locked option.

5. Click OK.

Optionally, choose Home⇨Cells⇨Format⇨Lock Cells. Because, by default, Excel locks all cells, choosing this option turns the Lock Cells option off. Click the option again to turn on the Lock Cells option.

**Figure 4-5:** Hide worksheet columns.

**Figure 4-6:** Unlocked cells can be edited in a protected worksheet.

# *Protect Worksheets*

1. Click the area on the sheet that you want to protect and then choose Review⇨Changes⇨Protect Sheet. The Protect Sheet dialog box appears, as shown in Figure 4-7.

2. Make sure the option Protect Worksheet and Contents of Locked Cells is checked.

3. Optionally, in the Password to Unprotect Sheet text box, type a password. For privacy reasons, only a series of dots appears.

4. From the Allow All Users of the Worksheet To box, select any options a user is allowed to change without unprotecting the worksheet.

    Deselecting the Select Locked Cells option doesn't allow an unauthorized user to even click a locked cell. All cells are considered locked unless you unlock them, as you see in the next section.

5. Click OK.

6. If you generated a password, a Confirm Password dialog box appears. Retype the password and then click OK again.

7. In the protected worksheet, attempt to change the value in a locked cell. Excel displays the error message shown in Figure 4-8.

8. To unprotect the worksheet, choose Review⇨Changes⇨ Unprotect Sheet.

9. Enter the password if prompted.

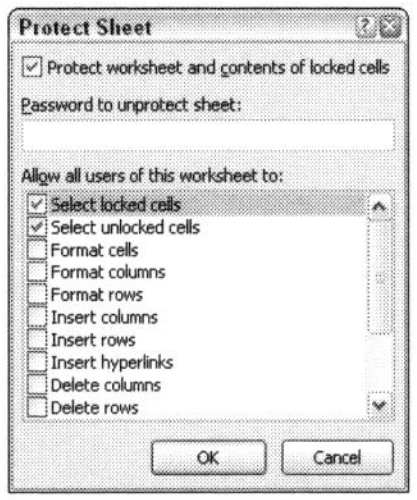

**Figure 4-7:** Protect a worksheet against accidental or unwanted changes.

**Figure 4-8:** Typing in a locked cell prompts an error message.

# Restrict User Data Entry

1. In an unprotected worksheet, choose Review⇨Changes⇨Allow Users to Edit Ranges. The Allow Users to Edit Ranges dialog box appears.

2. Click New. The New Range dialog box, shown in Figure 4-9, appears.

3. In the Title text box, type a short descriptive name, such as Qty Shipped or Price, for the data entry area.

4. In the Refers To Cells box, enter the range you want to allow users to edit. Begin the range with an equal (=) sign.

5. Enter a password that the user must type to gain access to the cell range. Passwords are optional, but without one, any user can enter data into the range.

6. Click OK. The Confirm Password dialog box appears.

7. Retype the password and then click OK. The Allow Users to Edit Ranges dialog box appears with the newly created range. (See Figure 4-10.)

8. Choose one of the following:

   • Click Protect Sheet to launch the Protect Sheet dialog box. (See "Protect Worksheets" earlier in this chapter.)

   • Click Apply and add another cell range.

   • Click OK to accept the changes and close the dialog box, but not protect the worksheet.

 Excel doesn't enable the feature until you protect the worksheet.

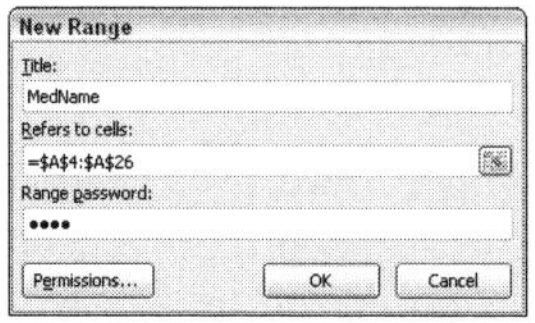

**Figure 4-9:** Allow specific users restricted cell range access.

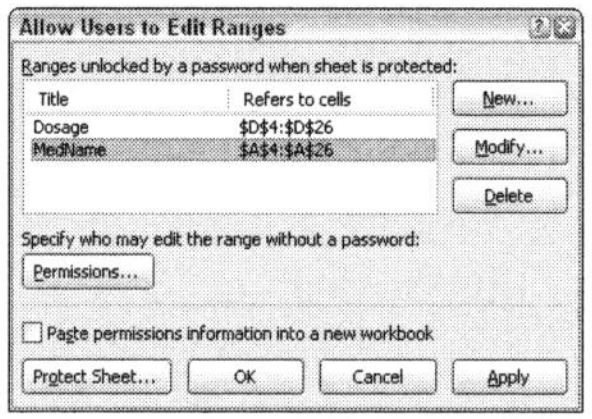

**Figure 4-10:** This dialog box displays restricted ranges.

# Enter Data in a Restricted Area

1. On a protected worksheet, in any cell with restricted access, begin typing data. The Unlock Range dialog box you see in Figure 4-11 appears.

2. Type the password. Passwords are case-sensitive.

3. Click OK. Excel allows access to the specific range.

4. Continue entering cell data as desired.

# Inspect for Private Information

1. Save the Workbook.

2. Choose Office Button⇨Finish⇨Inspect Document.

3. The Document Inspector dialog box appears.

4. Deselect any option you do not want to check.

5. Click Inspect. Excel inspects the document for the selected information.

6. When the inspection is complete, the Document Inspector reappears with information as in Figure 4-12.

7. Click the Remove All button next to any option you want removed. Excel removes the selected data. After removing the data, the Remove All button next to the option disappears.

8. Repeat Step 7 for any additional items you want to remove.

9. Click Close and save your file.

**Figure 4-11:** A password can be required to enter data into the range.

**Figure 4-12:** Inspect your workbook for hidden or personal information.

# Hide Cell Formulas

1. Select the cells containing formulas or information you want to hide.

2. Choose Home⇨Cells⇨Format⇨Cells. This displays the Format Cells dialog box.

3. Click the Protection tab and select the Hidden option.

4. Click OK. In Figure 4-13, although you see the results of the formula in cell F12, the formula bar does not display the actual formula.

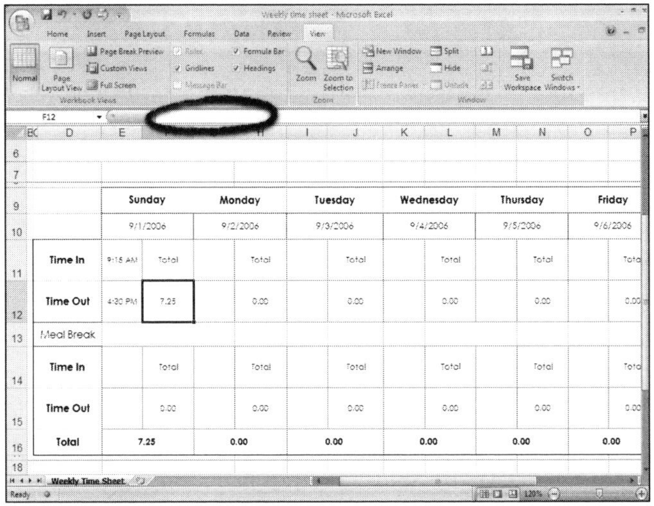

# Assign a File Password

1. Choose Office Button⇨Save As. The Save As dialog box opens.

2. Click the Tools button and then select General Options. The Save Options dialog box appears.

3. Type a password in the Password to Open text box if you want users to enter a password before they can open and view the workbook. (See Figure 4-14.)

4. Retype the password to open; then click OK. Retype the password to modify; then click OK. Click Save.

5. Open the password protected file, which displays the Password dialog box.

6. Type the Open password; then click OK.

7. If prompted, type the password to allow modifications and click OK. The protected file opens.

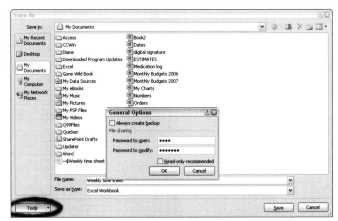

**Figure 4-13:** Keep cell data from appearing on the formula bar.

**Figure 4-14:** Protecting a workbook from unauthorized viewing or modifications.

# Part II
# Sprucing Up Your Spreadsheet

The 5th Wave          By Rich Tennant

"I've used several spreadsheet programs, but this is the best one for designing quilt patterns."

# Formatting Cells

*W*hoever said "Looks aren't everything" wasn't staring at an unformatted Excel spreadsheet. Columns often aren't wide enough, fonts are too small to read, dates display in an unusual manner, and when columns of data are stacked next to each other, sometimes the information overlaps.

Fortunately, Excel includes a plethora of features to make your data more presentable and easier to read. In fact, it has so many appearance-altering features, I had to break them up into two chapters! After you master the Excel formatting features in this chapter, you can.

➡ Change the font type, size, and style of text, values, or dates.

➡ Change the alignment of data in a cell from the standard left-aligned for text and right-aligned for values or dates.

➡ Turn values into currency or percentages.

➡ Create titles using the Excel Merge and Center button.

➡ Change column width and row height.

## Get ready to . . .

# Format Values

1. Select the cells you want to format. You can select a few cells, entire rows, entire columns, or the entire worksheet. (See Chapter 3 for information on selecting multiple cells.)

2. Choose Home➪Number➪Number Format. A list of options appears. Figure 5-1 shows values formatted in various Excel styles. Notice the different dollar sign placement in the Accounting and Currency types.

The Number group on the Ribbon also displays three icons you can use to quickly format as Accounting, Percentages, or Comma. The Accounting option has a drop-down list from which you can select different international currency symbols. Percentages add a percent sign and no decimal points. The Comma option adds two decimal places and a comma between the thousands. It does not include a dollar sign.

3. To remove digits to the right of the decimal point, choose Home➪Number➪Decrease Decimal. To add decimal digits, click the Increase Decimal button. Each click adds or removes a number to the far right of the decimal point and rounds the value in the cell. See Figure 5-2.

If you see a cell with values displaying #####, you need to widen the column width. See the next section.

Another method to select number formatting is using the Number dialog box launcher, which displays the Format Cells dialog box. Number format selections are on the Number tab.

Excel numbers can display up to 30 decimal places.

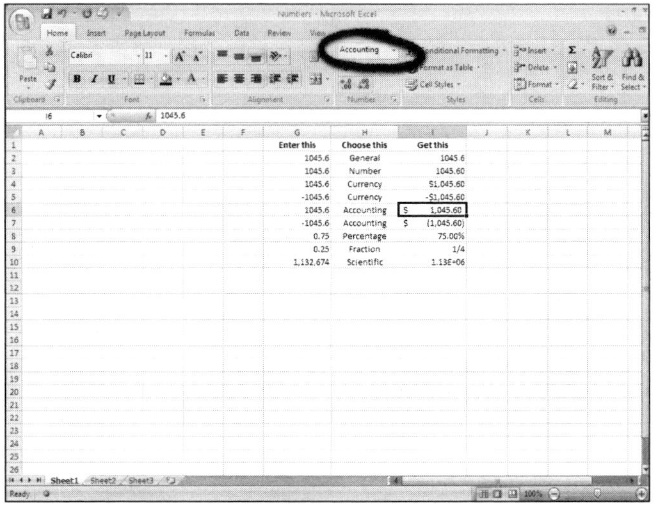

**Figure 5-1:** Numeric values formatted with different styles.

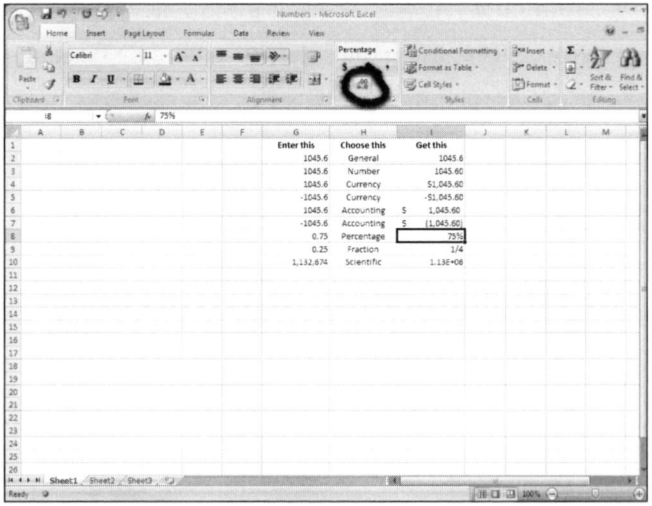

**Figure 5-2:** Easily add or remove decimal places.

# Adjust Column Width

**1.** To adjust the width of columns headings, highlight the ones to be widened. If you want to adjust a single column, click any cell in that column.

 If your worksheet contains many numbers, you can widen the columns to make the worksheet less cluttered. Columns that especially need widening are those containing cells with truncated text entries or numbers that Excel shows as #####.

**2.** Choose a method to adjust column width:

- To manually change the width of columns, position the mouse pointer on the right boundary of the column heading until it turns into a double-ended arrow. Drag until the column is the width that you want. As you move the pointer, a balloon message displays the new width. In Figure 5-3, I'm expanding column A.

 Excel displays cell width in characters and pixels instead of in inches. The minimum column width is 0 characters and the maximum is 255 characters.

- To set column width to a specific setting, choose Home⇨Cells⇨Format⇨Width. The Column Width dialog box, shown in Figure 5-4, appears. Type the exact width you want; then click OK.

- To automatically change the column width so it fits the widest entry, double-click the boundary on the right side of the column heading or choose Home⇨Cells⇨Format⇨AutoFit Selection. Excel sets the width slightly larger than the longest entry in the column.

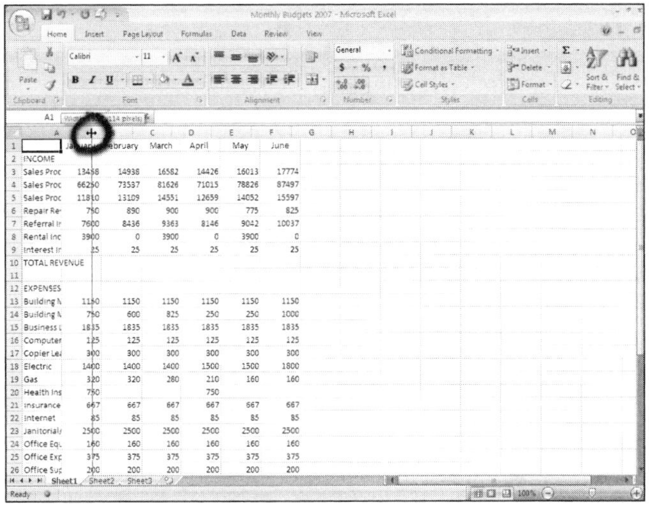

**Figure 5-3:** Manually changing column width.

 The default column width is 8.43 based on the default 11-point Calibri font. If you change the default font type or size, Excel may also change the standard column width. You can manually set a default column width by choosing Home⇨Cells⇨Format⇨Standard Width.

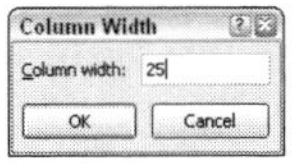

**Figure 5-4:** Set a specific column width.

# Change Row Height

1. Highlight the row headings whose height you want to adjust. If you want to adjust a single row, click any cell in that row.

2. Choose a method to adjust row height:

   • To manually change the row height, position the mouse pointer on the bottom boundary of the row heading until it turns into a double-ended arrow. Drag until the row is the height that you want. As you move the pointer, a balloon message displays the new height. In Figure 5-5, I'm increasing the height of rows 1 and 2.

    Excel displays row height in characters and pixels instead of in inches.

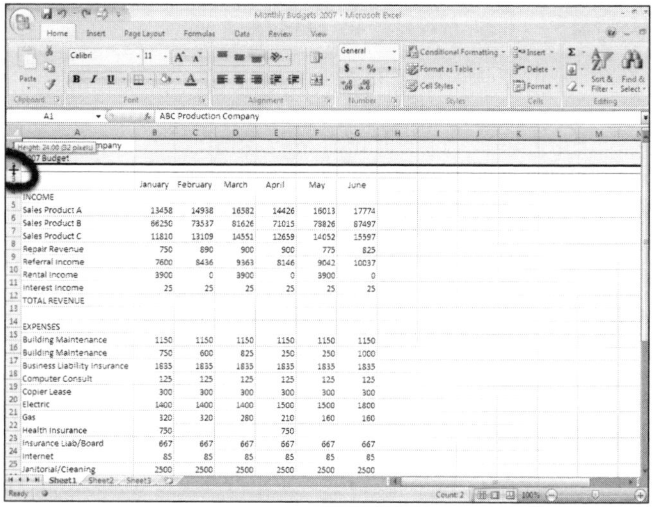

   • To set row height to a specific setting, choose Home⇨ Cells⇨Format⇨Height. The Row Height dialog box, shown in Figure 5-6 appears. Type the exact width you want; then click OK.

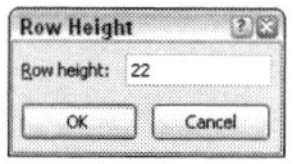

   • To automatically change the height of the row so it fits the tallest entry in the row, double-click the boundary on the bottom of the row heading or choose Home⇨Cells⇨Format⇨AutoFit. Excel examines the rows contents and sets the height slightly larger than the tallest entry.

    The default row height is 15 based on the default 11-point Calibri font. If you change the default font type or size, Excel may also change the standard row height. You cannot manually set a default row height.

**Figure 5-5:** Manually changing row height.

**Figure 5-6:** Enter the desired row height for the selected rows.

# Align Data Horizontally and Vertically

1. Select the cells you want to align.

2. Choose Home➪Alignment; then, select one of these alignment buttons:

   - Align Left: Horizontally aligns the data along the left edge of the cell.

   - Center: Centers the data horizontally in the middle of the cell. If you modify the column width, the data remains centered to the new column width. Cells B4 through G4 are center-aligned in Figure 5-7.

   - Align Right: Horizontally aligns the data along the right edge of the cell.

 Values formatted as Accounting can only display as right-aligned. You can change alignment on all other formatting styles.

   - Top Align: Aligns the data vertically along the top edge of the cell.

   - Middle Align: Centers the data vertically in the cell.

   - Bottom Align: This is the default option and aligns the data along the bottom edge of the cell. Notice the heading in Figure 5-8. Row 1 shows a top vertical alignment, whereas row 2 shows the default bottom alignment.

 Optionally, you can view additional alignment options and align both the horizontal and vertical alignment at the same time using the Format Cells dialog box. From the Home tab, click the Alignment group dialog box launcher. If necessary, click the Alignment tab and then set any desired alignment options; then click OK.

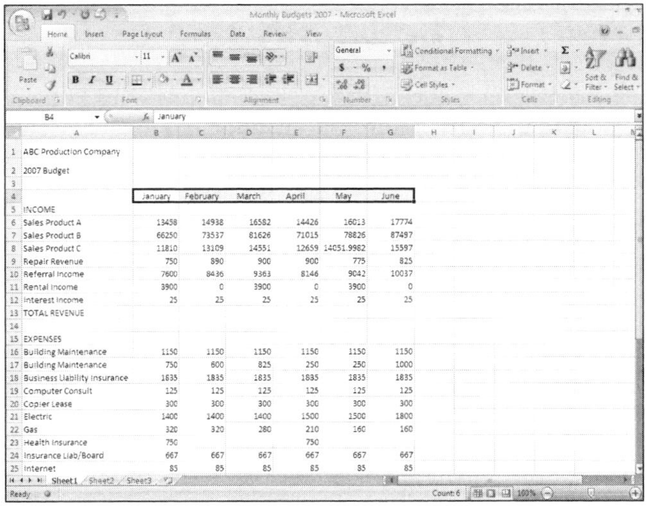

**Figure 5-7:** Align cell data horizontally.

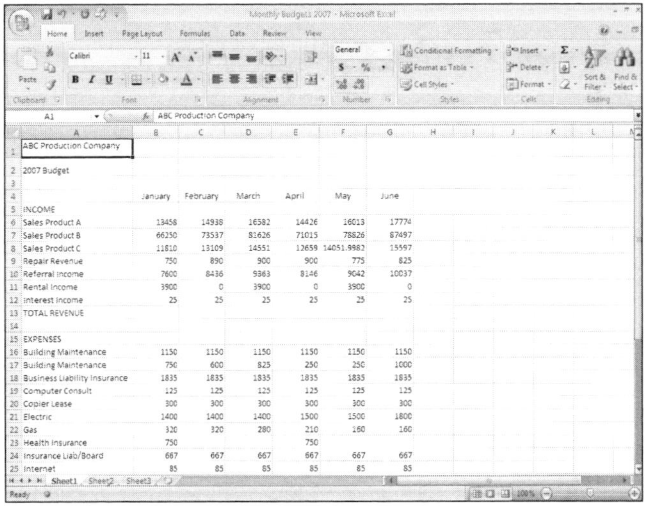

**Figure 5-8:** Vertical cell alignment.

# Create a Title by Merging Cells

1. Select the cell containing the data you want to merge and the cells you want to include in the merge. The data cell must be in the left cell of the selection and the other cells cannot contain data. This is shown in Figure 5-9.

2. Choose Home⇨Alignment⇨Merge and Center. All the selected cells merge into one larger cell, and the data is horizontally centered.

 If you select cells vertically and choose the Merge and Center command, Excel merges the cells and vertically bottom-aligns the data.

 After clicking Merge and Center, you can change the alignment. Click the Merge and Center button again to unmerge the cells from each other.

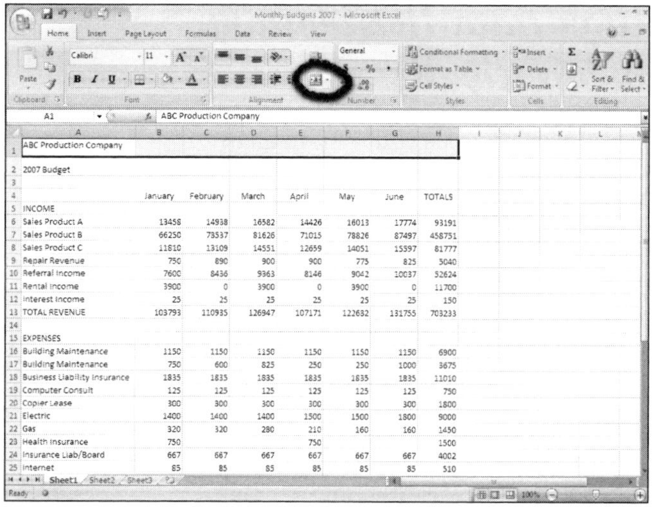

**Figure 5-9:** Merging cells can create a title for your worksheet.

# Change Font Color

1. Select the cells you want to format.

2. Choose Home⇨Font and click the Font Color drop-down arrow to select a color. Again, Excel's Live Preview feature, as you see in Figure 5-10, shows you the selected cells in the new font colors.

 Click More Colors to display the Colors dialog box from which you can select additional colors as well as create your own custom color.

Another method to select Font color is through the Font dialog box launcher, which displays the Format Cells dialog box. Font color selection is on the Font tab.

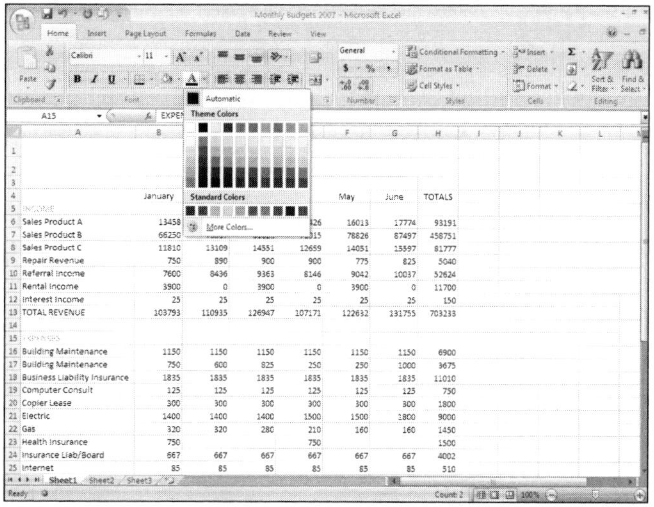

**Figure 5-10:** Choosing a font color.

# Select Font Attributes

1. Select the cells you want to format.

2. On the Home tab, open the Font drop-down menu and select a font. As you hover your mouse over a font face, Excel displays the selected cells in the different fonts.

3. From the Home⇨Font group, click the Font Size arrow and select a font size.

4. From the Home⇨Font group, click an attribute such as Bold, Italics, or Underline. (See Figure 5-11.)

# Apply Cell Background Colors

1. Select the cells to which you want to add background color.

2. From the Home tab, in the Font group, click the down arrow next to the Fill Color icon. A gallery of colors appears. (See Figure 5-12.)

3. Select the cell background color you want.

 Select No Fill to remove any cell background shading or choose More Colors to create your own shading color.

 A good combination to use with a black and white printer is a black background and a white font color.

**Figure 5-11:** Direct attention to certain cells by changing font attributes.

**Figure 5-12:** Choose a color for background shading.

# Wrap Text in a Cell

1. Select the cells you want to format.

2. Choose Home➪Alignment➪Wrap Text. As in Figure 5-13, if the selected text cells contain more text than will fit the width of the cell, Excel displays it on multiple lines. Notice that Excel automatically increases row height to accommodate the additional text lines.

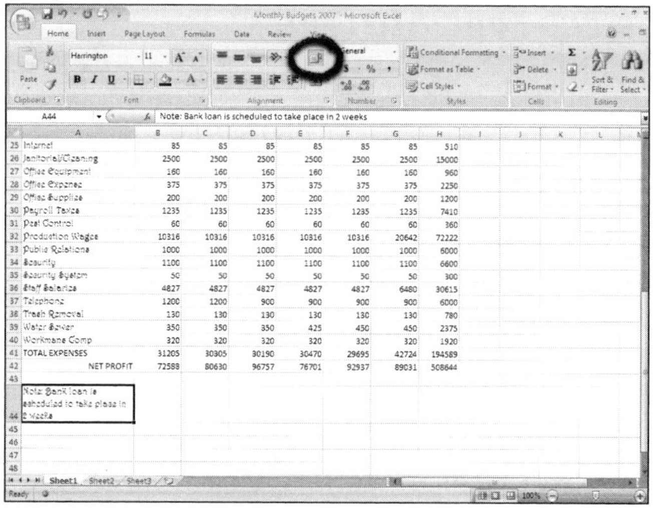

# Rotate Text

1. Select the cells you want to format.

2. Choose Home➪Alignment➪Orientation. A list of options appears:

   - Angle Counterclockwise: Angles the text in the cell from left bottom to right top.

   - Angle Clockwise: Angles the text in the cell from left top to right bottom.

   - Vertical Text: Centers the text and places one letter on top of the other.

   - Rotate Text Up: Places the text on the lower-right side of the cell and runs it vertically up the cell.

   - Rotate Text Down: Places the text on the lower-left side of the cell and runs it vertically down the cell.

3. Choose an option. The selected cells take the rotation you choose. In Figure 5-14, the cells are angled counterclockwise.

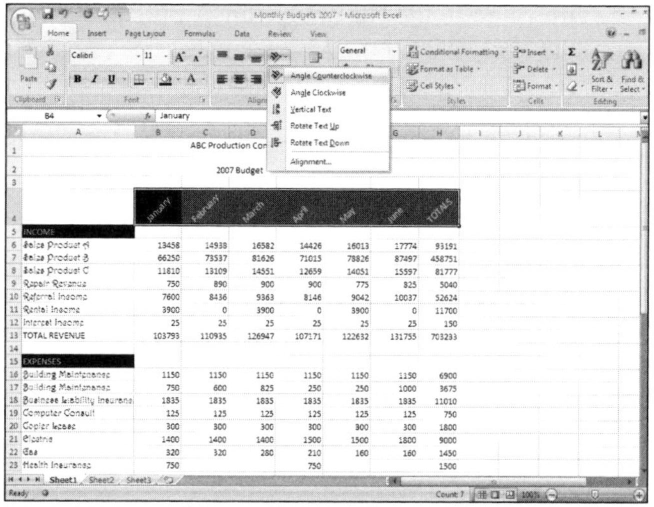

**Figure 5-13:** Worksheet cells with wrapped text.

**Figure 5-14:** Rotate cell data to add a special effect.

# Applying Additional Formatting Options

## Chapter 6

*I*n the previous chapter, you discovered many of the Excel features designed to change the cell data appearance. In this chapter, you discover a few more of the exciting Excel formatting utilities created especially to make your worksheet more interesting and easier to read:

➡ Save time with the Mini Toolbar and the context-sensitive menu.

➡ Liven up the worksheet with effective use of borders and lines.

➡ Format cells containing dates and discover ways to use dates in calculations.

➡ Reduce redundancy with the format painter.

➡ Effectively use predefined styles and themes that carry a single design through all office products.

➡ Specify conditional formatting to designate cell appearance if the cell value conditions are met.

## Get ready to . . .

# *Use the Mini Toolbar*

1. Right-click a cell or a group of cells. As you see in Figure 6-1, the Mini Toolbar and short-cut contextual menu appear.

 The Mini Toolbar contains many of the formatting commands available on the Home tab, making it unnecessary for you to actually switch to the Home tab.

2. Choose the formatting attribute you want to apply. The cells take the selected attributes, and the Mini Toolbar remains open for you to make additional selections.

3. Click any cell to close the Mini Toolbar.

# *Change the Default Font*

1. Click the Office Button and then click Excel Options.

2. If it is not already displayed, click Personalize. (See Figure 6-2.)

3. Click the Use This Font drop-down list.

4. Select the font type face you want to use in all new workbooks.

5. Open the Font Size drop-down menu and select the font size you want to use in all new workbooks. Click OK.

6. A message box appears. Click OK.

7. Exit and restart Excel.

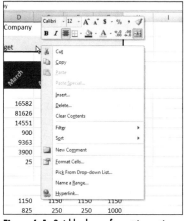

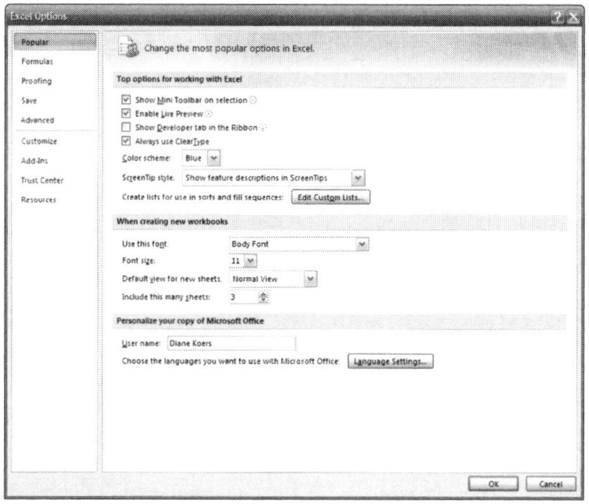

**Figure 6-1:** Quickly choose formatting options.

**Figure 6-2:** Select the font you use most often.

# *Place Borders around Cells*

1. To add a border, select the appropriate cells.

2. Choose Home⇨Font and then click the arrow next to the Borders button. A variety of border options, as you see in Figure 6-3, appears.

    The Borders tooltip button may display Bottom Border, Top Border, or whatever border was last used.

3. Select the border you want. Excel applies the border to the selected cells.

    For more border styles, colors, and options, click the More Borders option to open the Format Cells dialog box.

# *Work with Date Formats*

1. Enter a date into a cell. Depending on what you type, Excel probably displays the date in a different format. Figure 6-4 illustrates some date examples.

    Dates are actually numeric values, and you can use them in Excel calculations. See the next section.

2. From the Home tab, click the Number dialog box launcher, which displays the Format Cells dialog box.

3. Click the Date category. The right side of the screen displays a variety of different date formats.

4. Select a format for the selected cells.

5. Click OK.

 Optionally, click Short Date or Long Date from the Number Format drop-down list in the Number group on the Home tab.

**Figure 6-3:** Creating border lines for cells.

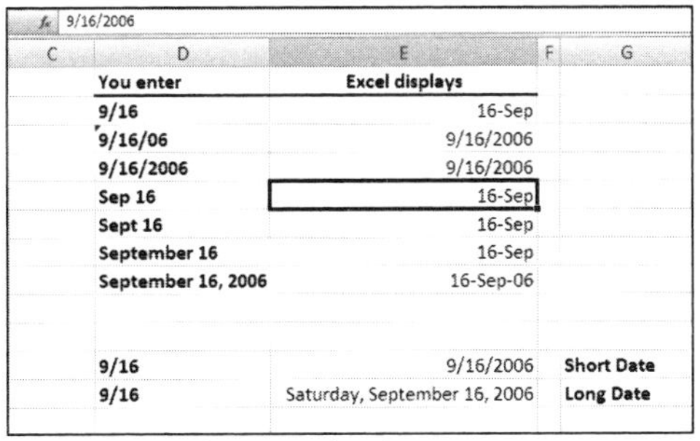

| You enter | Excel displays | | |
|---|---|---|---|
| 9/16 | 16-Sep | | |
| 9/16/06 | 9/16/2006 | | |
| 9/16/2006 | 9/16/2006 | | |
| Sep 16 | 16-Sep | | |
| Sept 16 | 16-Sep | | |
| September 16 | 16-Sep | | |
| September 16, 2006 | 16-Sep-06 | | |
| | | | |
| 9/16 | 9/16/2006 | Short Date | |
| 9/16 | Saturday, September 16, 2006 | Long Date | |

**Figure 6-4:** Excel automatic date formats.

# Use Dates in a Calculation

1. Enter a date into a cell. You can format the date any way you want.

2. Enter another date into another cell.

To have the cell dynamically display the current date, enter **=Now ( )**. To enter today's date as a static entry, press Ctrl+; (semicolon). To enter the current time as a static value, press Ctrl+: (colon).

3. To find the difference between the two dates, create a formula that subtracts one date from another. For example, if you put the first date in cell A1 and the other date in cell A2, then in cell A3 or wherever you want the difference to appear, enter **=A1-A2**. Excel returns a value, but it is formatted in a date pattern rather than in a numerical pattern (which is what you want). Your answer probably looks something like what you see in Figure 6-5.

To calculate the number of days between a specific date and the present time, enter the specific date in a cell such as A1 and then in another cell enter the formula **=A1-NOW()**.

4. With the answer cell (A3) selected, choose Home⇨Font⇨Number Format.

5. Select Number. Excel changes the date value to a numerical value. (See Figure 6-6.)

The reason Excel initially returned an unusual date is that dates are really serialized values beginning with day 0 at December 31, 1899. When you create a formula involving date formats, Excel naturally returns a date format. In the Figure 6-6, the first formula resulted in 1/10/1900, which is 10 days after December 31, 1899. Therefore, there are 10 days between the values in cells C4 and B4.

| | A | B | C | D | E |
|---|---|---|---|---|---|
| 1 | Planting Record | | | | |
| 2 | | | | | |
| 3 | Type | Date Planted | Date Germinated | # of Days | |
| 4 | Sunflower | 5/1/2006 | 5/11/2006 | 1/10/1900 | |
| 5 | Calendula | 5/1/2006 | 5/15/2006 | 1/14/1900 | |
| 6 | Poppy | 5/10/2006 | 5/28/2006 | 1/18/1900 | |
| 7 | Cornflower | 5/6/2006 | 5/18/2006 | 1/12/1900 | |
| 8 | Marigold | 4/18/2006 | 4/25/2006 | 1/7/1900 | |
| 9 | Zinnia | 4/23/2006 | 5/2/2006 | 1/9/1900 | |
| 10 | Nasturtium | 5/3/2006 | 5/13/2006 | 1/10/1900 | |
| 11 | | | | | |

**Figure 6-5:** Calculate the difference between two dates.

| | A | B | C | D | E |
|---|---|---|---|---|---|
| 1 | Planting Record | | | | |
| 2 | | | | | |
| 3 | Type | Date Planted | Date Germinated | # of Days | |
| 4 | Sunflower | 5/1/2006 | 5/11/2006 | 10 | |
| 5 | Calendula | 5/1/2006 | 5/15/2006 | 14 | |
| 6 | Poppy | 5/10/2006 | 5/28/2006 | 18 | |
| 7 | Cornflower | 5/6/2006 | 5/18/2006 | 12 | |
| 8 | Marigold | 4/18/2006 | 4/25/2006 | 7 | |
| 9 | Zinnia | 4/23/2006 | 5/2/2006 | 9 | |
| 10 | Nasturtium | 5/3/2006 | 5/13/2006 | 10 | |
| 11 | | | | | |

**Figure 6-6:** Change a date-formatted value to a numerical-formatted value.

# Copy Formatting

1. Click a cell containing formatting you want to copy.

2. Choose Home⇨Clipboard⇨Format Painter. The mouse pointer is a white plus sign along with a paintbrush like the one you see in Figure 6-7.

3. Click or drag across the cells you want to format. Excel immediately applies formats such as font, size, colors, borders, and alignment.

 Double-click the Format Painter tool to lock it in so you can paint additional cells without having to reselect the tool. Click the Format Painter tool again to unlock it.

 To quickly copy the width of one column to another column, select the heading of the first column, click the Format Painter tool, and then click the heading of the column where you want to apply the column width.

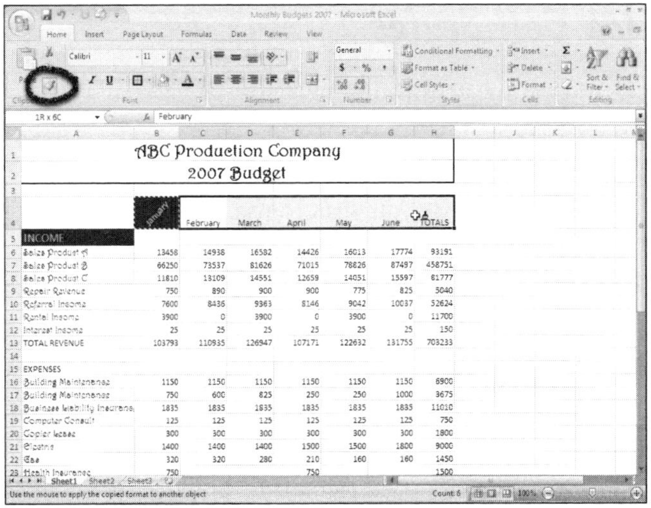

# Indent Data in Cells

1. Select the cells you want to indent.

2. Choose Home⇨Alignment⇨Increase Indent. Each Increase Indent click adds a small amount of space between the cell border and the data itself. (See Figure 6-8.) How Excel indents depends on how you format the cell:

   - If the data is left-aligned, Excel indents to the left.

   - If the data is right-aligned, Excel indents to the right.

   - If the data is centered, with the first click, Excel indents to the right; but subsequent clicks cause Excel to move the data to the left.

   Click the Decrease Indent button to remove indentation.

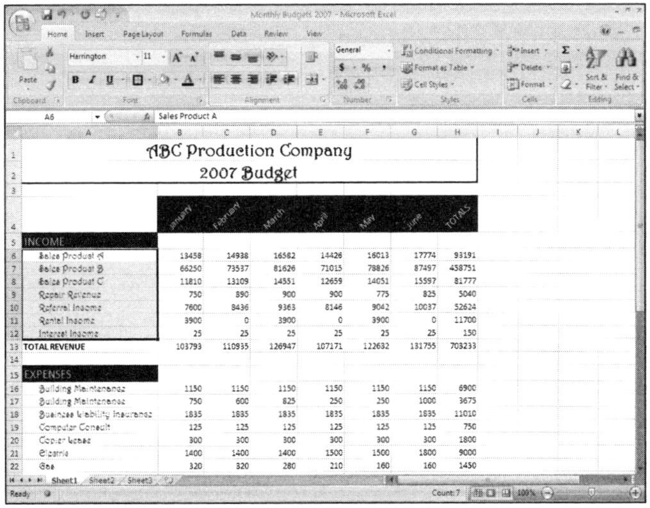

**Figure 6-7:** Use the Format Painter tool to duplicate formatting selections.

**Figure 6-8:** Indenting helps set data apart from other cells.

# Use Cell Styles

1. Select the cells you want to format.

2. Choose Home⇨Style⇨Cell Styles. In Figure 6-9, you see that Excel displays a gallery of predefined styles.

3. Select the style you want to use.

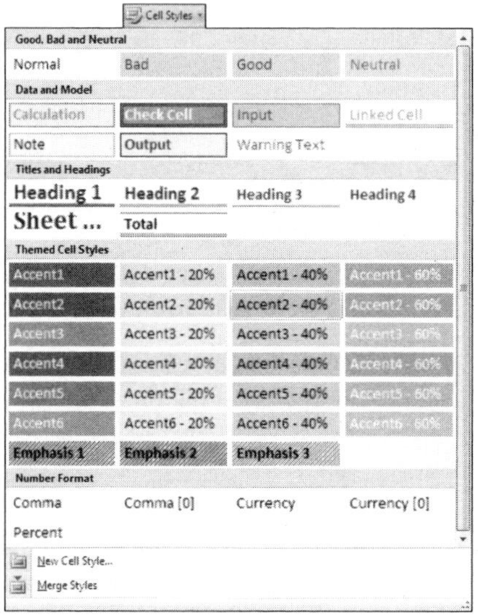

# Format Cells as a Table

1. Click anywhere in the data you want to format as a table.

2. Choose Home⇨Styles⇨Format as Table. A gallery of Excel-themed formats appears. (See Figure 6-10.)

    Themes are predefined style sets that appear across the entire Office suite, providing consistency in your work appearance.

3. Select the table style and theme you want to use. The Format as Table dialog box appears.

4. Confirm that the selected cells contain the data you want to format.

5. If the top row of your selection contains the headers, make sure the My Table Has Headers option is selected.

6. Click OK. Excel formats the table and applies filter arrows to each header. (See Chapter 14 for information about filtering.) The Table Tools Design tab appears.

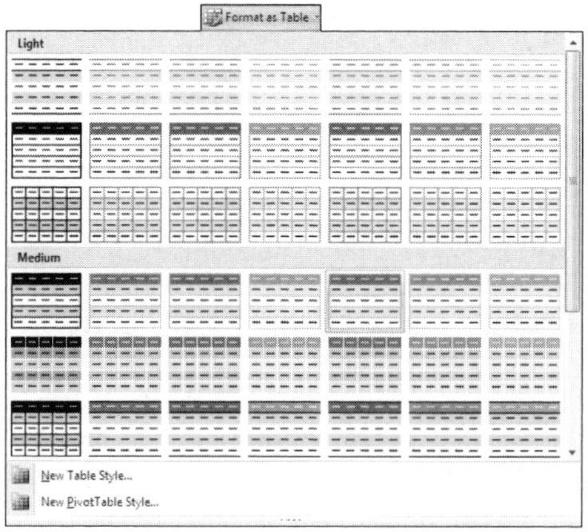

**Figure 6-9:** Select from many different cell styles.

**Figure 6-10:** Manage data better with an Excel table.

# Specify Conditional Formatting

1. Select the cells to which you want to apply conditional formatting.

    Reasons for using conditional formatting might include locating dates that meet a certain condition (such as falling on a Saturday or Sunday), specifying highest or lowest values in a range, or indicating values that fall under or over a specified amount.

2. Choose Home⇨Styles⇨Conditional Formatting⇨ Highlight Cell Rules.

3. Select the criteria you want to use. Criteria options include Greater Than, Less Than, Between, Equal To, Text That Contains, A Date Occurring, and Duplicate Values. A dialog box opens, where you can specify the value. In Figure 6-11, in order to see which items went over budget, you use the Greater Than criteria.

4. Enter the values you want to reference in the text box. The number of boxes depends on the criteria you selected in Step 3. You can type a value here, such as 500, or you can reference a cell address such as F13.

5. Click the drop-down arrow next to the format options so you can specify the format options to employ if the condition you specified is true. Live Preview shows you what your data will look like.

    Click the Custom Format option, where you can create your own format, selecting from font styles and color, numeric and other formats, borders, patterns, or background color.

6. Click OK. In Figure 6-12, you see formatting options applied to seven cells that meet the specified criteria of being greater than 0 (meaning, in this example, items over budget).

7. Repeat Steps 2 through 6 to apply any additional conditions.

 To clear conditional formats, go to the Home tab and choose Styles⇨ Conditional Formatting⇨Clear Rules⇨Selected Cells.

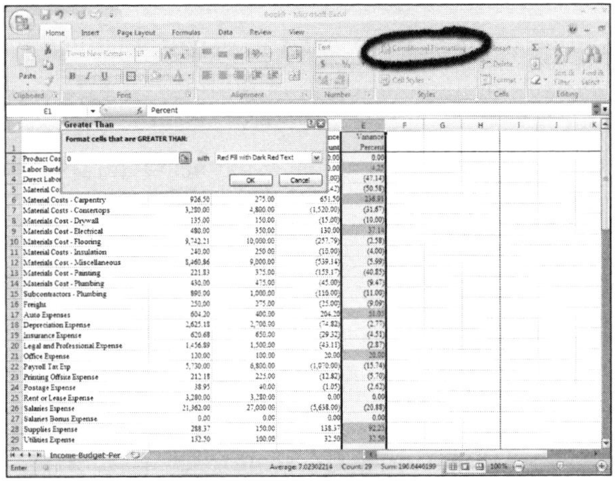

**Figure 6-11:** Specifying conditions for formatting options.

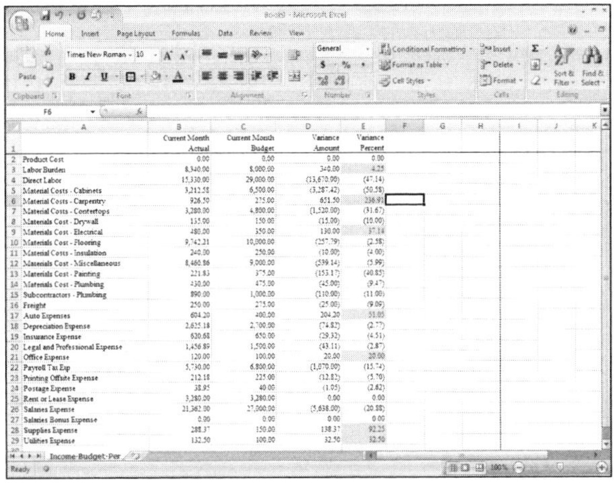

**Figure 6-12:** In this example, conditional formatting options include applying a font color change and a background color.

# *Add Data Visualizations*

1. Select the cells to which you want to apply formatting.

2. Choose Home⇨Styles⇨Conditional Formatting.

3. Select from the following options. (Figure 6-13 shows an example of all three data visualizations.)

   • **Data Bars:** A gradient-style bar helps you see the value of a cell relative to other cells. The length of the data bar represents the value in the cell, so a longer bar represents a higher value and a shorter bar represents a lower value. The data bars have six different color options designed to match Excel themes.

   • **Color Scales:** Designed to visually help you understand your data, color scales compare a range of cells by using two colors representing higher or lower values or three colors representing higher, middle, or lower values. The color scale bars come in eight different color themes, including red, yellow, and green. You can also create your own scheme by choosing More Rules under the Color Scales options.

   • **Icon Sets:** Icon sets help you classify data into three, four, or five categories with each icon representing a range of values such as higher, middle, and lower. As shown in Figure 6-14, icon sets include arrows, traffic lights, clocks, and even smiley faces.

 The icon size you see depends on the cell font size. You may need to adjust the column width to accommodate the icon.

 To clear visualization formatting, select the formatted cells and then choose Home⇨Styles⇨Conditional Formatting⇨Clear Rules⇨ Selected Cells.

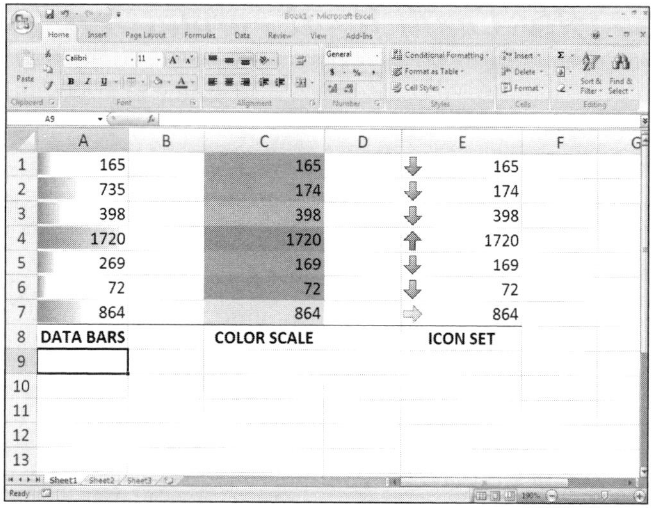

**Figure 6-13:** Using data visualizations.

**Figure 6-14:** Select the icon symbol you want to use to represent your data.

# Designing with Graphics

**S**ometimes, even after adding font and style attributes to cell data, you still want to call extra attention to specific areas. Maybe you'd like to add an arrow to point to a specific area. What? You can't draw a straight line? That's not a problem because with Excel, you don't have to be a gifted artist to draw.

Whether you want to draw circles, squares, lines, or arrows, Excel provides tools to assist you, making the drawing process fun and easy.

In this chapter, you discover how to:

- ➡ Draw arrows, shapes, and annotation boxes, plus add depth to your art using shading and dimension.

- ➡ Insert clip art, which is a collection of ready-made, computerized graphic illustrations.

- ➡ Insert a photograph or your company logo, making your viewers sit up and take notice of your worksheet.

- ➡ Use WordArt, stylized text objects, which add pizzazz to your worksheet.

- ➡ Manipulate and manage all the above mentioned graphic objects — by moving, resizing, cropping, rotating, recoloring, and using many other options.

## Get ready to . . .

# Illustrate with Arrows

1. Choose Insert➪Shapes. The Shapes gallery, shown in Figure 7-1, appears.

2. From the Lines category, select a line style. For this example, I select an arrow. The mouse pointer turns into a plus sign.

3. Click and drag the mouse in any direction. Begin wherever you want the back end of the arrow to appear.

4. Release the mouse where you want the arrow head to appear. A small thin arrow appears on the worksheet with a circle at each end, indicating the arrow is selected. (See Figure 7-2.)

 While the arrow is selected, Excel displays an additional worksheet tab called Drawing Tools Format.

5. Choose Drawing Tools Format➪Shape Styles➪Shape Outline. A list of options appears:

   • Theme or Standard Colors changes the arrow line color.

   • Weight displays a submenu, where you can select a different line thickness.

   • Dashes displays a submenu, where you can change the line style from a solid line to a dotted, dashed, or other style line.

   • Arrows displays a submenu, where you can select different arrowhead styles and sizes.

6. Click anywhere in the worksheet to deselect the arrow. Click the arrow again to reselect it.

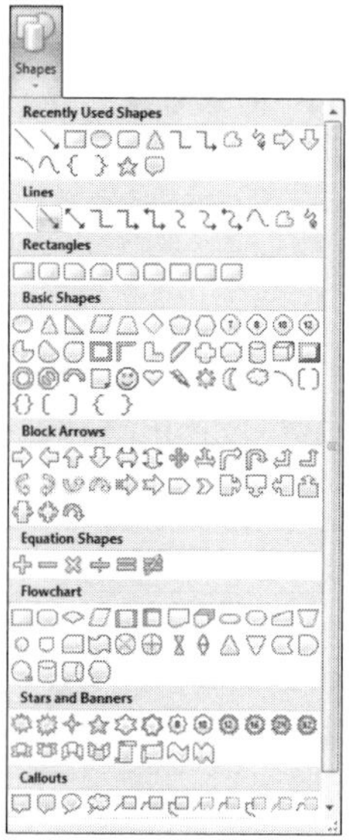

**Figure 7-1:** The Shapes gallery.

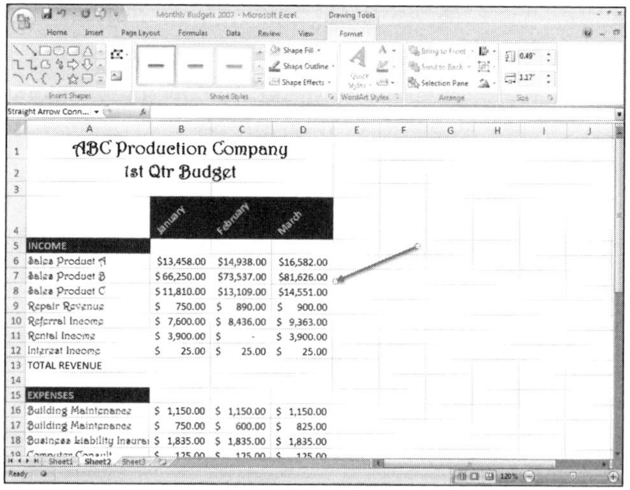

**Figure 7-2:** A drawn selected arrow.

# Draw Using Shapes

1. Choose Insert⇨Shapes. The Shapes gallery appears. Select a shape.

2. Click and drag the mouse in any direction. Release the mouse. The shape appears on-screen with eight selection handles around it, along with a rotation handle.

3. If you want the shape to contain text, with the shape still selected, begin typing the desired text.

4. Choose Drawing Tools Format⇨Shape Fill. A list of options appears:

   - Theme or Standard Colors: Changes the interior color.

   - No Fill: Shape becomes an outline without interior color.

   - Picture: Opens the Insert Picture dialog box, where you can select an image to display inside the shape.

   - Gradient: Displays a gallery of gradient fills.

   - Textures: Shows a gallery of texture fills (see Figure 7-3).

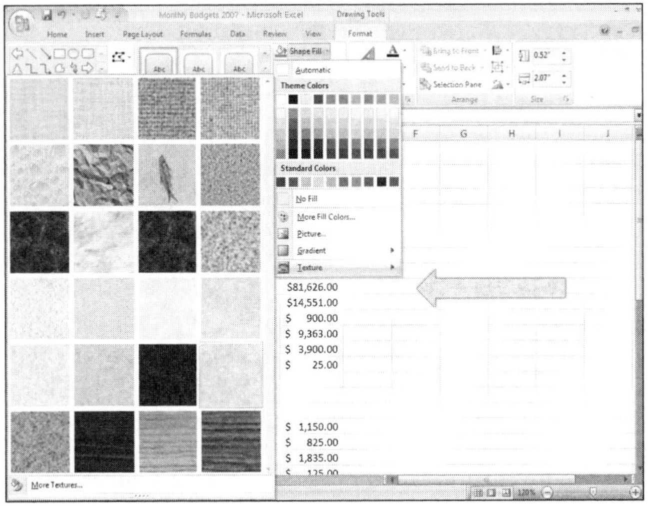

# Insert Saved Images

1. Choose Insert⇨Illustrations⇨Picture. The Insert Picture dialog box opens.

2. Locate and select the picture you want to place in the worksheet. (See Figure 7-4.)

3. Click Insert. Excel places the picture on the worksheet with selection handles surrounding the image.

**Figure 7-3:** Drawing shapes on an Excel worksheet.

**Figure 7-4:** Insert a logo or photograph.

# *Annotate with Text Boxes*

1. Choose Insert⇨Text⇨Text Box. The mouse pointer looks like an upside-down cross.

2. Click and drag diagonally on the worksheet to draw the box the approximate size you want. You can resize or move it later if necessary. You see a text box like the one shown in Figure 7-5. A blinking cursor appears inside the text box.

3. Type the desired text.

4. Click outside of the text box to deselect it.

5. Right-click the text box and choose Format Shape. The Format Shape dialog box (shown in Figure 7-6) opens. In this dialog box, choose any of these formatting options:

   • To add a background fill to the text box, click Fill and select an option from the right side of the dialog box.

   • To change the border that surrounds the text box, click Line and choose a line option.

   • To change the style of line surrounding the text box, click Line Style and choose any desired options.

   • To add a shadow around the text box, click Shadow and then select an option from the Presets drop-down list.

   • Make the text box three-dimensional with choices in the 3-D Format and 3-D Rotation sections.

   • From the Text Box option, select Resize Shape to fit text. As you add or remove text from the text box, the box expands or contracts to fit around the text.

6. Click OK when you finish making your selections.

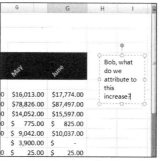

**Figure 7-5:** Annotate cells with text boxes.

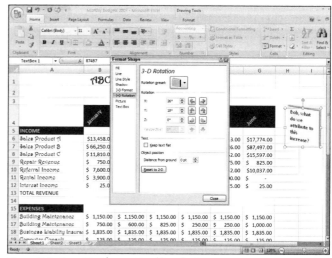

**Figure 7-6:** Format text box text to add emphasis.

# Add Clip Art

1. Choose Insert⇨Illustrations⇨ClipArt. The ClipArt task pane appears, as shown in Figure 7-7.

2. In the Search For box, type a brief description of the image type you want, such as food, buildings, animals, or people.

3. From the Search In list, choose where you want Excel to search.

   • My Collections: Includes searching in your private folders such as Favorites and My Documents.

   • Office Collections: Includes clip art, organized by category, installed with the Microsoft Office application.

   • Web Collections: Includes clip art from the Microsoft Office Online Web site.

4. Choose the type of image you want from the Results Should Be drop-down list. Excel can locate clip art, photographs, movies, or sound files.

 Click the plus sign next to any image type to further define the search options.

5. Click the Go button. Excel displays a number of images representing the art you specified.

6. Select the desired image. Excel places the image onto your worksheet, as shown in Figure 7-8.

 For thousands of additional pieces of free clip art, click Clip Art on Office Online.

7. Click the Close button to close the Clip Art task pane.

**Figure 7-7:** Searching for clip art.

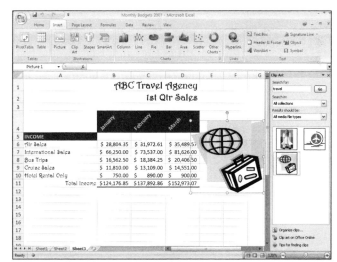

**Figure 7-8:** Placing clip art onto your worksheet.

# Create WordArt

1. Choose Insert⇨Text⇨WordArt. A gallery of options appears.

2. Select a style. A box appears on the worksheet.

3. Type the text you want. (See Figure 7-9.) The text shrinks to fit into the existing box, but you can resize it later.

4. Click the Drawing Tools Format tab.

 To change the style of any or all of the WordArt, highlight the portion you want to change and choose Drawing Tools Format⇨Quick Styles to make a selection.

5. Use the tools in the WordArt group to modify the WordArt text characteristics. All options include Live Preview, so as you pause your mouse pointer over any option, you see its effect on your WordArt object:

   • Text Fill changes the text color, gradient, or pattern.

   • Text Outline modifies the outer edges of the text.

   • Text Effects applies special effects such as shadow, reflection, rotation, and bevel.

6. To apply a background to the WordArt object, choose Drawing Tools Format⇨Shape Styles. Next, click the More button. A gallery of themed styles appears. (See Figure 7-10.)

7. Select a background option or click the Other Theme Fills arrow to select from several gradient options.

 To change multiple object characteristics, choose Drawing Tools Format⇨Shape Styles and then click the dialog box. The Format Shape dialog box opens.

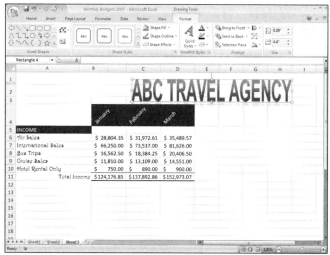

**Figure 7-9:** Add elaborate text with WordArt.

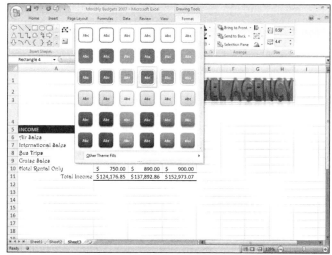

**Figure 7-10:** Apply WordArt enhancements.

# *Manipulate Graphics*

1. Select the object you want to modify. Selection handles appear around the object. Figure 7-11 shows a selected object.

2. Perform any of the following actions:

   - Delete: Press the Delete key on the keyboard.

   - Move: Position the mouse pointer over the object, but not on the handles. Click and drag the object to the desired location.

      Optionally, nudge a selected object using the up, down, left, or right arrow keys.

   - Resize: To resize an object, position the mouse pointer over one of the white selection circles and drag the circle until the object reaches the desired size. Use the top or bottom middle handle to resize the object height. Use the middle left or right handle to resize the object width. Use a corner handle to resize both the height and width.

      If you want to constrain the sizing when resizing an object, hold down the Shift key.

   - Rotate Shape: Position the mouse over the green rotation handle until the pointer turns into a circle. Then, drag the green rotation handle until the object rotates to the desired angle. (See Figure 7-12.) This does not apply to arrows.

   - Rotate Arrow: Drag either of the white selection handles in the direction you want to rotate.

 To constrain rotation to 15-degree angles, press and hold the Shift key while rotating the object.

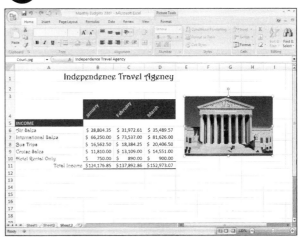

**Figure 7-11:** A selected object with eight selection handles and a rotation handle.

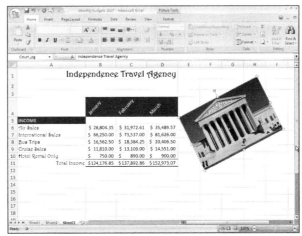

**Figure 7-12:** Use the rotation handle to rotate shapes or other objects.

# Crop an Image

1. Choose Picture Tools Format⇨Size⇨Crop.

2. Position the mouse over a corner of the image to display crop handles. A crop handle looks like an upside-down and backward letter L, as shown in Figure 7-13.

3. Click and drag a crop handle inward to crop out an area of the image.

4. Release the mouse button. Excel crops the image.

5. Continue cropping other edges of the image, as needed.

6. Click the Crop button again to turn off the Crop tool.

# Flip an Object

1. Select the object you want to flip.

2. Choose Picture Tools Format⇨Arrange⇨Rotate. A menu of choices appears. As you pause your mouse over a menu option, Excel previews the effect on the picture. (See Figure 7-14.)

3. Select from the following options:

   • Rotate Right 90°

   • Rotate Left 90°

   • Flip Vertical

   • Flip Horizontal

 Choose More Rotation options to display the Size and Properties dialog box, where you can set many options precisely including size, rotation, and cropping.

**Figure 7-13:** Removing undesired areas of a picture — in this example, the car on the left.

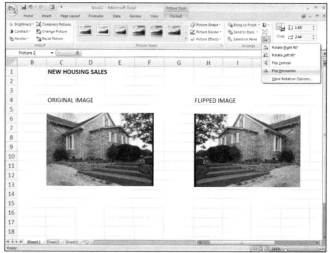

**Figure 7-14:** Flipping an object.

# *Align Multiple Graphics*

1. Select the first object and then hold down the Ctrl key and select any subsequent objects.

 For assistance in selecting multiple objects, select one object and then choose Drawing Tools Format⇨Arrange⇨Selection Pane.

2. Choose Drawing Tools Format⇨Arrange⇨Align. A list of options appears. (See Figure 17-15.)

3. Choose a menu option. Figure 7-16 shows three arrows aligned both center and middle. Some options include:

   • Align Left: Aligns two or more objects so their left edges are the same as the leftmost selected object.

   • Align Right: Aligns two or more objects so their right edges are the same as the rightmost-selected object.

   • Align Top: Aligns two or more objects so their top edges are the same as the highest-selected object.

   • Align Bottom: Aligns two or more objects so their bottom edges are the same as the lowest-selected object.

   • Snap to Grid: When active, using any of the align options aligns the objects to the closest grid intersection. When Snap to Grid is turned on, nudging an object with the arrow keys moves the object one gridline at a time. With Snap to Grid turned off, nudging an object moves it one pixel at a time.

   • View Gridlines: Turns the gridline display off and on in the Excel worksheet.

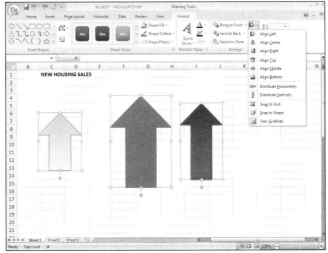

**Figure 7-15:** Select an alignment option.

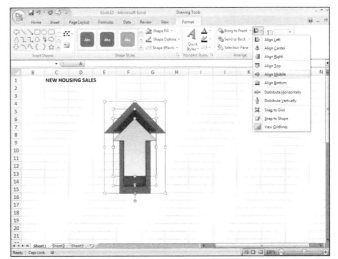

**Figure 7-16:** Three arrows aligned center and middle.

# Control Object Order

1. Select the object you want to move.

2. Choose Drawing Tools⇨Arrange⇨Bring to Front. A menu of options appears.

    Optionally, choose Send to Back to move a selected object behind another one.

3. Choose Bring Forward or Bring to Front. The selected object moves on top of the other object or objects. (See Figure 7-17.)

# Group Objects Together

1. Select two or more objects.

    An alternative way to select objects is to choose Home⇨Editing⇨ Find and Select⇨Select Objects. Next, use the mouse to draw an imaginary box around the objects you want to select. Click the Select Objects option again to turn off the feature.

2. Choose Drawing Tools Format⇨Arrange⇨Group. The selected objects become one object with a single boundary box around it. With grouped objects, any changes you make affect the entire object. In Figure 7-18, you see the rectangle, circle, and triangle grouped together as one.

    When you group objects, you combine them; therefore, any changes you make affect the entire object. Changes include move, resize, flip, rotate, crop and any style, shadow, or color changes. You can also create groups within groups to help you build complex drawings.

   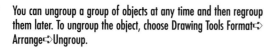 You can ungroup a group of objects at any time and then regroup them later. To ungroup the object, choose Drawing Tools Format⇨ Arrange⇨Ungroup.

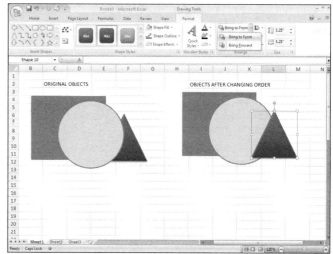

**Figure 7-17:** Rearranging the objects so the red triangle is on top of the yellow circle.

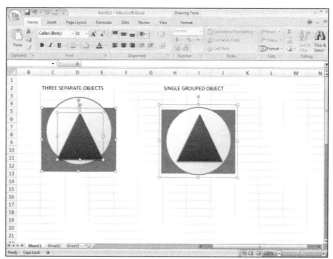

**Figure 7-18:** Combine multiple objects into one.

# Managing Workbooks

*L*et's begin by clearing up a couple of terms. A *worksheet*, sometimes called a *spreadsheet*, is a collection of cells that can have more than 1 million rows down and more than 16,000 rows across. Each cell of each sheet can contain more than 32,000 characters.

Secondly, a *workbook* is a collection of worksheets. By default, each time you create a new Excel workbook, it contains three worksheets. Each workbook however, can have an almost unlimited number of worksheets, limited only by your computer memory. The resulting possible number of cells in a single workbook is too huge to even dream about, but the fact remains you *could* create a single huge workbook. Realistically, however, you'll probably have a number of different workbooks, each with a number of worksheets.

Excel makes it easy to work with multiple worksheets. You can maneuver between the sheets by clicking a sheet tab. It even provides navigation buttons for situations when you have a lot of tabs. This chapter is primarily about working with multiple sheets. You discover how to insert, delete, move, and copy worksheets, rename the tabs that reference them, and create formulas that reference other worksheets or workbooks.

Finally, you discover how to create hyperlinks to jump to Web sites, other cells, or workbooks and how to create an instant e-mail.

## Chapter 8

### Get ready to . . .

# Insert Additional Worksheets

1. Choose Home⇨Cells⇨Insert⇨Insert Sheet. Excel automatically inserts a new blank worksheet on top of the currently selected sheet. (See Figure 8-1.) Excel automatically assigns the next number — such as Sheet4.

2. Click a different worksheet tab. That worksheet becomes the current sheet.

3. If your workbook has more worksheets than you can see at the bottom, click the First, Previous, Next, or Last navigation buttons in the bottom-left corner of the workbook.

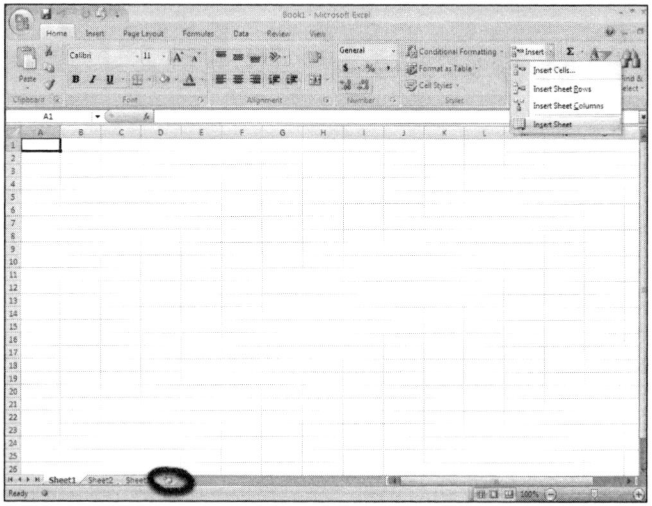

# Delete Worksheets

1. Choose Home⇨Cells⇨Delete⇨Delete Sheet. If any cells in the selected sheet have data in them, a warning message appears, as shown in Figure 8-2.

    A worksheet with no data in it will not display the warning message.

2. Click the Delete button.

    Use caution when deleting worksheets. The Undo feature does not work with the Delete Sheet function.

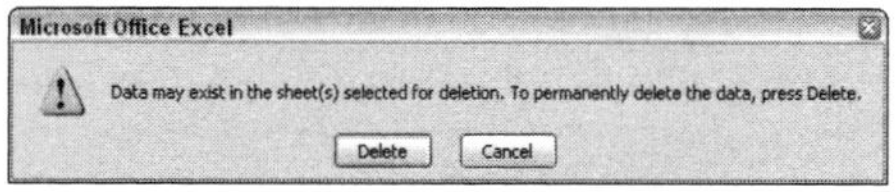

**Figure 8-1:** Inserting a new worksheet.

**Figure 8-2:** Delete an unwanted worksheet.

# Rename Worksheets

1. Click anywhere on the sheet you want to rename.

2. Choose Home⇨Cells⇨Format⇨Rename Sheet. The worksheet tab becomes highlighted. Leave it highlighted so that you can replace it with a new name.

3. Type a unique name for the worksheet, as shown in Figure 8-3. Remember that two worksheets in a single workbook cannot have the same exact name. Press Enter to accept the change.

 Be descriptive, but keep the name short. When you have lots of worksheets with long names, it can be more difficult to maneuver from one to the next.

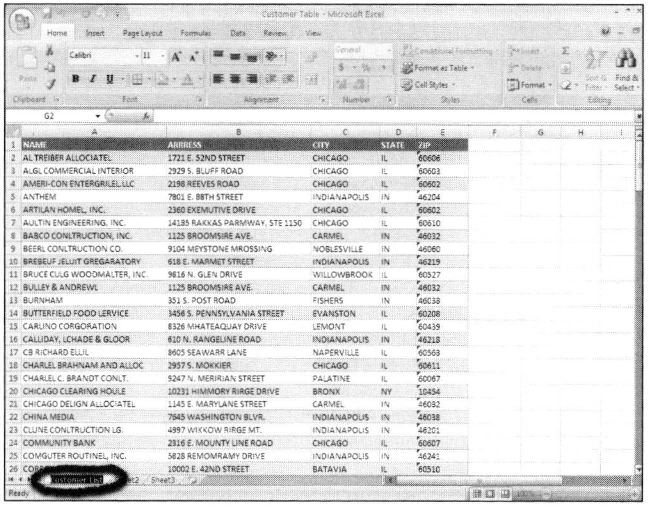

# Copy Worksheets

1. Click anywhere on the worksheet you want to duplicate.

2. Choose Home⇨Cells⇨Format⇨Move or Copy Sheet. The Move or Copy dialog box appears.

3. Check the Create a Copy box. (See Figure 8-4.)

4. Select where in the order of the worksheets you want the duplicate sheet placed.

5. Click OK. Excel duplicates the sheet and gives it the same name as the copied sheet, plus numbers it sequentially.

 To change the worksheet tab order, drag the worksheet tabs left or right.

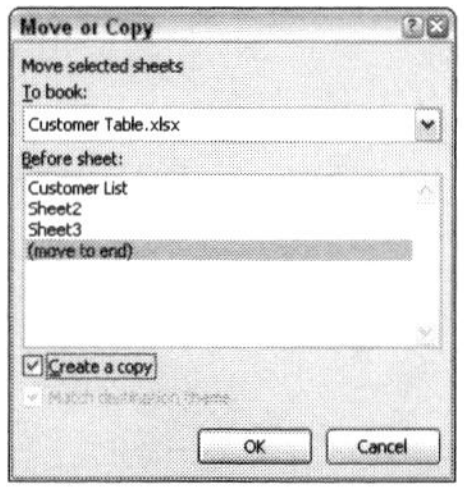

**Figure 8-3:** Rename a worksheet.

**Figure 8-4:** Duplicating a worksheet.

# *Move or Copy Worksheets to a Different Workbook*

1. Open the workbook to which you will move the worksheet.

2. Open the workbook that contains the worksheets you want to move.

3. Click anywhere on the worksheet you want to move. If you don't see the sheet you want, click the tab navigation buttons until you see it.

> If you want to move or copy multiple worksheets, hold down the Ctrl key and click additional tabs. If you want to move or copy all the existing worksheets to another workbook, right-click a sheet tab and choose Select All Sheets.

4. Choose Home➪Format➪Move or Copy Sheet. The Move or Copy dialog box opens.

5. Click the To Book drop-down list as in Figure 8-5 and select the workbook to which you want to move or copy the sheets.

6. If you want to duplicate the sheets to the other workbook, click the Create a Copy box.

7. Select where in the order of the existing worksheets you want the moved sheet placed.

8. Click OK. Excel moves or copies the worksheets to the other workbook. In Figure 8-6, the sheet named Customer List was moved from the Customer Table workbook to the Names and Address workbook.

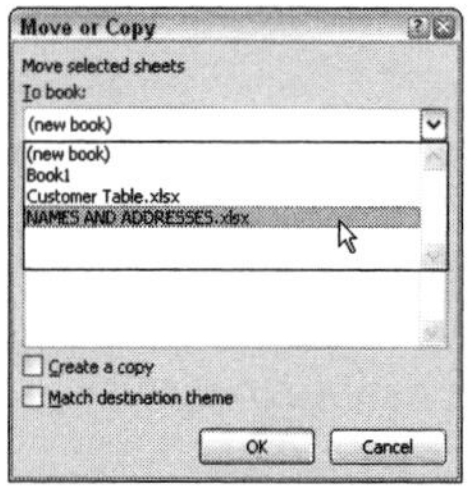

**Figure 8-5:** Select another workbook.

> If you chose to copy a sheet to another workbook in which a sheet has the same name, Excel keeps the same name but adds a sequential number to the end.

> You cannot copy or move a worksheet created in an Excel 2007 workbook to one created in an earlier version of Excel.

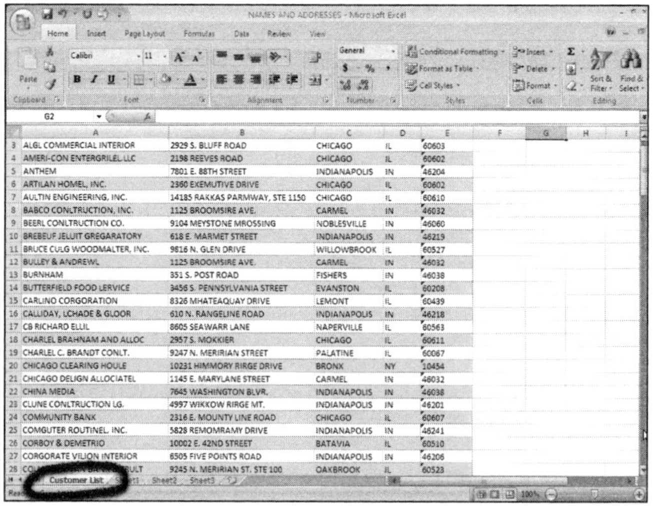

**Figure 8-6:** Move worksheets from one workbook to another.

# Hide and Unhide Worksheets

1. Click anywhere on the worksheet that you want to hide.

2. Choose Home⇨Cells⇨Format⇨Hide & Unhide⇨Hide Sheet. Excel hides the worksheet from view. All formula references to a hidden worksheet are still valid even when a worksheet is hidden.

 Optionally, right-click a worksheet tab and select Hide (or Unhide).

3. To unhide the worksheet, choose Choose Home⇨ Cells⇨Format⇨Hide & Unhide⇨Unhide Sheet. A dialog box, like the one in Figure 8-7, appears, listing all currently hidden worksheets in the active workbook.

4. Select the worksheet you want to unhide and click OK.

# Change Worksheet Tab Colors

1. To recolor the tab of a worksheet, click anywhere in that worksheet.

2. Choose Home⇨Cells⇨Format⇨Tab Color. The Tab Color gallery that you see in Figure 8-8 appears.

3. Select a color.

 Select No Color to remove a tab color.

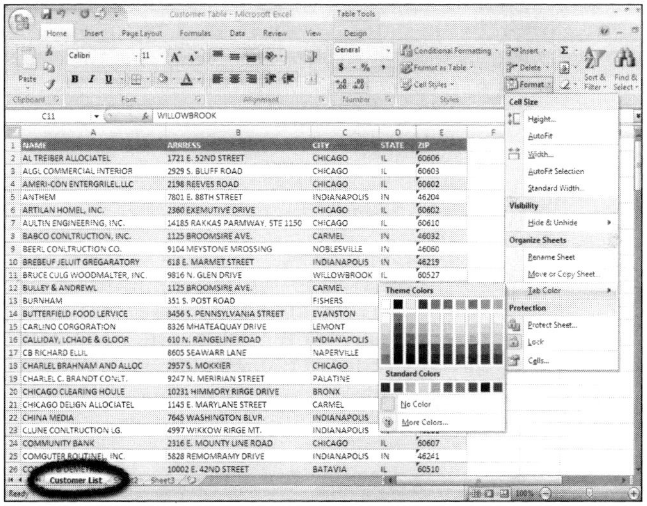

**Figure 8-7:** Select a worksheet to unhide.

 When a worksheet with a colored tab is the current worksheet, Excel does not display the tab color in full. It only displays a colored line under the tab name. The tab becomes full color when the worksheet is not the active one.

**Figure 8-8:** Make certain worksheets easy to locate by changing their tab colors.

# Generate References to Other Worksheets

1. Select the cell into which you want to enter a reference.

2. Perform one of the following actions:

   - To display a value located in another cell on the same worksheet, type the equal sign and then the cell address. For example, type **=B45**. If the value in B45 changes, the cell with the reference to B45 also changes.

   - To display a value located in a cell on a different worksheet but in the same workbook, type the equal sign. Next, click the worksheet tab containing the cell you want to reference and then click the actual cell you want to reference. Press the Enter key. Excel displays the equal sign, the worksheet name, an exclamation point, and the cell reference. (See Figure 8-9.)

   - To include a cell located on a different worksheet but in the same workbook in a formula, begin to type the formula. In the place where you want to position the distant cell reference, click the worksheet containing the cell and then click the actual cell. Follow this with the remainder of the formula. Figure 8-10 illustrates an example of a formula using a reference to a different worksheet.

   Formulas referencing other worksheets or other workbooks can also be compound formulas or used in a function.

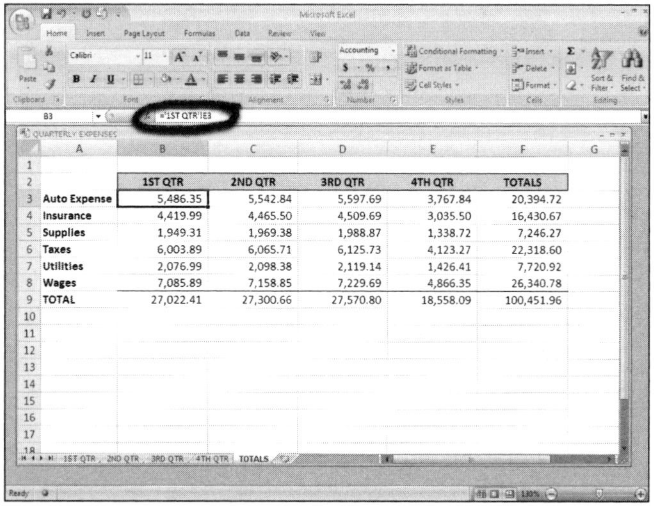

**Figure 8-9:** Creating a reference to another worksheet in the same workbook.

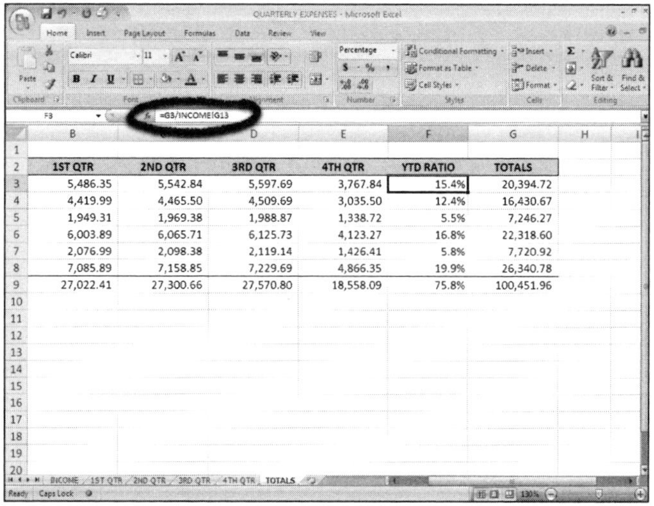

**Figure 8-10:** Including a reference in a formula.

# Cross-Reference Other Workbooks

1. Open the workbook to which you will refer. For simplicity sake, call this Workbook2.

2. Click the desired cell in the workbook where you want to create a reference. Call this Workbook1.

3. In Workbook1, begin the formula or reference with an equal sign.

4. If using a function or formula, enter any portion that you want to precede the cross reference.

5. Click the cell that you want to reference from Workbook2.

6. Finish the remainder of the formula or press the Enter key. Excel displays the equal sign, an apostrophe, and then the Workbook2 filename in brackets followed by the worksheet name, a closing apostrophe, an exclamation point, and then, the absolute cell reference. For example, *[Sales.xls]January'!$E$10* refers to the value in cell E10 of the sheet January in the Excel file named Sales. See Figure 8-11 for an example of a cross reference.

Excel uses absolute references (with dollar signs) when referring to other workbooks.

- When you open a workbook containing a cross reference, Excel displays a message such as the one shown in Figure 8-12, prompting you with a security alert so it can determine whether to update the cross-referenced cell. Click Enable Contents if you want Excel to check the originating workbook for changes to the referenced cell. You may see another confirmation message.

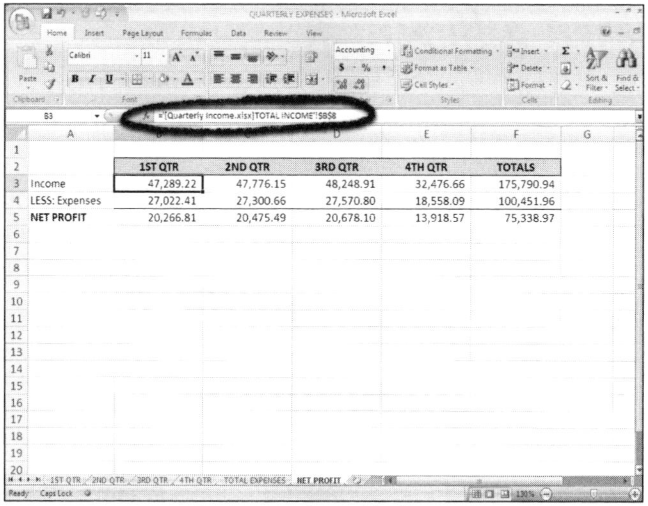

**Figure 8-11:** Create a reference to another workbook.

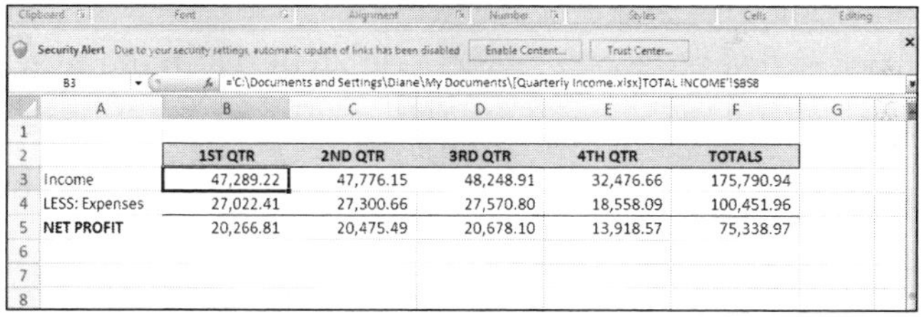

**Figure 8-12:** Updating a cross-referenced cell.

# Insert a Hyperlink

1. Select a cell or graphic object then choose Insert⇨ Links⇨Hyperlink. The Insert Hyperlink dialog box, shown in Figure 8-13, appears.

2. If you clicked a blank cell in Step 1, in the Text to Display box, you can type the text you want the cell to display. If you started with a cell already containing data or an object, you can change the displayed text.

3. Select an option:

   • If you want to link to a different file, locate and select the filename. When the user clicks the link, the referenced file will open.

   • If you want to link to a Web site, enter the Web address in the Address text box. When the user clicks the link, the Web browser opens to the referenced Web page.

   • If you want to link to a different cell in the current workbook, click the Place in This Document button, then specify which worksheet and cell location you want to reference. When the user clicks on this link, he or she is redirected to the specified cell address.

   • If you want to send an e-mail when the link is selected, click the E-mail Address button and then enter the recipient's e-mail address and a subject (Figure 8-14). When the user clicks the link, the user's e-mail program starts, as you also see in Figure 8-14.

4. Click OK.

**Figure 8-13:** Creating a Hyperlink.

 Click the ScreenTip button to enter text you want displayed, such as a prompt or hint that appears whenever the user pauses the mouse over the link.

 To remove a Hyperlink, right-click the link and select Remove Hyperlink.

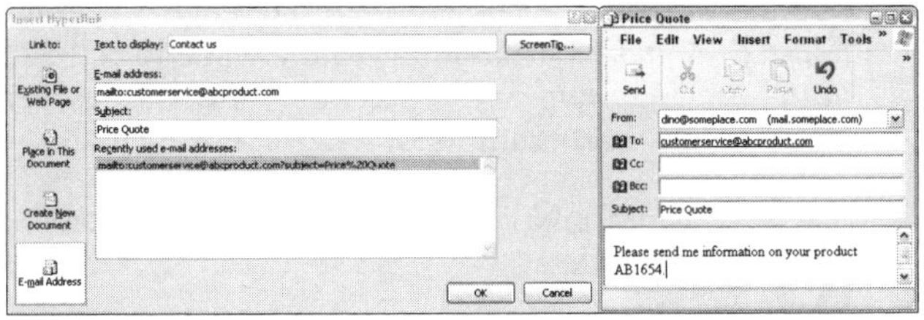

**Figure 8-14:** Create an e-mail via an Excel Hyperlink.

# Part III

# Viewing Data in Different Ways

The 5th Wave          By Rich Tennant

PROFIT
INCREASE
STRATEGY

"Look-what if we just increase the size of the charts?"

# Changing Worksheet Views

**S**omeone once wrote about the importance of seeing and being seen. Although I'm sure that quote referred to people, it also can apply to your Excel worksheets. You need to see them in many different contexts. That's what this chapter is about — seeing your workbook from different perspectives by using the following techniques:

➡ Viewing alternatives such as zooming in or out, displaying page breaks, or seeing the worksheet without the Ribbon and other screen elements.

➡ Splitting the screen to see multiple sections of a worksheet at the same time or viewing multiple worksheets together.

➡ Freezing portions of a worksheet so you can see category or row headings.

➡ Comparing two spreadsheets on the screen.

➡ Creating templates that can bring consistency, such as the company standards or personal preferences, to your workbooks.

➡ Monitoring specific cells for changes.

Go ahead, take a look!

## Get ready to . . .

# Zoom In or Out

1. Choose View⇨Zoom. The Zoom dialog box appears.

    Optionally, click the magnification box next to the Zoom controls. The magnification box and the Zoom controls are located on the status bar.

2. Select a magnification percentage from the Zoom dialog box as seen in Figure 9-1. A higher zoom setting makes the text appear larger so you see less on the screen; a lower setting shows more on the screen, but the data appears smaller. Zooming does not affect the printed data size. Click OK.

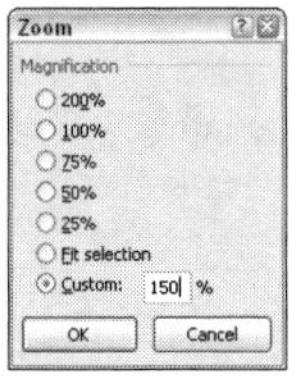

# Use the Zoom Controls

1. Click the Zoom In button on the Zoom Control. Excel increases the magnification percentage by 10% for each click of the Zoom In button. (See Figure 9-2.)

2. Click the Zoom Out button on the Zoom Control. Excel decreases the magnification percentage by 10% for each click of the Zoom Out button.

3. Click and drag the Zoom slider bar to the right. Excel increases magnification.

4. Click and drag the Zoom slider bar to the left. Excel decreases magnification.

**Figure 9-1:** Select a zoom percentage.

 Select the Custom option and enter your own setting from 10% to 400%.

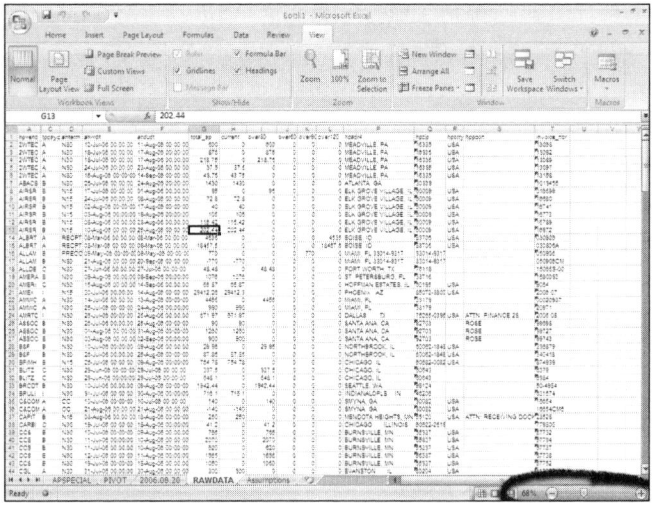

**Figure 9-2:** Using the Zoom Controls.

# Change Worksheet Views

1. Choose View➪Worksheet Views➪Page Layout View. As in Figure 9-3, the Page Layout view displays your worksheets on individual pages that correspond to printed pages. A ruler appears on the top and in the header and footer area. See Chapter 12 for more on headers and footers.

2. Choose View➪Worksheet Views➪Normal. Excel returns to the default Normal view, which shows one continuous page of columns and rows.

3. Choose View➪Worksheet Views➪Page Break Preview. A Welcome to Page Break Preview dialog box appears.

4. Click OK. The Excel mode changes to Page Break Preview, where Excel indicates page breaks with lines. (See Figure 9-4.) You can click and drag these lines to modify where pages break. See Chapter 12 for more on using page breaks.

5. Choose View➪Worksheet Views➪Full Screen. You see only the worksheet itself with its row and column headings, worksheet tabs, and the title bar. The Ribbon, Quick Access toolbar, and the Status bar are hidden.

6. Press the Escape key. Excel returns to Normal view.

 On the Status bar, next to the Zoom Controls, you find three icons you can use to quickly switch among the Normal, Page Layout View, and Page Break Preview modes.

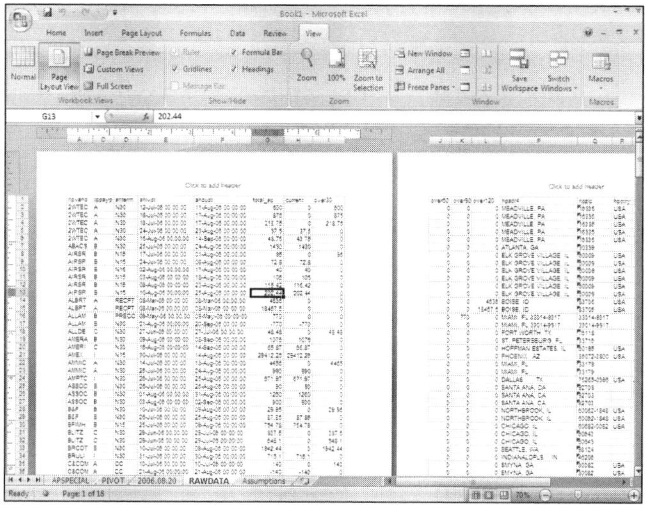

**Figure 9-3:** Page Layout View.

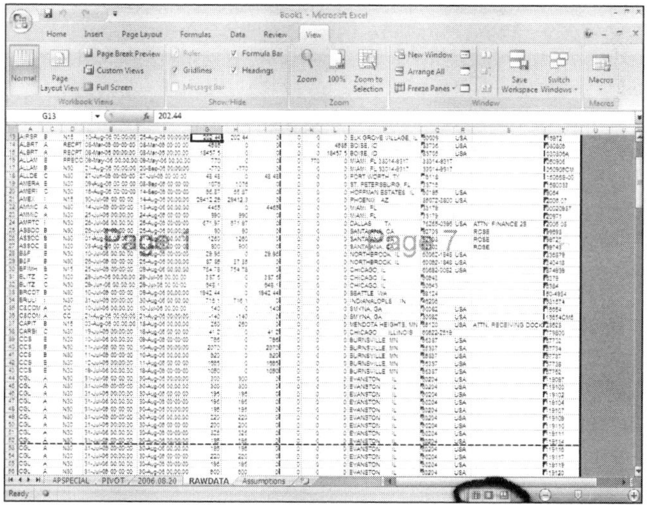

**Figure 9-4:** Page Break Preview.

# Freeze Worksheet Titles

*1.* Choose what you want to freeze:

- **Columns:** Select the column to the right of the columns you want to freeze. For example, click cell B1 to freeze only column A.

- **Rows:** Select the row below the rows you want to freeze. For example, click cell A4 to freeze rows 1, 2, and 3.

- **Columns and rows:** Click the cell below the rows and to the right of the columns you want to freeze. For example, click cell B2 to freeze both column A and row 1 (as shown in Figure 9-5).

 Freezing panes only affects the current worksheet. If you want to freeze other worksheets, you must select them individually and freeze them.

*2.* Choose View⇨Window⇨Freeze Panes⇨Freeze Panes. A thin black line appears to separate the sections. As you see in Figure 9-6, as you scroll down and to the left, row 1 and column A remain visible even though you see rows 190 through 218 in the bottom section and columns F through M on the right.

 Normally when you press the Ctrl+Home key, Excel takes you to cell A1. However, when Freeze Panes is active, pressing Ctrl+Home takes you to the cell just below and to the left of the column headings. However, you can still use your arrow keys or click your mouse to access any cell.

*3.* Choose View⇨Window⇨Freeze Panes⇨Unfreeze Panes to remove the freeze from row and column headings.

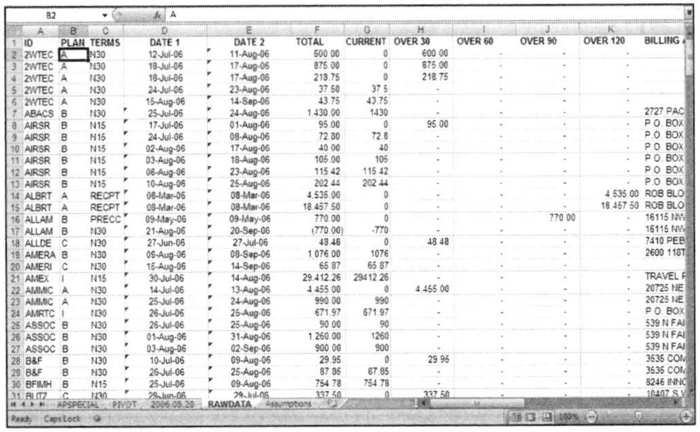

**Figure 9-5:** Cells above and to the left of the current cell will be frozen.

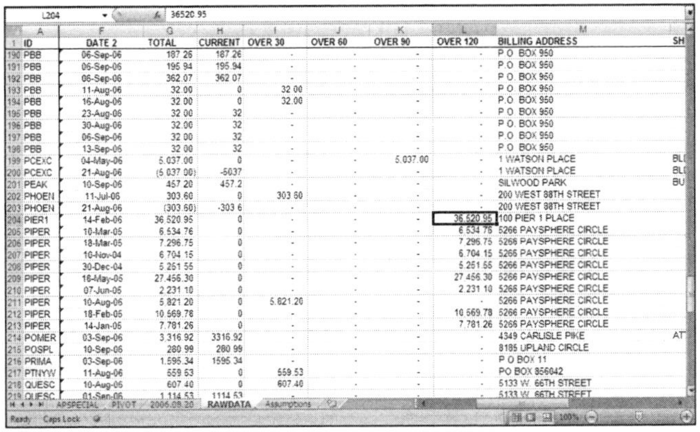

**Figure 9-6:** Keep titles visible by freezing the panes.

# Split the Excel Screen

1. Click anywhere in a row and column where you want to split your screen. This is usually somewhere around the middle of the screen.

2. Choose View➪Window➪Split. Excel splits the window horizontally into two or four panes each separated from other panes by bars. Each pane has its own set of scroll bars (see Figure 9-7).

3. Drag the horizontal split bar up or down or the vertical split bar left or right to resize the window sections.

 Optionally, double-click any part of the bars that divide the panes to remove that particular split.

4. Choose View➪Window➪Split again to remove the split.

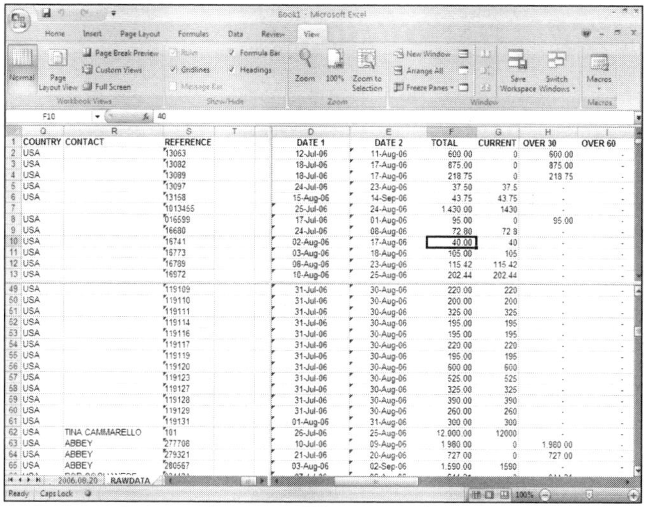

# Arrange Windows

1. Open two or more workbooks.

2. Choose View➪Window➪Arrange. The Arrange Windows dialog box, shown in Figure 9-8, appears.

3. Make a selection:

   - **Tiled** arranges the open workbook windows so they do not overlap each other.

   - **Horizontal** places the open workbook windows horizontally on top of each other.

   - **Vertical** lays the open workbook windows side by side.

   - **Cascade** arranges the windows so that they overlap each other, keeping the title bar visible.

4. Click OK.

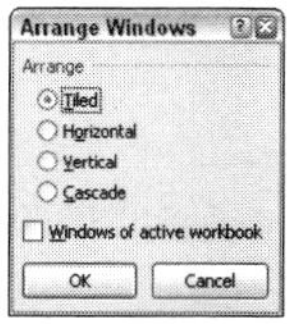

**Figure 9-7:** Splitting a window to view different areas of the worksheet simultaneously.

**Figure 9-8:** Arranging to see multiple worksheets.

 Maximize the workbook to return it to a larger size.

# Compare Worksheets

1. Open two workbooks.

2. Choose View⇨Window⇨View Side by Side. The two workbooks are split horizontally on the screen as shown in Figure 9-9.

3. Scroll down or across a worksheet. Notice the other worksheet scrolls simultaneously.

4. Choose View⇨Window⇨Synchronous Scrolling to turn off the option to scroll the worksheets independently.

5. Choose View⇨Window⇨Reset Window Position, if you want to reset the workbook windows to the positions they were in when you first started comparing workbooks.

6. Choose View⇨Window⇨View Side by Side to return the windows to Normal mode.

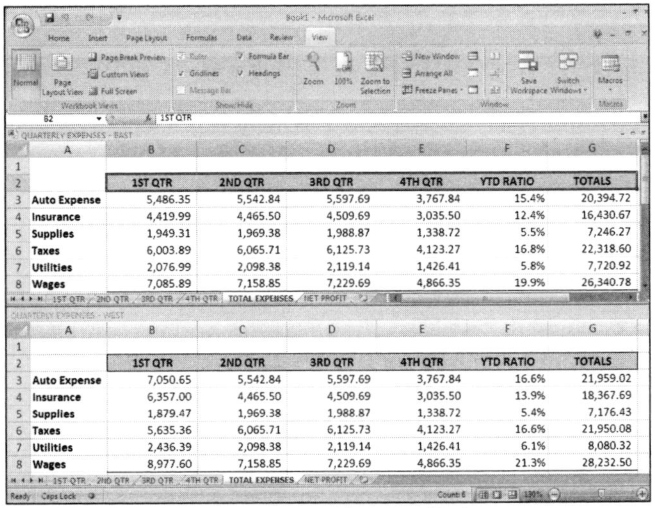

# Save as a Template

1. Create an Excel workbook. Templates can store formatting, worksheet layouts, data, formulas, and much more.

2. Choose Office Button⇨Save As. The Save As dialog box appears.

3. Type a name for the template in the File Name text box.

4. Choose Template from the Save As Type drop-down list. Excel automatically saves the template in the default template location (see Figure 9-10). Click Save and close the workbook.

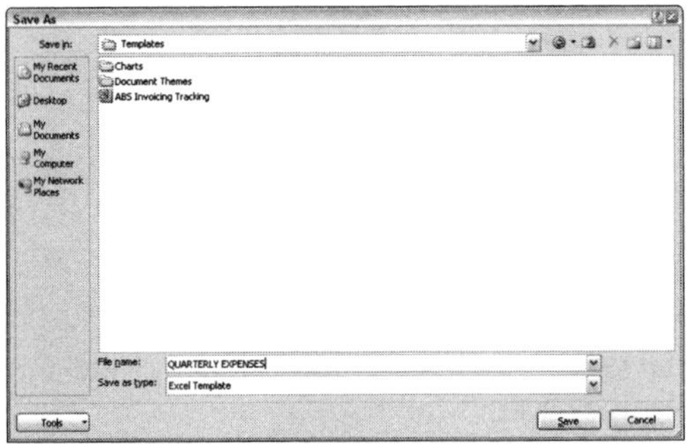

**Figure 9-9:** Comparing data between two different workbooks.

**Figure 9-10:** Saving a template.

## Open a Template

1. Choose Office Button⇨New. The New Workbook dialog box opens.

Using the Ctrl+N shortcut doesn't work here. It automatically creates a new standard blank worksheet, not one from a specially saved template.

Click any category in the Microsoft Office Online area to view a great collection of mostly free templates.

2. Click My Templates.

3. Click Create. The New dialog box displaying your customized templates appears. (See Figure 9-11.)

4. Select the template you want to use.

5. Click OK.

## Create a Workbook from an Existing File

1. Choose Office Button⇨New. The New dialog box opens.

2. Click New from Existing.

3. Click Create. The New from Existing Workbook dialog box. shown in Figure 9-12, appears.

4. Locate and click the workbook you want to open.

5. Click Create New. Excel opens a copy of the workbook. The filename in the title bar shows the same name as the original with a number after it.

**Figure 9-11:** Create a new file based on a template.

**Figure 9-12:** Use an existing file as a template.

When you choose to save the workbook, the Save As dialog box automatically opens, prompting you for a filename.

# Monitor Cells in the Watch Window

1. Choose Formulas⇨Formula Auditing⇨Watch Window. The Watch Window opens.

2. Click Add Watch. The Add Watch dialog box in Figure 9-13 appears.

3. Select the cell or cells you want to watch or manually type the cell reference address.

4. Click Add. Excel adds the cells to the Watch Window, including any values or formulas within the cells. If you scroll away from the original cells, the Watch Window always displays the cell contents. (See Figure 9-14.)

5. Repeat Steps 2 through 4 to add another watch area to the Watch Window. You can add watches with cells on the same worksheet, a different worksheet, or a different open workbook.

6. As necessary, perform the following actions:

   - To remove a cell from the Watch Window, click the cell name and then click Delete Watch. Excel immediately removes the cell from the window.

   - To move the Watch Window, click and drag the window's title bar anywhere on-screen.

   - To resize the columns within the Watch Window, position the mouse pointer over a column in the Watch Window and drag to resize the column.

7. When finished, click the Watch Window's Close button.

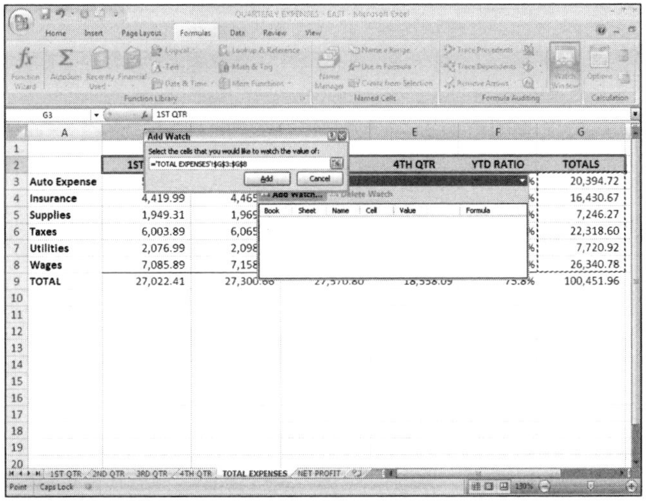

**Figure 9-13:** Add an area you want to watch.

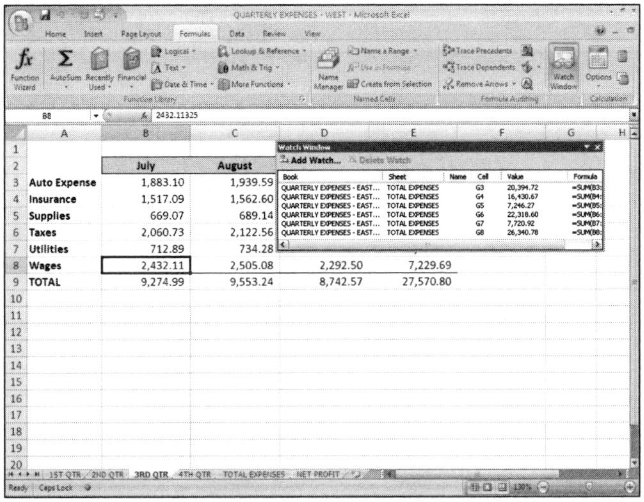

**Figure 9-14:** The Watch Window stays active no matter what area of the workbook you are using.

# Sorting Data

Sometimes worksheets become quite large, making locating particular pieces of information time-consuming and difficult. If your data is in an array, you may find the data easier to view if it is sorted in a particular manner.

Perhaps you have multiple worksheets, and you want to locate every occurrence of a specific value. Or, maybe you're just a neat freak and want everything to be in a particular order. Excel contains features to help your arrange your worksheets in an easy-to-manage sequence.

In this chapter, you discover how to:

➠ Sort your data in ascending or descending order using either the toolbar or the Excel Sort dialog box.

➠ Perform a secondary sort if the primary sort has multiple matches.

➠ Sort data containing days of the week or month names.

➠ Create a customized list of frequently used names or terms.

➠ Locate cells containing data you specify, whether the data is part of a formula or a resulting cell value.

➠ Quickly replace data containing certain information with another specified set of data.

➠ Locate all cells with a particular style of formatting and easily replace them with a different format.

## Chapter 10

### Get ready to . . .

# Use the Toolbar to Sort

1. For the easiest sorting, create a list in contiguous order and with headings specifying the contents of each column. Figure 10-1 illustrates an ideal data array.

2. In the column you want to sort by, click any cell containing data.

 If the data is in a connected list, you do not have to select it first. If it's not, you must first select the entire list. If Excel finds unselected data in columns next to the selected data, it may prompt you for more information.

3. Choose Data⇨Sort & Filter⇨Sort A to Z. (If the current cell contains a value, the button says Sort Smallest to Largest.) Excel sorts the entire list in ascending order.

 Sorting text data in ascending order sorts text A-Z; sorting numeric information in ascending order sorts low to high (1-10); and sorting dates in ascending order places the earliest date first.

 Excel sorts in the following pattern: numbers, spaces, special characters which are ! " # $ % & ( ) * , . / : ; ? @ [ \ ] ^ _ ` { | } ~ + < = > and, finally, alphabetic letters.

4. Choose Data⇨Sort & Filter⇨ Sort Z to A (or Largest to Smallest). Excel sorts the entire list by descending order. Figure 10-2 shows the Name column sorted in descending order (from highest to lowest).

 If Excel incorrectly sorts a cell that contains a value, make sure the cell is formatted as a number and not as text.

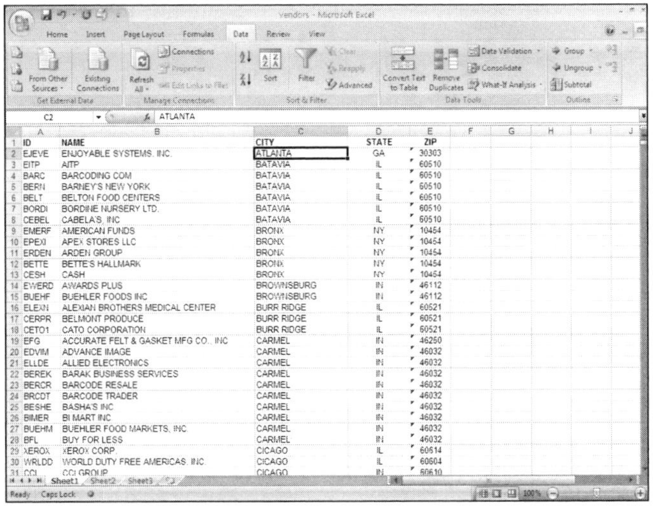

**Figure 10-1:** Data for sorting.

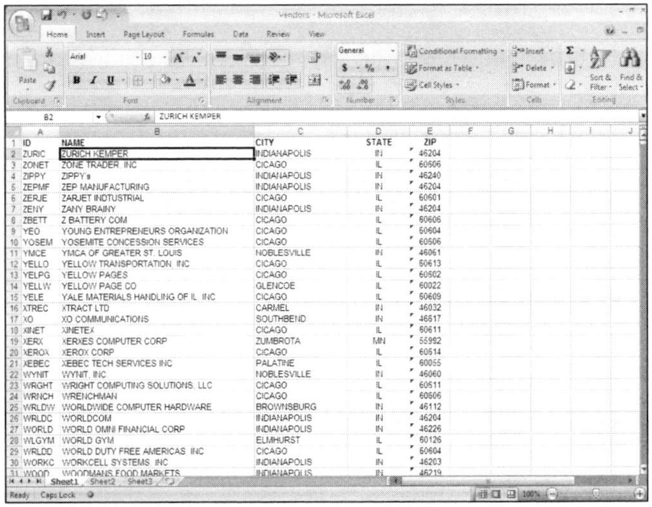

**Figure 10-2:** A sorted data array.

Sorting text data in descending order sorts text Z-A; sorting numeric information in descending order sorts high to low (10-1); and sorting dates in descending order places the latest date first.

# Work with the Sort Command

*1.* Select or click in the list of data you want to sort.

 Select only a single column of data if you want to sort that column independently of the rest of the data.

*2.* Choose Data⇨Sort & Filter⇨ Sort. The Sort dialog box opens. (See Figure 10-3.)

*3.* If your data includes column headings, make sure the My Data Has Headers option is checked. If the data doesn't include column headings, deselect the option.

 Excel does not include header rows in the sort process.

*4.* From the Sort By drop-down list, select the column by which you want to sort. (See Figure 10-4.)

*5.* From the Sort On drop-down list, choose Values. (I discuss the other options later in this chapter.)

*6.* From the Order drop-down list, select how you want to sort the data:

- Choose A to Z or Z to A to sort text values.

- Choose Smallest to Largest or Largest to Smallest to sort numeric data.

- Choose Oldest to Newest or Newest to Oldest to sort by dates.

*7.* Click OK.

**Figure 10-3:** The Sort dialog box.

**Figure 10-4:** Select the sort column.

 Click the Options button if you want to make the sorting case-sensitive (noncapitalized words before capitals).

Excel sorts data in the following order: numbers, special characters, and finally alphabetic characters. Blanks are always placed last.

# Sort by Multiple Criteria

1. Select or click in the list of data you want to sort.

2. Choose Data⇨Sort & Filter⇨ Sort. The Sort dialog box opens.

3. If your data includes column headings, make sure the My Data Has Headers option is checked. If the data doesn't include column headings, deselect the option.

    Although the most common sort is by rows (top to bottom), you can also sort by columns (left to right). In the Sort dialog box, click the Options button and then, under the Orientation section, choose Sort left to right. Finally, click OK.

4. Set up the primary sort criteria as in the previous section.

    Excel sorts dates formatted with slashes such as 11/22/68, as numeric data. Dates with the day or month spelled out must be sorted differently. See the later section, "Sort by Day, Month, or Custom List."

5. Click the Add Level button.

6. In the Then By section, select the secondary column you want to sort by if two or more items are identical in the first Sort By option. See Figure 10-5.

7. Select how you want to sort the second data criteria. Repeat as needed.

    To delete an entry, select the sort entry and choose Delete Level. You must keep at least one sort entry in the list.

8. Click OK. Excel performs the sort process. Figure 10-6 illustrates data rows sorted first by State and then by City.

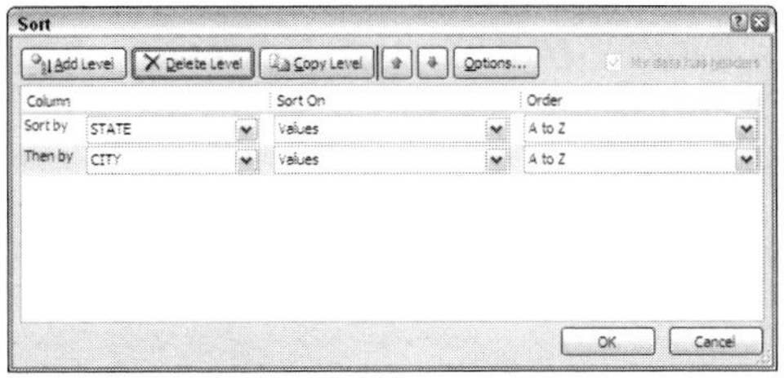

**Figure 10-5:** Select a second sort criteria.

During an Excel sort, apostrophes (') and hyphens (-) are ignored, unless two text strings are the same except for a hyphen. In that situation, the text with the hyphen is sorted as the latter.

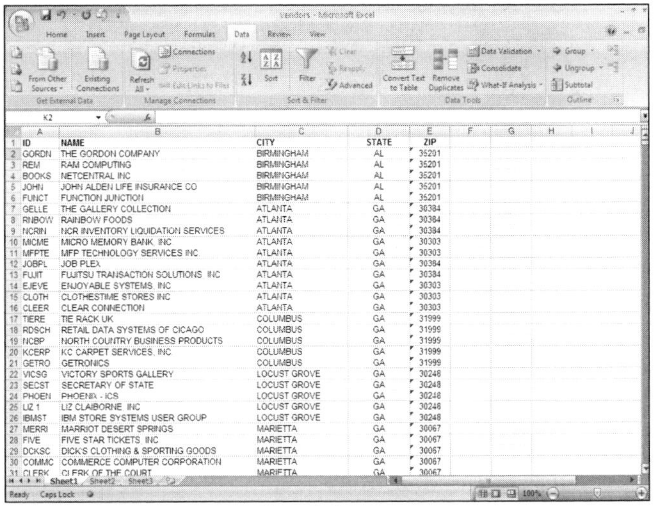

**Figure 10-6:** A data array sorted by multiple criteria.

# Create a Customized List

**1.** Choose Office⇨Excel Options. The Excel Options dialog box appears.

**2.** Choose Personalize

**3.** Click Edit Custom Lists. The Options dialog box opens. Excel provides two ways to create a custom list:

 A custom list can contain text or text mixed with numbers. Use custom lists to speed up data entry for commonly used terms such as sales people, regions, or products.

- To create a list from items you have already entered into the worksheet, click the worksheet icon next to the Import button. The Options dialog box collapses. Highlight the worksheet cells containing your list and then press Enter. The Options dialog box reappears. Click the Import button. The data you selected appears in both the List Entries box and the Custom Lists box (see Figure 10-7).

- To type your own list without entering it into the worksheet first, click New List from the Custom Lists section. Type your list in the List Entries text box as you see in Figure 10-8, separating each list item with a comma, and then click the Add button.

**4.** Click OK twice.

 You can now use the AutoFill feature with the custom list by typing one list entry and using AutoFill to enter the other list entries. See Chapter 2.

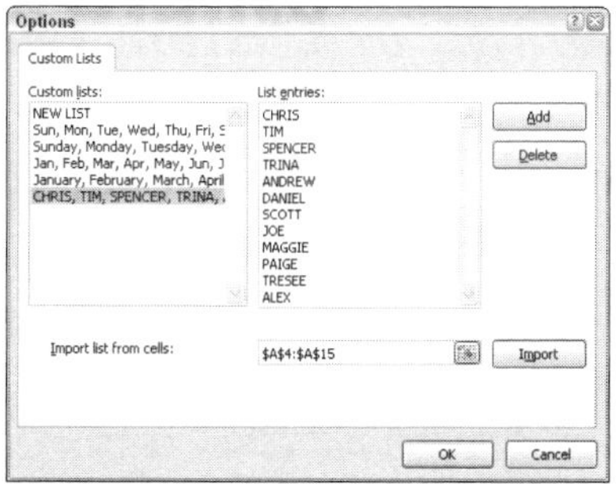

**Figure 10-7:** Create your own custom lists from data in your worksheet.

 To edit a custom list, from the Custom Lists tab select the list that you want to edit. Make any changes in the List entries box and then click Add. To delete a customized list, select the list and then click Delete. You cannot edit or delete the Excel-provided fill series such as months and days.

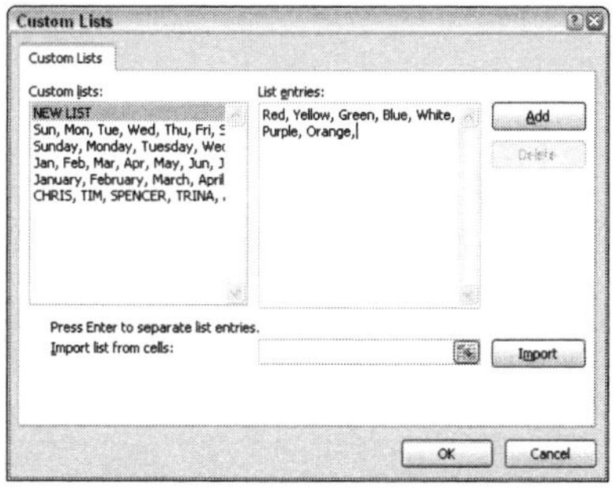

**Figure 10-8:** Manually create a customized list.

# Sort by Day, Month, or Custom List

1.  Select or click in the list of data you want to sort.

2.  Choose Data⇨Sort & Filter⇨ Sort. The Sort dialog box opens.

3.  If your data includes column headings, make sure the My Data Has headers option is checked. If the data doesn't include column headings, deselect the option.

4.  Select your first sort criteria field.

5.  From the order drop-down list, select Custom List. The Custom List dialog box appears.

6.  Select the Custom List (see Figure 10-9) you want to sort by.

7.  Click OK. The Sort dialog box reappears.

8.  Set up any secondary or additional sort criteria. Click OK.

# Remove Duplicate Records

1.  Select or click in the list of data you want to work with.

2.  Choose Data⇨Data Tools⇨Remove Duplicates. The Remove Duplicates dialog box appears. (See Figure 10-10.)

3.  Check or uncheck the columns you want Excel to examine.

4.  Click OK. Excel looks for and removes duplicates. A message tells you how many duplicates were removed (if any) and how many unique values remain.

5.  Click OK.

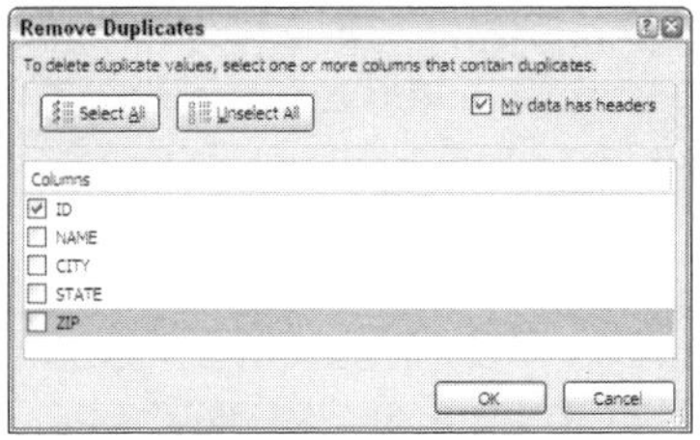

**Figure 10-9:** Sorting by weekday.

 By default, Excel sorts days and months alphabetically, not by date.

**Figure 10-10:** Let Excel find the duplicates for you.

# *Sort by Cell Format*

1. Select or click in the list of data you want to sort.

 Sorting by cell format is helpful when you have specified conditional formatting conditions. It can sort all items meeting your conditions to the top or bottom of the data table.

2. Choose Data⇨Sort & Filter⇨Sort. The Sort dialog box opens.

3. If your data includes column headings, make sure the My Data Has Headers option is checked. If the data doesn't include column headings, deselect the option.

4. Select your first sort criteria field.

5. In the Sort On drop-down list, select one of the following:
   - **Cell Color:** Choosing this option sorts the cells based on the cell background formatting.
   - **Font Color:** Choosing this option sorts the cells based on the font color of the cell contents, regardless of background formatting.

6. Click the Order drop-down list. Several options, including Automatic and each color you used in your selected field, appear.

7. Select the cell color or font color you want to sort by.

8. Choose whether you want the formatted cells to appear at the top of the data range or at the bottom of the data range. (See Figure 10-11.)

9. Add any additional sort criteria.

10. Click OK. In Figure 10-12 you see the data sorted with the formatted cells at the top.

**Figure 10-11:** Sort by formatting.

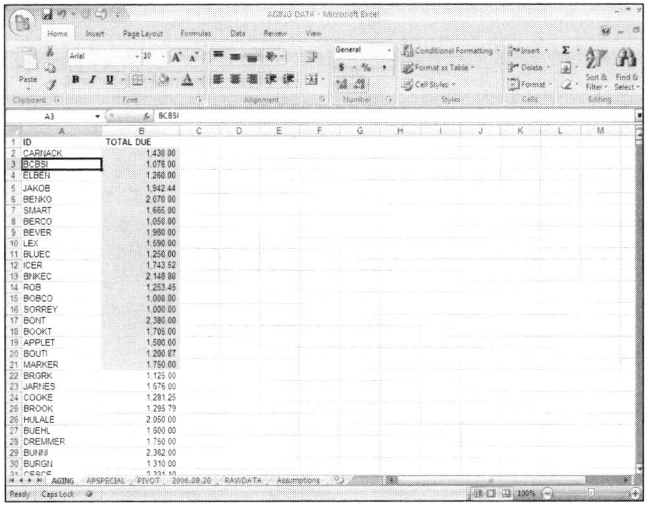

**Figure 10-12:** Data sorted by formatting.

# Search for Data

1. Choose Home➪Editing➪Find & Select➪Find. The Find and Replace dialog box appears.

2. In the Find What box, enter the value or word you want to locate.

3. Click the Options button and specify any desired options. (See Figure 10-13.)

   - **Within:** Search just the current worksheet or the entire workbook.

   - **Search:** Select whether to search first across the rows or down the columns.

   - **Look In:** Select whether you want to search through the values or formula results, through the actual formulas, or if you want to look in the comments.

   - **Match Case:** Check this box if you want your search to be case-specific (for example, **BOBCAT** instead of **BobCat** or **Bobcat**).

   - **Match Entire Cell Contents:** Check this box if you want your search results to list only the items that exactly match your search criteria.

4. Click Find Next. Excel jumps to the first occurrence of the match (see Figure 10-14). If this is not the entry you are looking for, click Find Next again. Excel advises you if it does not locate the data you are searching for.

5. Click Close when you have located the entry you want.

**Figure 10-13:** The Find and Replace dialog box.

**Figure 10-14:** Excel finds data based on search specifications.

 Select Formulas when you are looking for a formula that references a specific cell address.

# *Find All Data Occurrences*

1. Choose Home⇨Editing⇨Find & Select⇨Find. The Find and Replace dialog box appears.

2. In the Find What box, enter the value or word you want to locate.

3. Click Options and specify any desired options.

4. Click Find All. The Find and Replace dialog box expands, showing a list of each cell entry that contains your data (see Figure 10-15).

# *Locate Cells Based on Format*

1. Choose Home⇨Editing⇨Find & Select⇨Find. The Find and Replace dialog box appears.

2. Click Options. Verify that these options are the ones you want to use.

3. Click Format. The Find Format dialog box, shown in Figure 10-16, appears.

4. Select any formatting options on which you want to search. You can choose any combination of options.

5. Click OK. A preview of the formatting appears in the Preview box.

6. In the Find What box, enter the value or word you want to locate. Leave this blank if you want to locate only cells with the specified formatting, regardless of the cell contents.

7. Click the Find or the Find All button. Then click Close.

**Figure 10-15:** Find All results.

**Figure 10-16:** Find cells based on Format options.

# Use the Replace Command

1. Choose Home➪Editing➪Find & Select➪Find. The Find and Replace dialog box appears with the Replace tab on top. (See Figure 10-17.)

    If you want to replace data in only certain cells, rows, or columns, select the desired area before you open the Find and Replace dialog box.

2. In the Find What box, enter the data you want to locate.

3. In the Replace With box, enter the data with which you want to replace the found data.

4. Click Find Next to locate the first found occasion or click Find All to display a list of all occurrences.

    You can sort the results of a Find All search by clicking a column heading.

5. If you want to use the replacement data, click Replace. Excel performs the replacement and locates the next occurrence.

6. If you want to replace all occurrences at the same time, click Replace All. Excel displays an information box, like the one in Figure 10-18, indicating the number of replacements made.

7. Click OK.

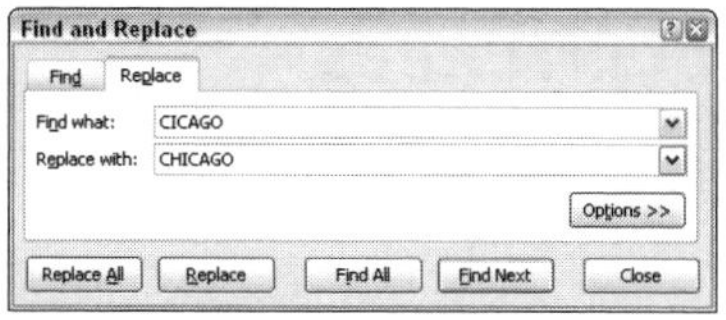

**Figure 10-17:** Exchange data with the Find and Replace feature.

**Figure 10-18:** Making global replacements.

 If you want to look for data that also has specific formatting, click the Format button and match the formatting you are searching for.

 Just as with the Find data, you can specify that the replacement data must have specific formatting.

# Creating Charts

# Chapter 11

*W*hoever said a picture is worth a thousand words is most certainly referring to a chart. Let's face it. . . we *like* looking at pictures more than we like looking at sheets of data. Charts, sometimes referred to as *graphs*, provide an effective way to illustrate your worksheet data by making the relationships between numbers easier to see. The chart turns numbers into shapes and enables you to compare the shapes to each other.

If you've ever spent hours drawing a chart on graph paper, you'll really appreciate the ease with which you can create dozens of different chart styles using your Excel data. And you don't really have to draw a thing! With just a few decisions on your part and a few clicks of the mouse, you have a two- or three-dimensional illustration of your data.

Charts let you get your thoughts across with simplicity and strength and, because different charts may cause you to draw varied conclusions, they also prod you to ask questions about what you are seeing. Whatever the idea you are trying to convey, charts make it easier.

In this chapter, discover how to

➠ Quickly and easily create a chart

➠ Modify a chart whether in appearance or content

➠ Work with a three-dimensional chart

## Get ready to . . .

# Create a Basic Chart

1. Select the data (sequential or nonsequential) you want to plot in the chart. See Figure 11-1 for an example of sequential data selected for a chart.

2. Press the F11 key. Excel immediately adds a new sheet called Chart1 to your workbook with the data plotted into a column chart. Each subsequent chart page is numbered sequentially such as Chart2, Chart3, and so forth. Figure 11-2 shows you the various elements that can make up a chart.

 Some newer keyboards use a different function for the F11 key. If your F11 key does not produce a chart, use the Insert tab as explained in the next section.

 Throughout this chapter you learn how to edit the look and style of a chart.

- **Title:** A descriptive name for the overall chart. By default, titles are not added in a basic chart, but you can add them later manually or by using the Chart Wizard.

- **X or Category axis:** Column or row headings from your selected data, which Excel uses for Category axis names. In a column chart, the categories display along the bottom. In other charts (such as a bar chart), the category axis displays along the left side.

- **X Axis Title:** A descriptive name for the Category axis. By default, a category label is not added in a basic chart, but you can add one later manually or with the Chart Wizard.

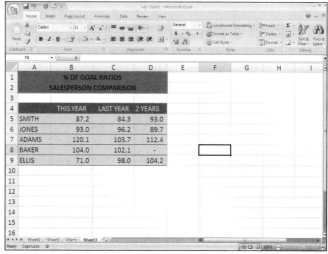

**Figure 11-1:** Select data for a chart.

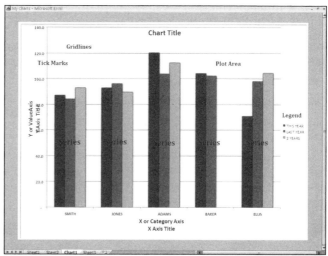

**Figure 11-2:** Viewing chart basics.

- **Y or Value axis:** A scale representing the zero or the lowest and highest numbers in the plotted data. The Value axis is usually located on the left side on a column chart or on the bottom on a bar chart.

- **Y Axis Title:** A descriptive name for the values. By default, a value label is not added in a basic chart, but you can add one later manually or by using the Chart Wizard.

- **Legend:** The box, usually located on the right, identifies the patterns or colors that are assigned to the chart data series. Notice in Figure 11-3 how the legend explains that one shade of color represents January, another shade is for February, and the third color shade is for March.

- **Tick marks:** The small extensions of lines that appear outside of the gray area and represent divisions of the value or category axis.

- **Gridlines:** These lines extend from the tick marks across the chart area to allow you to easily view and evaluate data.

- **Series:** Excel uses the worksheet cell values to generate the series. Each element, called a *data marker*, represents a single worksheet cell value. Related data markers make up a data series and have the same pattern or color. In Figure 11-4, you can see the comparison of the data values to the y-axis and the series values.

- **Plot area:** The background that represents the entire plotted chart area.

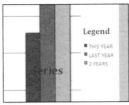

**Figure 11-3:** A chart legend.

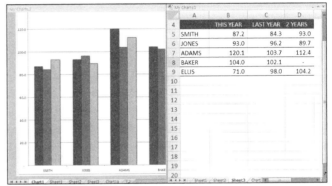

**Figure 11-4:** Data displayed in a data series.

| | A | B | C | D |
|---|---|---|---|---|
| 4 | | THIS YEAR | LAST YEAR | 2 YEARS |
| 5 | SMITH | 87.2 | 84.3 | 93.0 |
| 6 | JONES | 93.0 | 96.2 | 89.7 |
| 7 | ADAMS | 120.1 | 103.7 | 112.4 |
| 8 | BAKER | 104.0 | 102.1 | - |
| 9 | ELLIS | 71.0 | 98.0 | 104.2 |

To delete this chart, right-click the Chart tab and select Delete. When Excel asks for a confirmation, click Delete again.

# *Insert a Chart*

**1.** Select the data you want to plot in the chart.

 Typically, if you are selecting values such as monthly figures, you don't want to include totals in your chart.

**2.** Choose Insert⮕Charts, and then select the arrow beneath the chart style you want: Excel can create many different chart types; each compares data in a different manner. (See Figure 11-5.) Some of the most commonly used chart types include the following:

- **Column:** Column charts compare values to categories using a series of vertical columns to illustrate the series.

- **Bar:** Bar charts, like column charts, compare values to categories, but use a series of horizontal bars to illustrate the series.

- **Line:** Line charts are similar to bar charts but use dots to represent the data points and lines to connect the data points.

- **Pie:** This chart compares parts to a whole. Usually a pie chart only has one data series. Figure 11-6 illustrates data appropriate for a pie chart.

- **Area:** Area charts display the trend of each value, usually over a specified period of time.

- **X-Y Scatter:** These charts include two value axes, one showing a set of numerical data along the x-axis and the other showing data along the y-axis.

**Figure 11-5:** Select the chart type appropriate for your data.

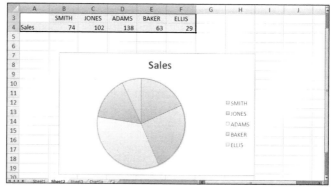

**Figure 11-6:** Create a pie chart from this data.

 Click a chart type to see a sample and an explanation of the chart.

- **Surface:** Shows trends in values in a continuous curve.

- **Doughnut:** Displays data similarly to a pie chart; it compares parts to a whole, but contains multiple series.

- **Stock**: Stock charts are usually (but not exclusively) used to illustrate the fluctuation of stock prices. In a stock chart, the data order is very important and usually the row headings are High, Low, and Close; or Open, High, Low, and Close. See Figure 11-7 for an example of a stock chart.

- **Radar:** Displays changes in values relative to a center point by comparing the cumulative values of multiple data series.

- **Bubble:** These charts are similar to scatter charts, but compare three sets of values by displaying a series of circles.

- **Cylinder, Cone, and Pyramid**: Excel uses these three chart types to create a column or bar chart using three-dimensional cylindrical, conical, or pyramid shapes.

3. Choose a chart subtype. Depending on the chart type, some chart subtypes show the data series next to each other; others show the data elements stacked on top of each other. Some charts are two-dimensional, and others are three-dimensional. As you see in Figure 11-8, Excel creates the chart on the worksheet where your data resides.

 You'll soon discover how you can change the chart location to its own sheet. But just in case you don't like your changes, make sure to save your worksheet, which also saves your chart, before modifying chart attributes.

**Figure 11-7:** A stock chart and its data.

 The chart is a graphic object. See Chapter 7 to revisit how to resize or delete it.

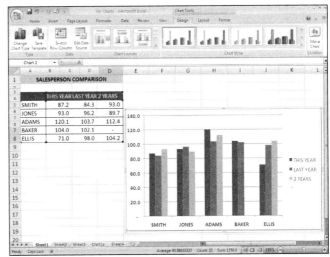

**Figure 11-8:** Creating an Excel chart.

# Change the Chart Type

1. Click the chart to select it, whether it appears on its own sheet or on a data worksheet. A Chart Tools tab with three subtabs appears.

2. Choose Chart Tools Design⇨Type⇨Change Chart Type. The Change Chart type dialog box appears.

3. Select the different chart type and subtype you want. (See Figure 11-9.)

4. Click OK. Excel modifies the existing chart.

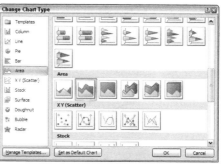

**Figure 11-9:** Select a different chart type or subtype.

# Adjust the Chart Location

1. Click anywhere on the chart that you want to move.

2. On the Design tab, choose Location⇨Move Chart. The Move Chart dialog box appears. (See Figure 11-10.)

3. Select a location:

   • **New sheet**: Creates a new worksheet and places the chart on the sheet.

   • **Object in**: Moves the chart to an existing sheet in the workbook. Click the drop-down arrow to select the worksheet to which you want to move the chart.

4. Click OK. Your chart is moved to the location you've specified.

**Figure 11-10:** Switch a chart from one location to the other.

To move the chart to a different location on the current worksheet, position the mouse over the edge of the chart and drag it to a new location.

# Display a Chart Title

1. Click anywhere on the chart you want to modify.

2. Click Chart Tools Layout⇨Labels⇨Chart Title. A list of options appears:

   - **None**: The default choice; it means you don't want to display a title. Also use this option to remove a chart title you don't want.

   - **Centered Overlay Title**: Centers the title over the chart but retains the existing size of the chart.

   - **Above Chart**: Centers the title over the chart but adds room at the top so the title doesn't interfere with the chart itself.

3. Make a selection. A box with the words *Chart Title* (as you see in Figure 11-11) appears on the chart.

4. Double-click the Chart Title and drag across the words *Chart Title*. The words become highlighted.

5. Type the desired title. The text you type replaces the words *Chart Title*.

6. Click anywhere outside of the chart title to deselect it.

7. Optionally, choose Chart Tools Layout⇨Labels⇨Chart Title, More Title Options. The Format Chart Title dialog box in Figure 11-12 appears.

8. Select Fill and then choose any desired background options for the chart title. Excel's Live Preview feature lets you view various options without first selecting them.

9. Select Line, Line Style, and other title options, including color, shadows, 3-D formatting, and much more.

10. Click OK.

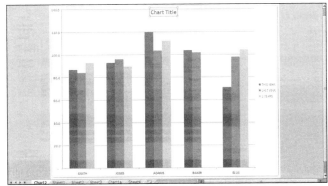

**Figure 11-11:** Add a title to your chart.

**Figure 11-12:** Select additional options for the chart title.

 You can't apply 3-D formatting or select a shadow if your title doesn't have a border line around it.

# Customize the Chart Legend

1. Click anywhere on the chart you want to modify.

2. Click Chart Tools Layout⇨Labels⇨Legend.

3. Select a placement for the legend or click None to turn off the chart legend. (See Figure 11-13.)

4. Click Chart Tools Layout⇨Labels⇨Legend⇨More Legend Options.

5. The More Legend Options box offers the same type of formatting options as the Chart Title. Choose any desired options. Click OK.

# Add a Data Table

1. Click anywhere on the chart you want to modify.

 Data tables can be added to charts on a regular worksheet, but it isn't a common practice because the worksheet itself already displays the data.

2. Click Chart Tools Layout⇨Labels⇨Data Table. Options include a choice not to show a data table, show a data table but not show a chart legend, or to show a data table and include the chart legend.

3. Make a Data Table selection.

4. Select the Show Data Table option.

5. Click OK. A data table, as seen in Figure 11-14, displays at the bottom of the chart showing the actual values.

**Figure 11-13:** Placing the chart legend.

 Data tables display the chart values in a grid beneath the chart. They are very helpful if a reader needs to see exact values along with a graphical display, such as when using a 3-D chart.

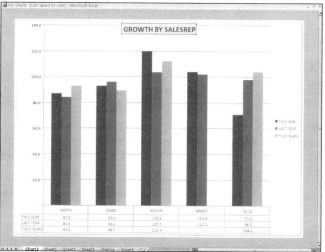

**Figure 11-14:** Display the data table.

# Show Data Labels

1. Click anywhere on the chart that you want to modify.

2. Choose Chart Tools Layout⇨Data Labels. A menu of data label placement options appears.

3. Select a placement option. Figure 11-15 shows the data labels with a placement of Outside End.

4. Choose Chart Tools Layout⇨Data Labels⇨More Data Label Options. The Format Data Labels dialog box appears.

5. If you don't want the data label to be the series value, choose a different option from the Label Options area (such as the series or category names).

6. In the Number option, select a number style for the data labels.

7. Select any additional options and then click OK.

# Select a Chart Color Style

1. Click anywhere on the chart you want to modify.

2. Choose Chart Tools Design⇨Chart Styles and click the More button, which displays the Chart Styles gallery seen in Figure 11-16.

3. Select a chart theme. Scroll down . . . there's more at the bottom.

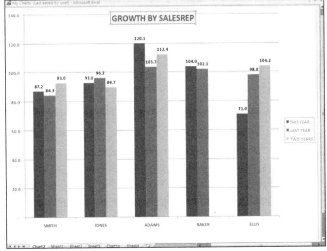

**Figure 11-15:** Data Labels.

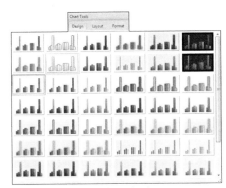

**Figure 11-16:** Select a chart color theme.

# Change Axis Options

1.  Click anywhere on the chart that you want to modify.

2.  Choose Chart Tools Layout⇨Labels⇨Axis Titles.

3.  Select Primary Horizontal Axis Title or Primary Vertical Axis Title.

4.  Choose an Axis title location. For the Horizontal axis, your choice is only Below the Axis (or None). For the Vertical axis, you have the option to rotate the title, run it vertically along the axis, or run it horizontally. I don't recommend the horizontal option because it takes up a great amount of chart space. In Figure 11-17, you see both a Vertical and a Horizontal Axis title.

5.  Highlight the axis text and replace it with your desired text.

6.  Choose Chart Tools Layout⇨Axes. Two options are available:

    *   **Axes**: Choose this option to change the way Excel displays either the horizontal or vertical axis. You can choose not to display an axis or you can change the value representation along the vertical axis. Click the More option to change choices such as axis-number formatting. (See Figure 11-18.)

    *   **Gridlines**: Choose this option to change the way the gridlines display along the chart background. You can add, change, or remove horizontal or vertical gridlines. You can also select More Options to modify the gridline color.

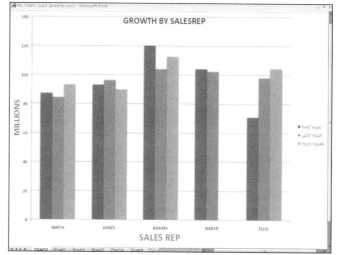

**Figure 11-17:** For further information on your data, add an axis title.

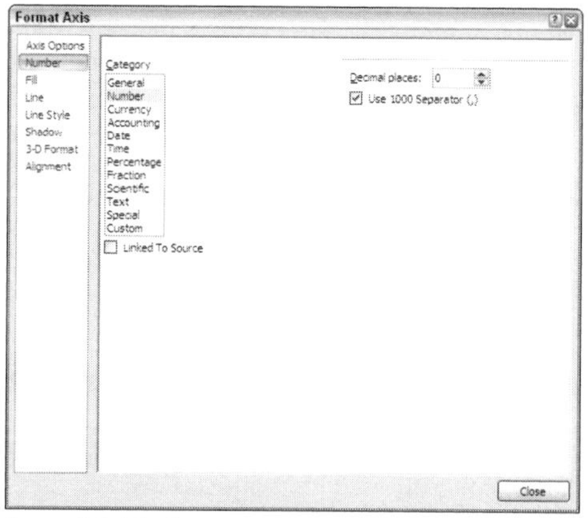

**Figure 11-18:** Changing axis options.

# *Enhance a 3-D Chart*

1. Click anywhere on the 3-D chart you want to modify.

2. Choose Chart Tools Layout⇨Background⇨3-D View. The Format Chart Area dialog box, shown in Figure 11-19, appears. The options you see depend on the chart type.

3. From the 3-D Rotation option:

   - Click the x-axis left or right rotation arrows or enter the degree of left/right rotation (between 0 and 360) you want for the chart in the Rotation box. This rotates the pie slices left or right.

   - Click the y-axis up or down rotation arrows or enter the degree of up/down rotation.

   - Click the Perspective up or down arrows to change the "camera" view or the view from the top. You can optionally type the elevation angle (between 10 and 80) in the Elevation text box.

4. From the 3-D Format option:

   - Choose a Rotation Preset option to select a bevel style for the top or bottom of the chart border.

   - Change the thickness of the bars or height of pie slices by entering a value (between 5 and 500) in the Height box.

   - Change the Depth option to deepen series bars and the chart floor. This option does not apply to pie charts. Values range from 0 – 2000.

5. Click Close. The chart appears on-screen, rotated to the angles you selected. Figure 11-20 shows a 3-D pie chart before and after changing the elevation and rotation.

**Figure 11-19:** Rotate a three-dimensional chart.

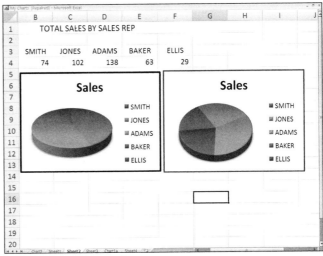

**Figure 11-20:** Enhance a pie chart.

# Place a Picture in a Data Series

1. Right-click the series or data point you want to modify. A shortcut menu appears.

2. Choose Format Data Series. The Format Data Series dialog box appears.

3. Click the Fill option. Fill options appear on the right side. Select Picture or Texture Fill.

4. Click File. The Insert Picture dialog box appears.

5. Locate and select the picture you want to use. Click Insert. The Format Data Series dialog box reappears.

6. Click OK. Figure 11-21 illustrates a pie chart where two series were replaced with graphic images. Data labels were also added for clarity

**Figure 11-21:** Liven up charts with graphic images.

 To quickly add or delete a series to a chart located on the same worksheet as the data, click anywhere on the chart that you want to edit. Notice that Excel surrounds the chart with selection handles and marks the source data in the worksheet with a colored border. Click and drag the corner handle of the worksheet source range to add or subtract cells.

# Adjust Chart Data

1. Click anywhere on the chart that you want to modify.

2. Choose Chart Tools Design⇨Data⇨Edit Data Source. The Edit Source Data dialog box opens with the current chart data selected in the worksheet (see Figure 11-22).

3. Click and drag in the worksheet to select the new data range. The Edit Data Source dialog box collapses so you can easily see your data.

4. Release the mouse button. The Edit Data Source box reappears.

5. Click OK. The Edit Data Source dialog box closes.

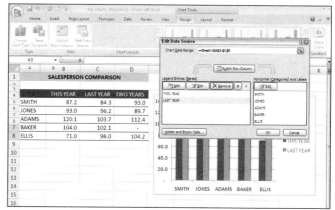

**Figure 11-22:** Change the chart data selection.

# Printing Workbooks

*W*hen you finish compiling your worksheet, you'll probably want to print a hard copy or e-mail a copy to someone else. This chapter shows you a number of Excel tools you can use to improve your document layout, including headers, footers, page orientation, and margins.

Also, before you print or give your Excel file to someone else, you should check it for spelling errors. You want to eliminate typos that scream to the world, "I can't spell." Excel includes a built-in dictionary you can use to check your workbooks for misspellings; however, it can't read your mind. If you type *too* instead of *two*, Excel probably won't indicate an error. But, combine the spell check with careful proofreading, and it becomes a very helpful tool.

When you are printing, Excel assumes you want to print the entire worksheet area unless you specify otherwise. You discover in this chapter how to tell Excel exactly what you want to print. This chapter also includes these topics:

→ Working with page breaks

→ Adjusting the paper size

→ Making a worksheet fit when you must get a few last rows or columns on a single page

→ Printing gridlines or row and column headings on the page, as well as other options for printing your worksheet or chart

# Chapter
## 12

## Get ready to . . .

# *Spell Check*

**1.** Choose Review⇨Proofing⇨Spelling. The Spelling dialog box opens, and Excel highlights the cell where it finds the first potential misspelling and also suggests possible changes (as shown in Figure 12-1).

 Spell Check reviews all cell values, comments, embedded charts, text boxes, buttons, and headers and footers, but it does not check protected worksheets, formulas, or text that results from a formula.

**2.** Select one of the following options:

- **Change or Change All:** Choose one of the suggestions; then click Change to change just this spelling mistake or select Change All if you think you made the mistake more than once.

- **AutoCorrect:** Have Excel, in future workbooks, automatically correct the mistake with the selected replacement.

- **Ignore Once:** Click this button if you don't want to change the spelling of the highlighted instance.

- **Ignore All:** Click this button if you don't want to change the spelling of any identical instances.

- **Add to Dictionary:** Add a word, such as a proper name or medical or legal term, to Excel's built-in dictionary so that Excel won't flag it as a potential error in the future.

**3.** After you select an option, Excel proceeds to the next error; when all potential mistakes are identified, Excel asks you to click OK (as shown in Figure 12-2).

**Figure 12-1:** Use the spell check to correct errors.

**Figure 12-2:** The completed spell check message box.

## Preview Before Printing

1. Click the Office Button.

2. Click the arrow next to Print and select Print Preview.

3. From the Print Preview screen (shown in Figure 12-3), select from the following options:

   - If you have multiple pages, click the Next Page or Previous Page buttons to view additional pages.

   - Click the Zoom button to enlarge the view. Click a second time to reduce the view.

   - Click the Print button to display the Print dialog box.

   - Click the Page Setup button to display the Page Setup dialog box.

   - Click the Show Margins button to display the page margins; then drag any margin line to manually set margin sizes. Click the Margins button again to turn off the margin lines.

4. Click the Close Print Preview button to return to Normal view.

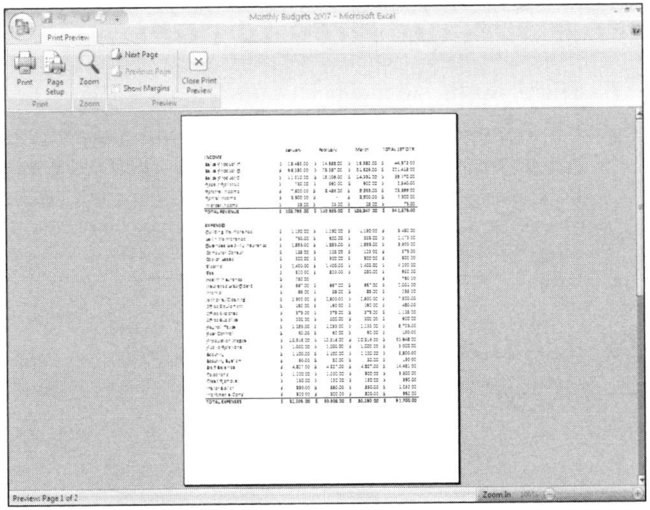

## Add a Manual Page Break

1. Click a cell in the row where you want the new page to begin.

2. Choose Page Layout⇨Page Setup⇨Breaks⇨Insert Page Break. Dotted page break lines, similar to the ones shown in Figure 12-4, appear.

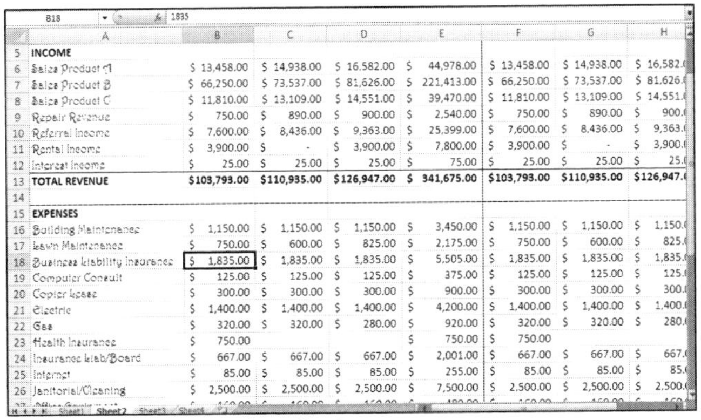

**Figure 12-3:** Print Preview options.

**Figure 12-4:** Insert a manual page break.

# Set a Specific Area to Print

1. Highlight the area you want to print. See Figure 12-5.

2. Choose Page Layout⇨Page Setup⇨Print Area⇨Set Print Area. Dotted lines appear around the print area. When you print the worksheet, only the area contained within the dotted lines prints. See "Print Worksheets or Charts," later in this chapter.

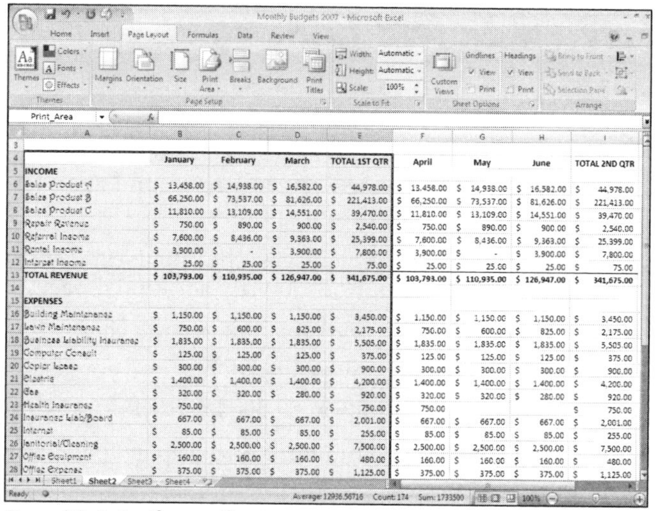

# Adjust the Paper Orientation and Size

1. Choose Page Layout⇨Page Setup⇨Orientation.

2. Select whether you want a Portrait or Landscape orientation.

3. Choose Page Layout⇨Page Setup⇨Size. A drop-down list of paper sizes appears.

4. Select a paper size. The paper size choices you see depend on the printer you use. The two most common US choices are Letter, which is 8.5 inches by 11 inches, and Legal, which is 8.5 inches by 14 inches. (See Figure 12-6.)

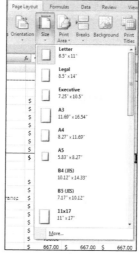

**Figure 12-5:** Specify a specific print area.

**Figure 12-6:** Select a paper size.

# Make Worksheets Fit Better on a Page

1. Choose Page Layout⇨Scale to Fit.

2. Click the Scale to Fit dialog box launcher. The Page Setup dialog box opens.

3. From the Scaling area, make a selection from the options seen in Figure 12-7:

   - **Adjust To:** Enlarge or shrink the printed font size by setting a percentage option between 10 and 400.

   - **Fit To:** Force Excel to a specified number of pages wide and high.

    Don't try to shrink the document too much. Because Excel shrinks the font, trying to fit too much on a page can make the document typeface too small to read.

4. Click OK.

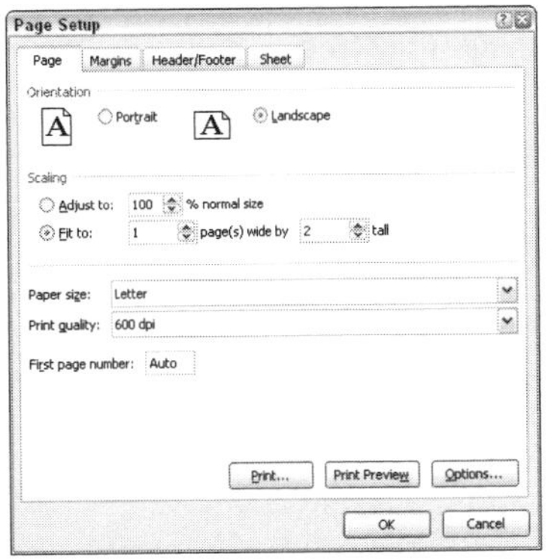

# Set Page Margins

1. Choose Page Layout⇨Page Setup⇨Margins. Figure 12-8 shows a list of margin options.

2. Select from the margins options shown or choose Custom Margins to open the Page Setup dialog box that enables you to set your own margin options. Click OK.

    From the Page Setup dialog box, click the option Horizontally and/ or the option Vertically in the Center on Page section to center the worksheet on the page, regardless of the margins.

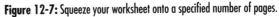

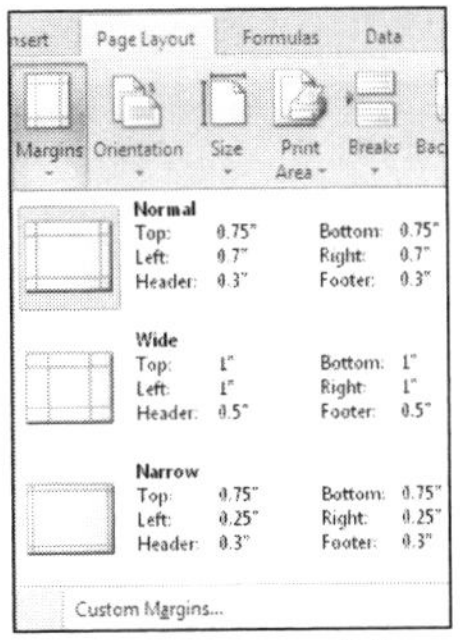

**Figure 12-7:** Squeeze your worksheet onto a specified number of pages.

**Figure 12-8:** Set worksheet page margins.

 The default worksheet margins are the Normal settings, which are .75 inch on both the top and bottom and .70 inch on the left and right sides.

# Specify Repeating Rows and Columns

1.  Choose Page Layout⇨Page Setup⇨Print Titles. The Page Setup dialog box opens.

2.  On the Sheet tab, type a dollar sign ($) followed by the row numbers or column letters you want to print as titles in the Print Titles section. Entering **$1:$1**, as you see in Figure 12-9, repeats row 1 at the beginning of each page. Click OK.

Click the worksheet icon on the right to collapse the Page Setup dialog box so you can select the rows or columns you want to include. Click the button again to return to the Page Setup dialog box.

# Print Gridlines and Row and Column Headings

1.  Choose Page Layout⇨Sheet Options.

2.  Choose from the following options:

    -   **Gridlines⇨Print:** Check this option to print the gridlines surrounding each cell in the worksheet.

    -   **Headings⇨Print:** Check this option to print the row numbers or column letters around the worksheet. Figure 12-10 illustrates a worksheet printed with gridlines and row and column headings.

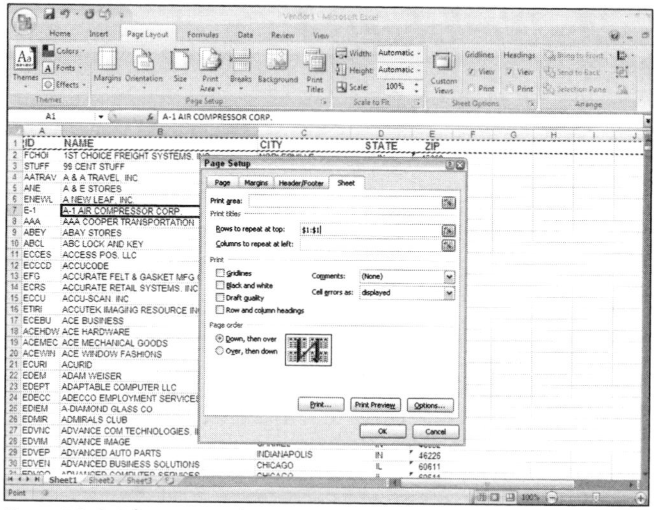

**Figure 12-9:** Select rows or columns to repeat at the top of each page.

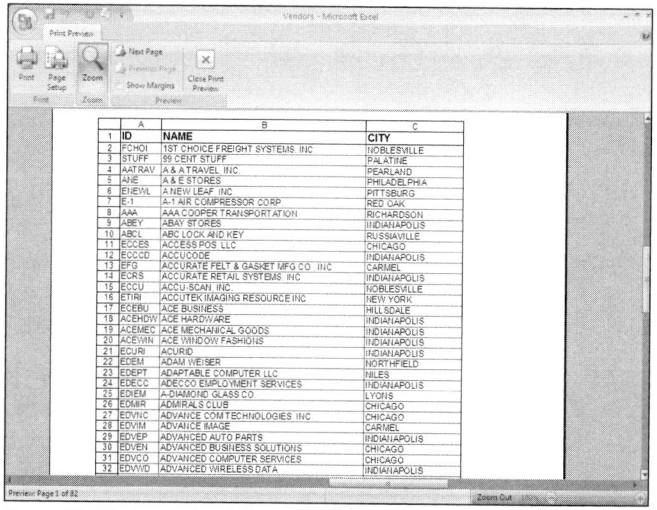

**Figure 12-10:** A printed worksheet with column and row headings and gridlines.

## *Add a Standard Header or Footer*

1. Choose View⇨Worksheet Views⇨Page Layout View. You see the header area of your worksheet.

2. Choose Header & Footer Tools Design ⇨Auto Header or Auto Footer. A list of predefined headers or footers appears as you see in Figure 12-11.

3. Select the header or footer you want to use.

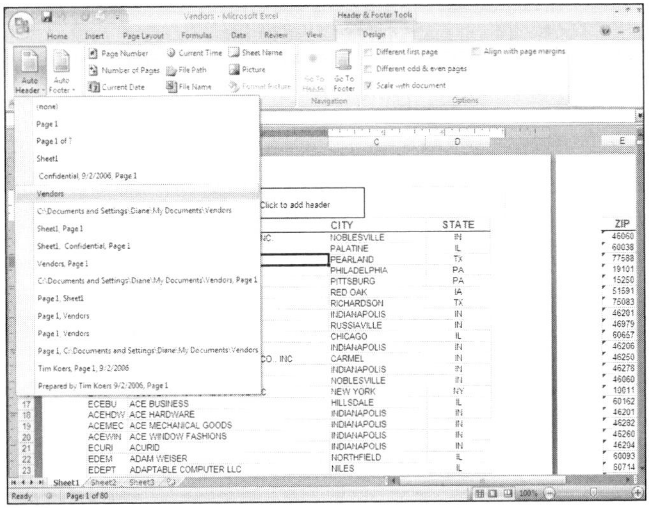

## *View Other Header and Footer Options*

1. Choose View⇨Worksheet Views⇨Page Layout View.

2. Choose Header & Footer Tools Design.

3. From the Options group, select any of the options shown in Figure 12-12:

   - **Different first page**: If you choose this option, Excel won't print the header or footer on the first page.

   - **Different odd and even pages**: Choose this option if you want a different header or footer for the odd-numbered pages of the document.

   - **Scale with document**: This option is selected by default and tells Excel to use the same font size and scaling as the worksheet. If you want the header and footer font size and scaling independent of the work-sheet scaling, clear this check box.

   - **Align with page margins**: Choose this option to align the header and footer with the left and right margins of the worksheet.

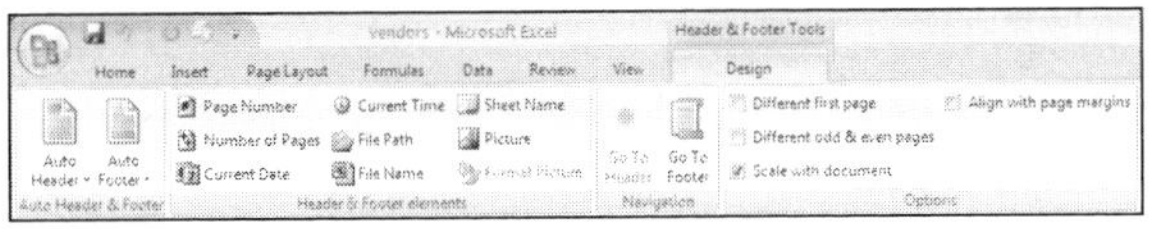

**Figure 12-11:** Insert the worksheet name in the header or footer.

**Figure 12-12:** Additional Header and Footer options.

# Create a Custom Header or Footer

1. Choose View⇨Worksheet Views⇨Page Layout View.

 Click Go To Footer to jump to the footer area.

2. In any desired header or footer section, type the text you want for the header (or footer). As you see in Figure 12-13, you can format the header and footer text just as you would any cell data.

3. Click any options from the Header and Footer Elements group:

   - **Page Number:** Insert a code that indicates the page number.

   - **Number of Pages:** Insert a code that indicates the total number of pages.

   - **Current Date or Current Time:** Insert the print date or time of day. See Figure 12-14.

   - **File Path, File Name, or Sheet Tab Name:** Include file information.

   - **Picture:** Insert a graphic image such as a company logo.

   - **Format Picture:** Resize, rotate, or crop a header or footer graphic image.

6. Click OK.

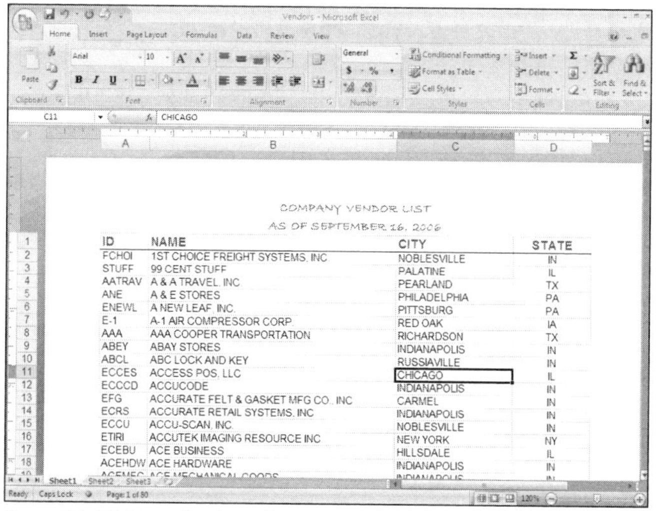

**Figure 12-13:** Format header or footer text.

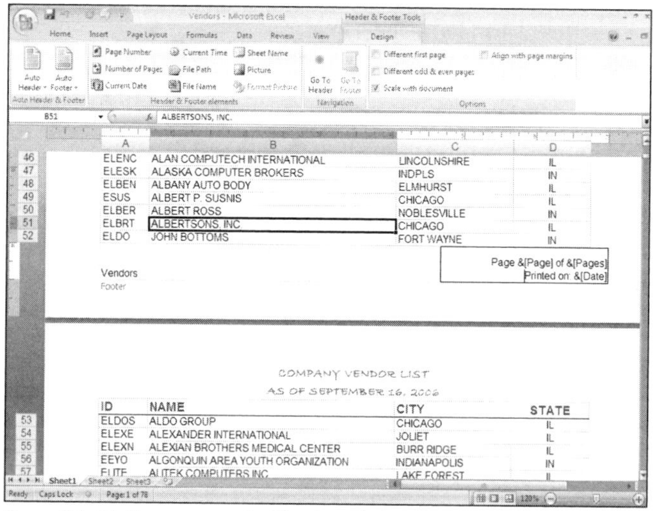

**Figure 12-14:** Create a customized header or footer.

# *Print Worksheets and Charts*

1. Choose Office➪Print. The Print dialog box, shown in Figure 12-15 appears.

    Optionally, print the worksheet immediately by clicking the Print button on the Quick Access toolbar.

2. Choose from the following options:

   • **Name:** Select a printer different than the default printer.

   • **Print Range:** Specify whether to print the entire worksheet as determined by the print area or whether to print only specific pages.

   • **Copies:** Select the number of copies you want to print.

   • **Print What:** Choose whether to print the current worksheet, a preselected area, or the entire workbook.

3. Click OK.

# *E-Mail a Workbook*

1. Choose Office➪Send➪E-Mail. As you see in Figure 12-16, your e-mail program launches with the worksheet as an attachment.

    Recipients must have Excel installed on their systems to open the workbook file.

2. Enter the recipient e-mail information and any additional text in the body of the message.

3. Click Send.

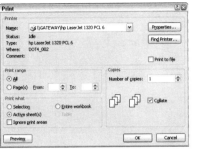

**Figure 12-15:** Select from a plethora of print options.

**Figure 12-16:** E-mail Excel information to others.

# Part IV

# Analyzing Data with Excel

The 5th Wave          By Rich Tennant

BANK MGR

"Our customer survey indicates 30% of our customers think our service is inconsistent, 40% would like a change in procedures, and 50% think it would be real cute if we all wore matching colored vests."

# Working with Outlines

*W*hen you are working with a large worksheet, it is sometimes difficult to look at the big picture your data presents to you. You can use Excel to automatically calculate subtotal and grand total values from rows containing related data (sometimes called a *database*). When you create subtotals, Excel outlines the list so that you can display or hide the detail rows for each subtotal.

A couple of other database terms you should become familiar with are *fields* and *records*. *Fields* break down your database list into manageable pieces by using Excel columns. For example, an address database might include fields such as name, address, and phone number. *Records* are the rows containing the individual pieces of information you enter. In an address database, for example, a single row contains all the information about a specific person.

Before you use the subtotal function, you must first sort your list so that the rows you want to subtotal are grouped together. You can then calculate subtotals and perform other mathematical calculations for any columns that contain numbers. You can also count the number of items in a selected field.

If your data is not in a database format, you can still group sections to create a quick way to display or hide them as necessary. Similarly to the way it does subtotals, Excel displays groups in an outline format. In this chapter, I take a look at the extensive subtotaling, grouping, and outlining features contained in Excel. I also show you how to create a data entry form screen for faster data entry. By default, Excel 2007 doesn't include the Form command you need for this, but I'll show you how to add it to your Quick Access toolbar.

## Get ready to . . .

# Add the Form Button

1. Choose Office Button➪Excel Options.

2. Click Customization.

3. From the Choose Commands From drop-down list, select Commands not in the Ribbon.

4. Click Form.

5. Click Add. Excel places the Form command in the right-hand column. (See Figure 13-1.)

6. Click OK. Excel places the Form command in the Quick Access toolbar.

**Figure 13-1:** Making the Form command accessible.

# Create a Data Entry Screen

1. Enter the column headings for your database. When you create the data entry screen, the column headings appear as field names.

2. Click in any table heading cell and then choose Form from the Quick Access toolbar.

3. Click OK if a message box appears. If you already have records entered into the database, Excel does not display the message box. Instead, Excel displays a data form with the headings shown as field names. See Figure 13-2.

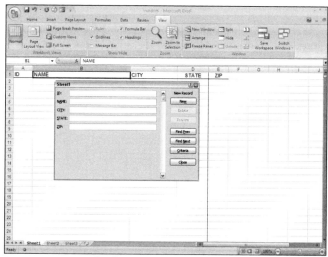

**Figure 13-2:** Create a data form.

**4.** Enter the information for the first record and press the Tab key to move from field to field (see Figure 13-3).

 Press Shift+Tab key to move back to the previous field.

**5.** Click New. Excel adds the record to the database and displays another blank screen ready for the next record.

**6.** Click Close when you finish entering data.

 You can reopen the database form at any time by clicking the Form button on the Quick Access toolbar.

## *Manage Records through the Form Screen*

**1.** Choose Form from the Quick Access toolbar. The Form window opens.

 The active cell must be somewhere within the database headings or data.

**2.** Click Find Next. The form displays the next record in your database.

**3.** Click Find Prev. The previous record in your database appears.

**4.** If you want to delete the current displayed record, click the Delete button. The warning message you see in Figure 13-4 appears.

**5.** Click OK if you want to delete the record. Use caution. This action cannot be undone!

 Click the New button to display a blank form where you can enter a new record.

 To quickly look for specific records, click Criteria and then enter data you want to locate in the applicable field. Click Find Prev or Find Next to navigate through the matches. Click the Criteria button again to change the search criteria.

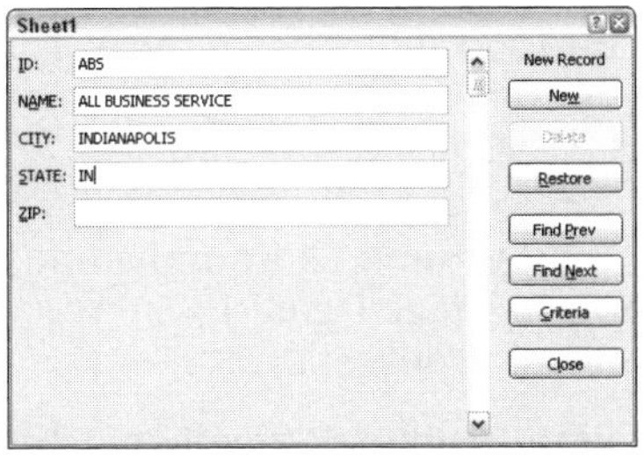

**Figure 13-3:** Enter database records with a form.

**Figure 13-4:** Deleting unwanted records.

# *Generate a Subtotal*

1. Sort the field to use for generating subtotals. For example, if you want to know the total sales by salesperson, you sort by the salesperson field. See Chapter 10 for sorting instructions.

2. Choose Data⇨Outline⇨Subtotals. The Subtotal dialog box appears.

3. Select the field you want to subtotal from the At Each Change In drop-down list.

4. Select a function from the Use Function drop-down list.

5. Select the fields you want to subtotal from the Add Subtotal To drop-down list. (See Figure 13-5). You can select more than one field to subtotal.

6. Check the Replace Current Subtotals box if you already have previous subtotal calculations. Excel replaces the previous subtotals with the new ones.

7. Check the Page Break between Groups box if you want Excel to begin each subtotaled group on a new page.

8. Remove the check from the Summary below Data box if you want Excel to place the subtotals at the top of each group instead of under each group.

9. Click OK. Excel performs the subtotal. Figure 13-6 shows sales subtotaled by Name.

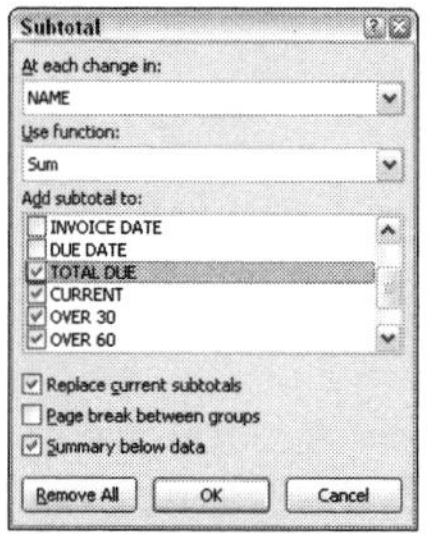

**Figure 13-5:** Select fields to calculate.

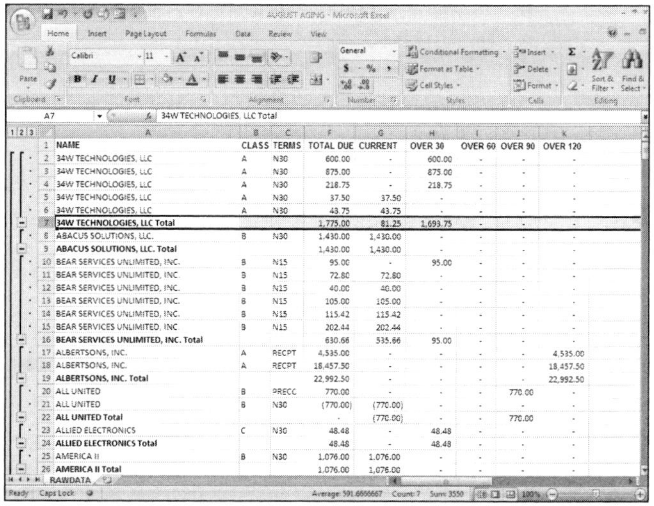

**Figure 13-6:** A subtotaled worksheet.

# Collapse Subtotal Headings

1. Create subtotals of your data (see the "Generate a Subtotal" section, earlier in this chapter).

2. Hide and show data using the following methods:

   - **See only the grand total:** Click the 1 on the subtotal headings.

   - **See the subtotal categories and amounts (the detail is hidden):** Click the 2 on the subtotal headings (the column on the left side of the worksheet). (See Figure 13-7.)

   - **Show all the detail and subtotals:** Click the 3 on the subtotal headings. Excel displays the individual worksheet rows.

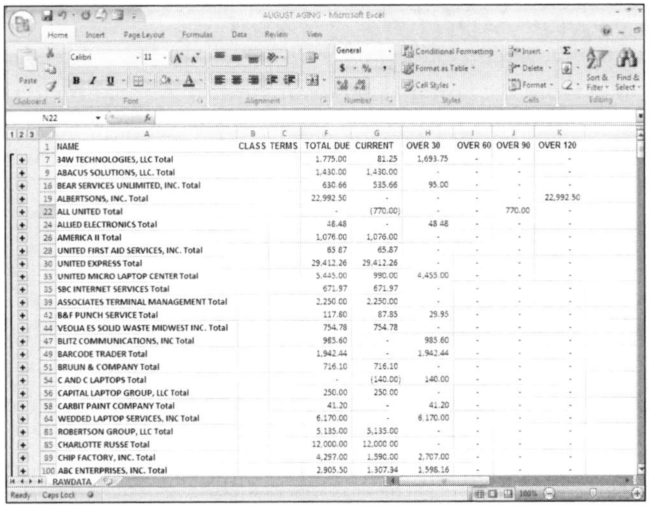

# Control Individual Subtotals

1. Create subtotals for your data (see the "Generate a Subtotal" section, earlier in this chapter).

2. Click the Hide Detail button (minus sign) next to any subtotal row. As shown in Figure 13-8, the selected subtotal detail collapses. The detail data for Bear Services is not lost, only hidden.

3. Click the Show Detail button (plus sign) next to any subtotal row. The detail data for the selected row appears.

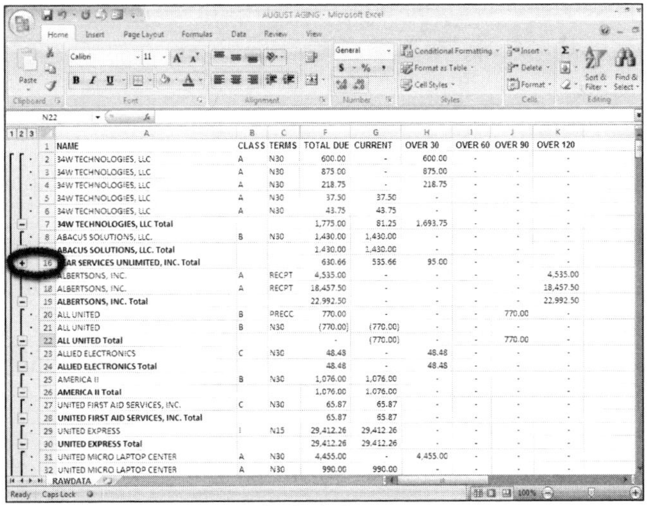

**Figure 13-7:** Collapse and expand entire subtotal sections.

**Figure 13-8:** Collapse and expand individual sections.

# Create Multiple Subtotals

1. From the Sort dialog box, first select the column to use for generating primary subtotals and then the column for generating secondary subtotals. For example, if you want to subtotal sales by state and then by city, you first sort by state and then by city. See the example in Figure 3-9.

2. Choose Data➪Outline➪Subtotal to display the Subtotals dialog box.

3. Select the primary field you want to subtotal from the At Each Change drop-down list.

4. Select a function from the Use function drop-down list. Use Count for this example.

5. Select the fields you want to subtotal from the Add Subtotal To drop-down list.

 You can select multiple fields to subtotal. For example, in a sales tracking worksheet you might want to total the sale, the sales tax, and the shipping amount.

6. Click OK. Excel summarizes the data by the first selected field.

7. Choose Data➪Outline➪Subtotal. Excel again displays the Subtotal dialog box.

8. Select the secondary field you want to subtotal, the type of function, and the fields you want to subtotal. In this example, I want a count of the City field.

9. Remove the check mark from the Replace Current Subtotals box.

10. Click OK. Figure 13-10 illustrates the vendor list subtotaled first by State and then by City.

 As you perform additional subtotaling, Excel adds additional levels. In Figure 13-10, four heading levels are displayed. Level 1 displays only the grand totals, level 2 displays the count by State, level 3 shows the count by City, and level 4 displays the detail.

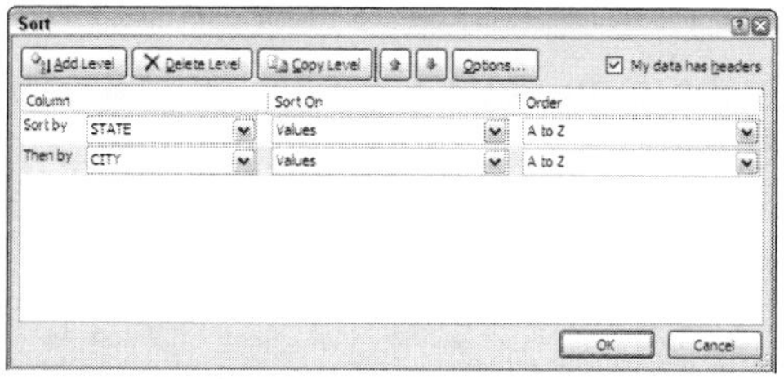

**Figure 13-9:** Select the fields you want to sort and then subtotal.

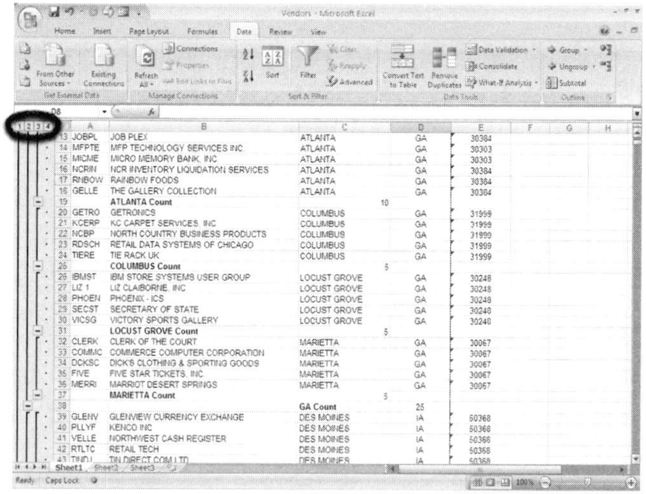

**Figure 13-10:** Click the heading levels to expand or collapse the subtotals.

# Copy Subtotals

1. Hide any unwanted Detail buttons by clicking the Expand or Collapse buttons.

2. Select the data you want to copy.

3. Choose Home⇨Find & Select⇨ Go To Special. The Go To Special dialog box opens (see Figure 13-11).

4. Select the Visible Cells Only options. White lines appear around the selected cells.

5. Click OK.

6. Choose Home⇨Clipboard⇨Copy. A marquee appears around the selected cells.

7. Select the first cell of the group in which you want to place the copied data.

8. Choose Home⇨Clipboard⇨Paste. Excel duplicates only the subtotaled values, not the formulas or hidden cells.

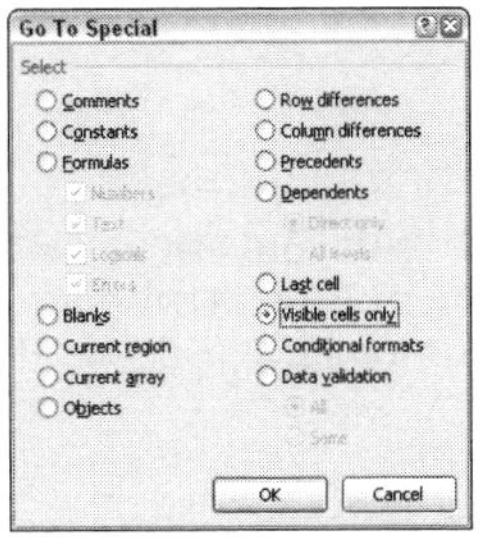

# Remove Subtotals

1. Choose Data⇨Outline⇨Subtotals. The Subtotal dialog box appears. (See Figure 13-12.)

2. Click Remove All. Excel removes all subtotal information from the database, including the Expand and Collapse icons from the left side of the worksheet. Your data remains in the order you last sorted it.

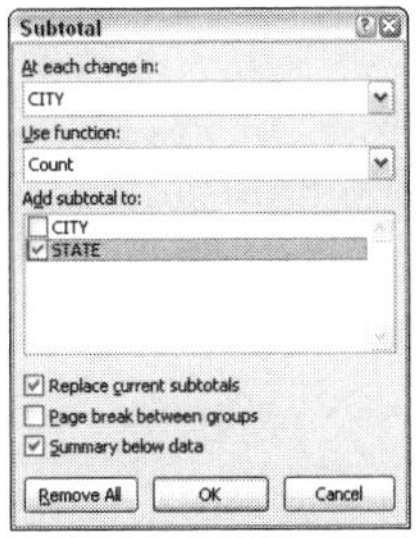

**Figure 13-11:** The Go To Special dialog box.

You can also use for the Go To Special box if you want to select only cells with constant values or only those containing formulas.

**Figure 13-12:** Remove subtotals from the database.

The copy subtotal process also works if you have your data in outline format. See more about outlining later in this chapter.

# Use AutoOutline

1. Choose Data⇨Outline⇨Group⇨AutoOutline. Figure 13-13 illustrates a worksheet with outline headings for both rows and columns. Row outline symbols are on the left, and column outline symbols are at the top of the worksheet

   AutoOutline works by evaluating summary formulas that reference cells in the detail cells. The summary formulas must be adjacent to the detail. Based on the information in the summary functions, it creates all the possible outlines pertaining to the layout of your data.

   You can create and apply formatting to an outline before or after you create the outline. See Chapter 5.

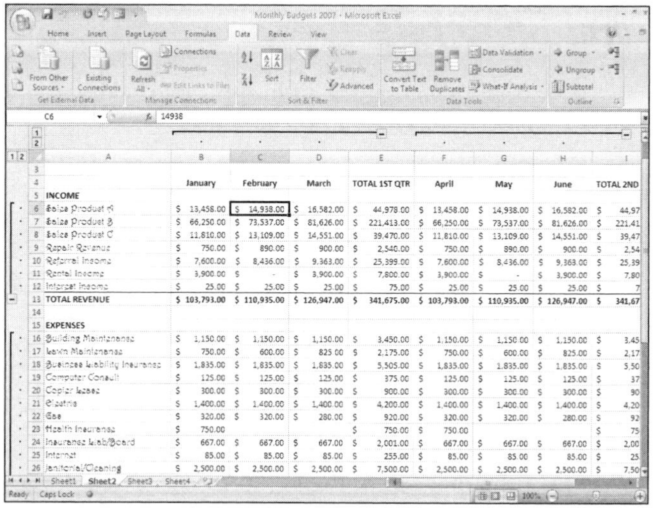

2. To expand the outline, click the Show Detail buttons to the left of the rows or above the column headings. (See Figure 13-14.)

3. To collapse the outline, click the Hide buttons to the left of the rows or above the column headings.

   When you print an outlined worksheet, Excel prints the worksheet as it is shown on the screen. Hidden detail does not print.

4. To remove the AutoOutline, choose Data⇨Outline⇨ Ungroup⇨Clear Outline.

   To hide an outline without removing it, display all the data by clicking the highest number in the outline symbols and then choose Office⇨Excel Options. From the Advanced tab, remove the check from Show Outline Symbols if an outline is applied.

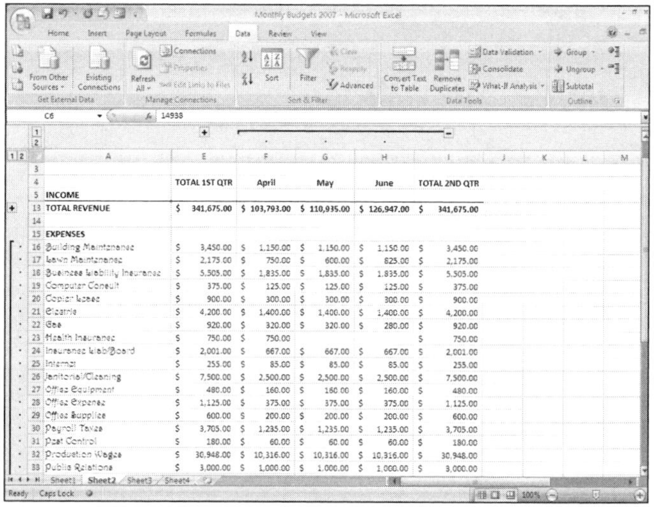

**Figure 13-13:** A worksheet with outline headings.

**Figure 13-14:** Click the plus or minus buttons to hide or display parts of the workbook.

# Form an Outline Group

1. Highlight the rows that you want to group.

2. Choose Data⇨Outline⇨Group. In Figure 13-15, you see all the file cabinets in the asset list grouped together.

    Optionally, to create a group, select the rows or columns then press Alt+Shift+right arrow.

    Use the Hide or Show Detail buttons to hide or display the group detail.

3. Repeat Steps 1 and 2 until you have created all the levels you want in the outline. A worksheet can have up to eight outline levels.

    Grouped areas cannot be immediately adjacent to other grouped areas. If you create a group then create another group directly next to it, Excel doesn't create two groups; it creates one larger group.

# Remove Items from a Group

1. Select the rows or columns you want to remove from the group. If you want to remove an entire group, select all the rows or columns in the group.

2. Choose Data⇨Outline⇨Ungroup. Excel removes the rows or columns from the group and if the rows or columns you delete are in the middle of a group, Excel breaks the group into two smaller groups. See Figure 13-16 where the file cabinets are broken from one group into two smaller groups.

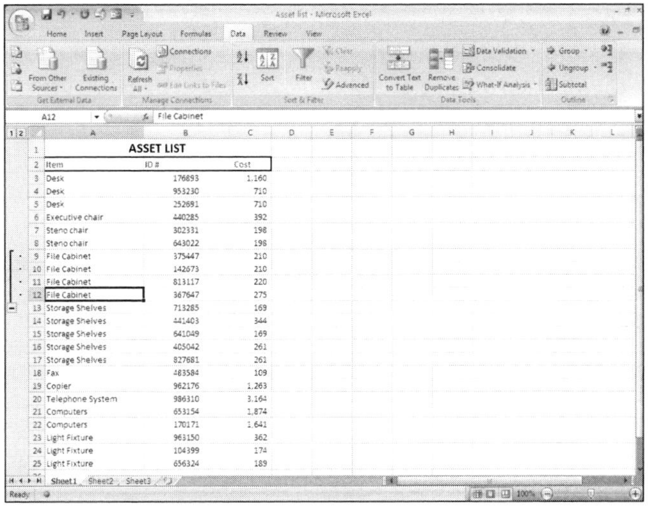

**Figure 13-15:** Create a manual group.

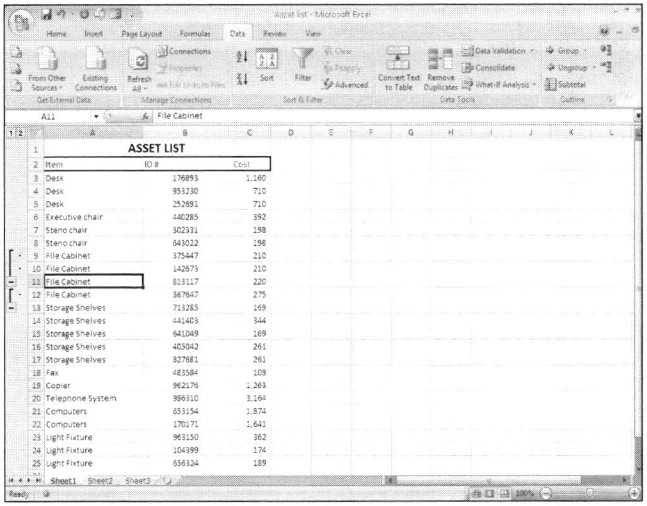

**Figure 13-16:** Splitting up groups.

# Filtering Data

After you create an Excel database and assemble a large amount of data, you probably want to analyze it. You may want to ask yourself questions about your data. "Who are my best customers?" "Which inventory items are provided by a specific supplier and cost less than a certain amount?" "Which employees work the least amount of hours?" Excel includes several tools you can use to answer these questions and study your data so you can make better decisions.

*Filtering* means that Excel can pull out specific records for review. This provides you with an easy way to break down your data into smaller, more manageable chunks. Filtering does not rearrange your data; it simply temporarily hides records you don't want to review so you can clearly examine those you do.

You can create your filtered database just by typing in the Excel screen. You can also use an Excel data entry screen, but it isn't required.

This chapter is devoted to the different ways you can filter your data including

➡ Using AutoFilter, which allows you to select key pieces of data.

➡ Selecting records by using more than one condition.

➡ Displaying only the top *x* number of records.

➡ Using multiple filtering to locate records that either match all criteria or meet one or the other criteria.

➡ Performing advanced filtering to designate a specific area of your worksheet to manage your criteria selections.

## Chapter 14

# Create an AutoFilter

1. After clicking anywhere in your database, choose Data⇨ Sort & Filter⇨Filter. Excel displays a filter arrow in each database column.

    Optionally, choose Home⇨Sort & Filter⇨Filter.

    In Chapter 4, you discovered you could choose Home⇨Styles⇨ Format as Table. After you selected a style, your table automatically appeared with filter arrows.

    The AutoFilter feature is unavailable for protected worksheets.

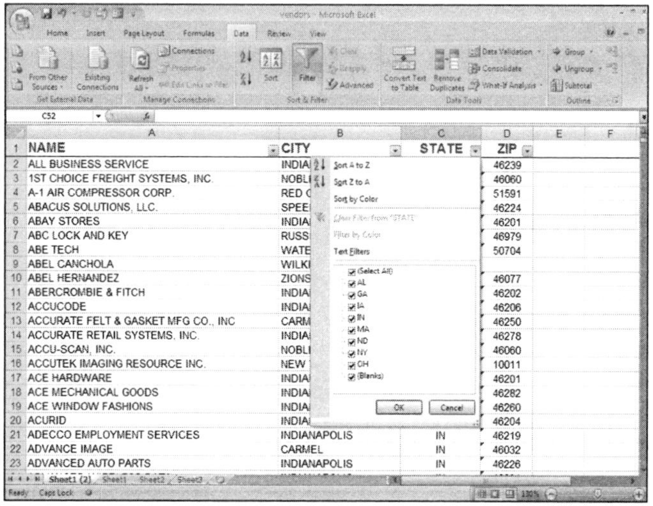

**Figure 14-1:** AutoFilter selections.

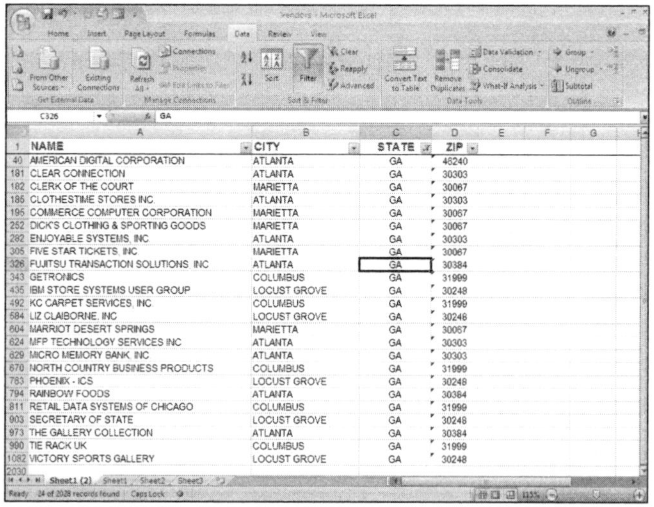

2. Click the arrow in the column heading from which you want to find a common value. Excel displays a drop-down list, which includes one of each unique entry (up to 10,000 entries) in the selected column (as you see in Figure 14-1).

3. Remove the check mark from Select All. All items become unselected.

4. Click the entry you want to filter and then click OK. Excel displays only the records that match your choice. In Figure 14-2, for example, you see only the vendors from Georgia.

    The filter arrows on filtered columns take on a different appearance to indicate that a filter is in use.

**Figure 14-2:** Filter by state.

# Remove Filtering

1. From the column containing filtering, click the filter arrow and choose Clear Filter from *"field name"* (see Figure 14-3).

    Optionally, click the Select All option.

2. Click OK. The filtering is removed from the selected field.

3. When you finish filtering your data, choose Data➪Sort & Filter➪Filter to turn off the AutoFilter.

# Search for Blank or Non-Blank Cells

1. Make sure the AutoFilter option is on and your database columns contain filter arrows.

2. Click the arrow in the column heading where you want to find a blank cell.

3. Remove the check mark from Select All. All items become unselected.

4. Scroll to the bottom of the list and check the (Blanks) entry. It should be the only one selected.

5. Click OK. Excel displays only the records with blank cells in the column you selected (as you can see in Figure 14-4).

 To filter for nonblank values, make sure Select All is chosen in the AutoFilter menu at the top of the list of values. Then, at the bottom of the list, remove the check mark from (Blanks).

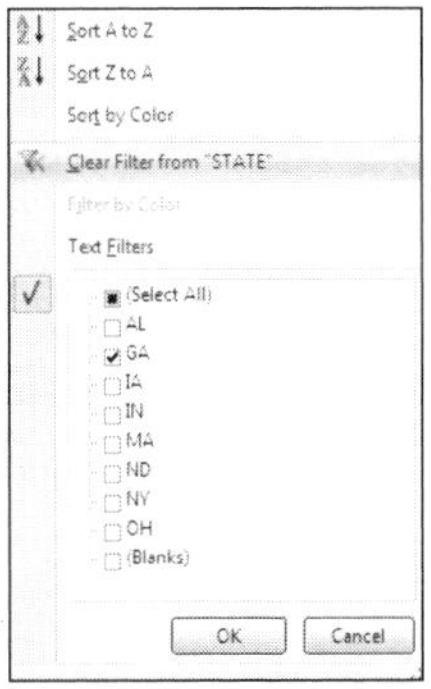

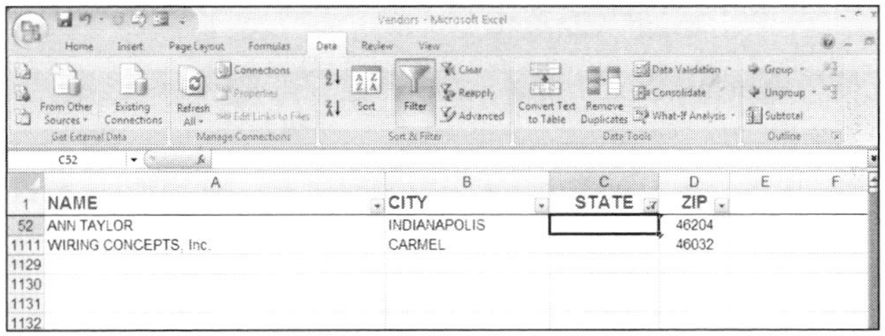

**Figure 14-3:** Remove a filter.

**Figure 14-4:** Locate records with blank values.

 You can turn the AutoFilter on and off as often as you need to.

# Perform a Secondary Filter Selection

1. Make sure the AutoFilter option is on and your database columns contain filter arrows.

2. Click the column arrow by which you want to filter data first.

3. Choose the data you want to filter. In Figure 14-5, you see only selections that display *Atlanta* in the *City* column. Note, however, that there is an Atlanta in GA, IN, OH, and NY.

4. To further isolate specific items, click the filter arrow at the top of another column.

5. Select the field by which you want to perform the second filter. In Figure 14-6, the primary option was to filter by the city of Atlanta. I now apply the state of GA as the secondary filter (because, in Step 3, four states had a city named Atlanta).

6. Repeat Steps 4 and 5 to further filter by as many fields as necessary.

7. When you're finished working with your filtered data, choose one of these options:

   - **Return to the first filter:** Click the second filter column arrow and choose a different second filter.

   - **Return to the first filter only:** Click the second filter column arrow and choose Clear Filter from *"field name."*

   - **Return to viewing all records:** Choose Data⇨Sort & Filter⇨Clear.

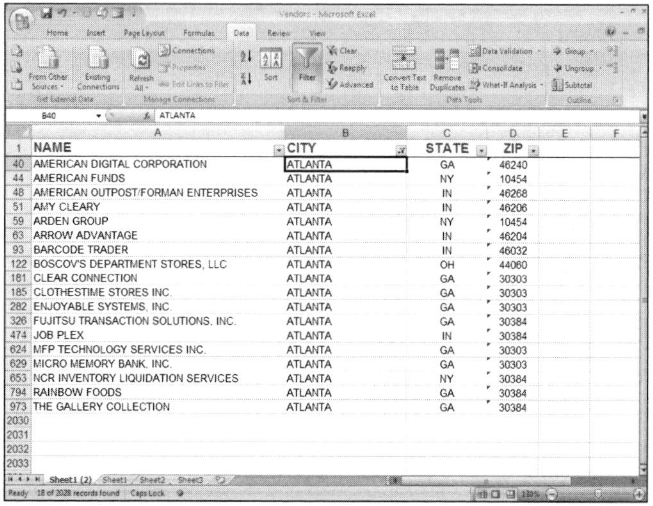

**Figure 14-5:** Select the first filter.

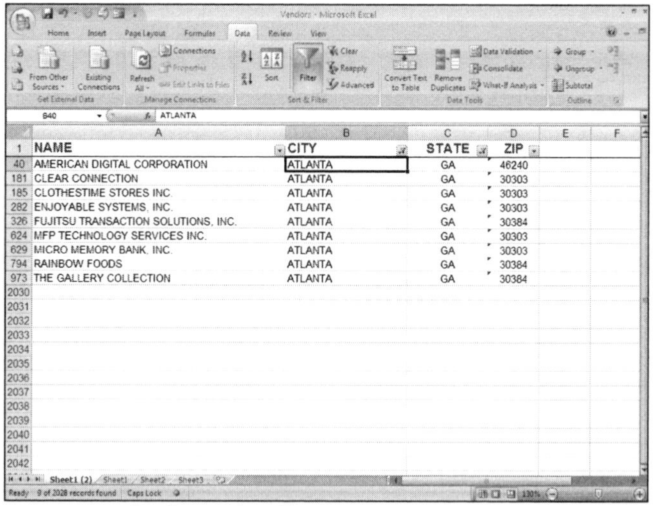

**Figure 14-6:** Select the second sort filter.

# Use a Comparison Filter for Text

1. Click the filter arrow for the text column by which you want to filter data.

2. Click Text Filters. A submenu of comparison filters like the one in Figure 14-7 appears.

   - **Equals** or **Does Not Equal**: Equals locates all records in which the selected field cells exactly match or don't match the text you specify. For example, if you look for records matching "Boston" only the records with Boston appear. Records containing New Boston, Boston Hill, Indianapolis, Bostonia, Atlanta, or Chicago do not appear. If you chose Does Not Equal you might see New Boston, Boston Hill, Indianapolis, Bostonia, Atlanta, and Chicago, but not Boston.

   - **Begins With** or **Ends With**: Locates all records in which the selected field cells begin or end with the text you specify. If you chose Begins With, Boston Hill, Bostonia, and Boston display, but not New Boston, Indianapolis, Atlanta, or Chicago. If you chose Ends with, you would see the records for Boston and New Boston but not Boston Hill, Bostonia, Indianapolis, Atlanta, or Chicago.

   - **Contains or Does Not Contain**: Locates all records in which the selected field text contains or doesn't contain the text you specify. The text could be at the beginning, the middle, or the end of the field cell value.

3. Make a selection. The Custom AutoFilter dialog box you see in Figure 14-8 appears.

4. In the first list box on the right, type the data you want to filter.

5. Click OK to display the filtered records.

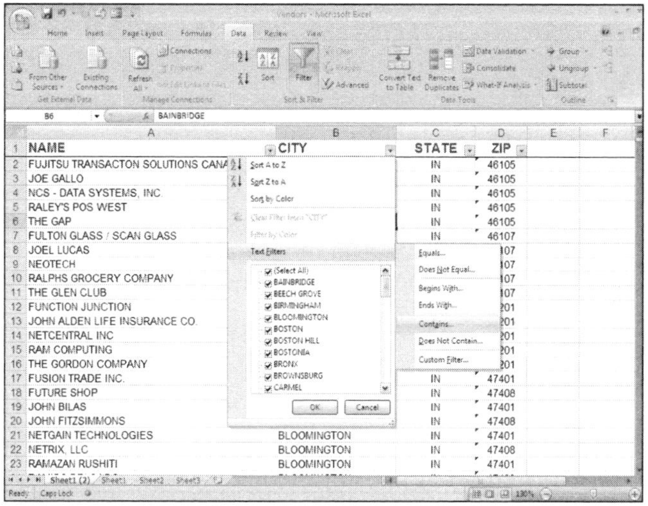

**Figure 14-7:** Comparison filters.

 The comparison filter you selected appears in the Line description box, but you can click the drop-down list and select a different comparison function.

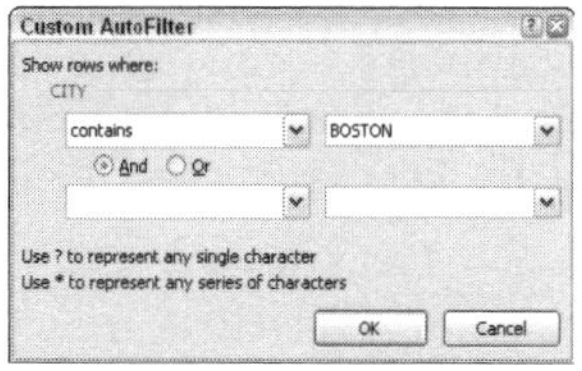

**Figure 14-8:** The Custom AutoFilter dialog box.

# Choose Additional Comparison Criteria

1. Follow Steps 1 through 4 from the previous section, "Use a Comparison Filter for Text."

2. Select the And or the Or option. Choosing "And" means that both criteria must be met, and choosing "Or" means that either criteria can be met.

3. From the drop-down list, select a second comparison filter.

4. Enter the second comparison filter value. Figure 14-9 shows an example.

5. Click OK to display the filtered records.

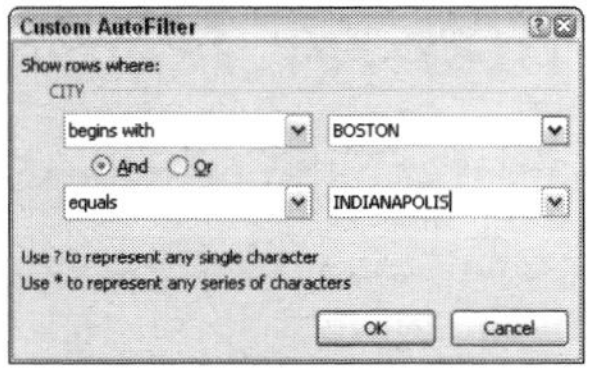

# Use a Comparison Filter for Numbers

1. Click the filter arrow for the numeric column by which you want to filter data.

2. Click Number Filters. A submenu of comparison filters like the one in Figure 14-10 appears. Some of the choices included are: Equals, Does not Equal, Greater than, Greater than or Equal To, Less Than, Less Than or Equal To, and Between.

3. Select a comparison filter to display the Custom AutoFilter dialog box.

4. Enter your filter criteria and then click OK.

**Figure 14-9:** Choosing multiple comparison criteria.

**Figure 14-10:** Choosing multiple comparison criteria.

 If you need to locate cells that share some of the characters you entered, but not others, you can use a wildcard character. Entering one or more question marks finds single characters and entering an asterisk finds any number of characters. For example: if you enter **Bos???**, you would find Boston, Bosnia, Bosart, Boshel . . . any word that begins with Bos but only has six characters.

# Filter for the Top or Bottom Numbers

1. Click the filter arrow for the numeric column by which you want to filter data.

2. Click Number Filters.

3. Choose Top 10. In Figure 14-11, you see the Top 10 AutoFilter dialog box.

4. From the first option, select whether you want the Top (highest) or Bottom (lowest) values.

5. In the second option, select the number of items you want to see (from 1 to 500).

6. In the third option, select whether you want to filter the items by their names or by their percentiles. For example, choose to list the top 10 customers per their sales dollars, or list the top 10% of your customer base.

7. Click OK. Excel displays the records that match your criteria.

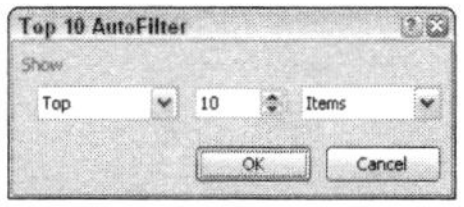

# Filter for the Above or Below Average Values

1. Click the filter arrow for the numeric column by which you want to filter data.

2. Click Number Filters.

3. Choose Above Average or Below Average to filter by numbers that meet either condition. In Figure 14-12, only the records with values below the total average appear.

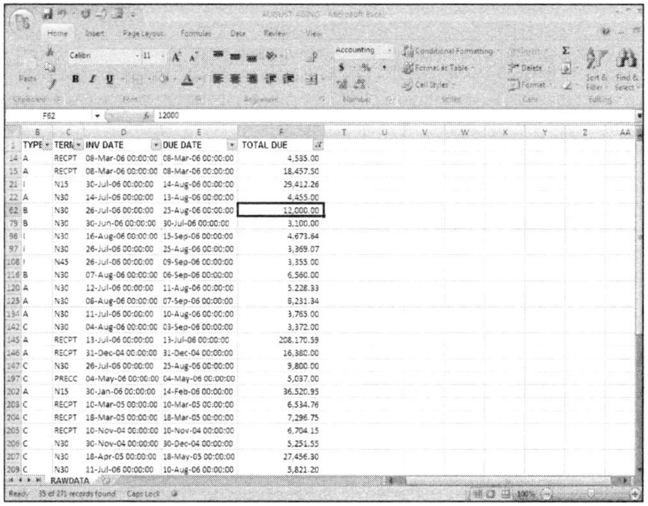

**Figure 14-11:** The Top 10 AutoFilter dialog box.

**Figure 14-12:** Looking for Averages.

Top and Bottom values are based on the original range of cells and not on any filtered data subset

Excel calculates the averages by taking the *total* of all the cells in the field and averaging them — not by using any filtered data subset.

# Filter by Date or Time

1. Click the filter arrow for the date column by which you want to filter data.

2. Click Date Filters. You see an extensive list of date filters like the ones shown in Figure 14-13.

3. Select a date filter. If you select a Common filter, you see the Custom AutoFilter dialog box. If you selected a dynamic filter, Excel immediately applies the filter.

 To filter by a date range, select Between.

4. In the box on the right, enter a date or time and click OK.

 Optionally, click the Calendar button to select a date.

# Filter by Color

1. Click the filter arrow for the column by which you want to filter data.

2. Select Filter by Color. A submenu of color options like the one you see in Figure 14-14 appears. You can filter by Cell (background) Color or by Font Color. The submenu you see depends on the color choices in your data.

3. Select an option. Excel displays the database using the filter you requested.

**Figure 14-13:** Filtering by dates.

**Figure 14-14:** Filtering by cell background or font color.

 Years and quarters always start in January of the calendar year.

# Use Advanced Filtering

1. Make sure the AutoFilter is turned off (Data⇨Sort & Filter⇨Filter).

2. Select the first for rows of the worksheet.

3. Choose Home⇨Cells⇨Insert⇨Insert Sheet Rows.

4. Select the database header row.

5. Choose Home⇨Clipboard⇨Copy or press Ctrl+C. A marquee appears around the copied area.

6. Click cell A1, the first cell of the first blank row.

7. Choose Home⇨Clipboard⇨Paste, which copies the header row of your database to the first blank row (Row 1). You now have a criteria range ready to enter filter selections. (See Figure 14-15.)

8. In the first blank row of the criteria range, enter the data you want to match. For example, if you want to locate any entries for the state of California, type **California** under the State heading.

9. Enter any additional filter criteria:

   - **Create an And filter:** If you want Excel to find data that meets more than one restriction, enter the desired additional criteria in another field on the first criteria row.

   - **Create an Or filter:** Enter the filter data on the second row of the criteria range. See Figure 14-16 where I've added criteria to both the State and Totals columns.

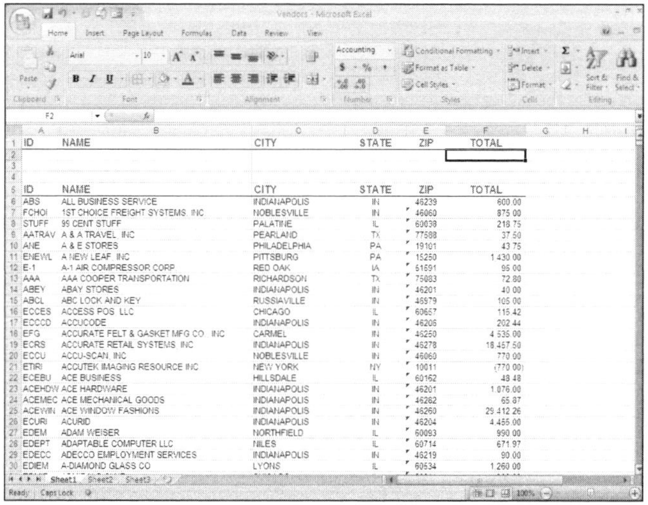

**Figure 14-15:** Insert blank rows for a criteria range.

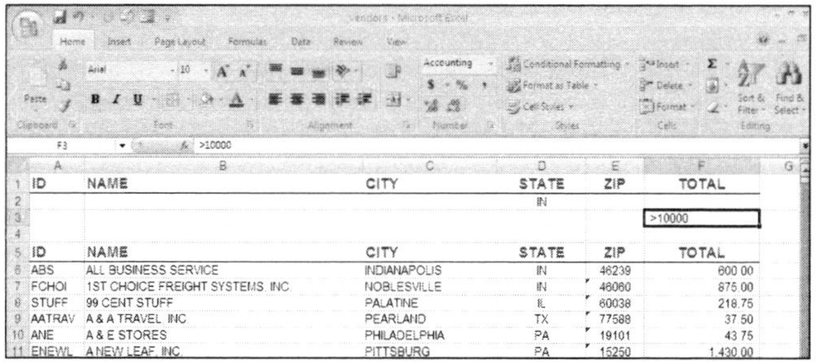

**Figure 14-16:** Enter your criteria.

Although you could just retype the header row, using the Copy and Paste features protects you against typing errors. The criteria area header row must exactly match the database header row.

You can use Greater Than, Greater Than Or Equal to, Less Than, or Less Than Or Equal To as operators in your criteria range. For example, to find sales greater than or equal to 100, enter >=**100** in the Sales criteria row.

**10.** Click any cell in the main part of the database.

**11.** Choose Data➪Sort & Filter➪Advanced. Excel displays the Advanced Filter dialog box.

**12.** Select the Filter the List, In Place option in the Actions section.

**13.** Verify the database range in the List Range box.

**14.** Enter the criteria range. Excel provides two different ways to do this:

- Type the criteria range including the header row, but **not any blank rows**. For example, in Figure 14-17, the criteria range is A1: F2.

 Be sure to specify only the rows that contain filtering information. If you include blank rows in your criteria range, Excel includes them in the filtering process. The effect is that no data is filtered out, so all records are returned.

- Click the Collapse button to the right of the Criteria Range box and highlight the entire criteria range, again including the header row but not any blank rows. Press Enter to return to the Advanced Filter dialog box.

**15.** Click OK. Excel places the results of your search in place of your original database (as shown in Figure 14-18). In this example, I asked for those vendors in the state of IN who *and* had an amount greater than 10,000.

**16.** When you're ready to view all data records, choose Data➪Sort & Filter➪Clear.

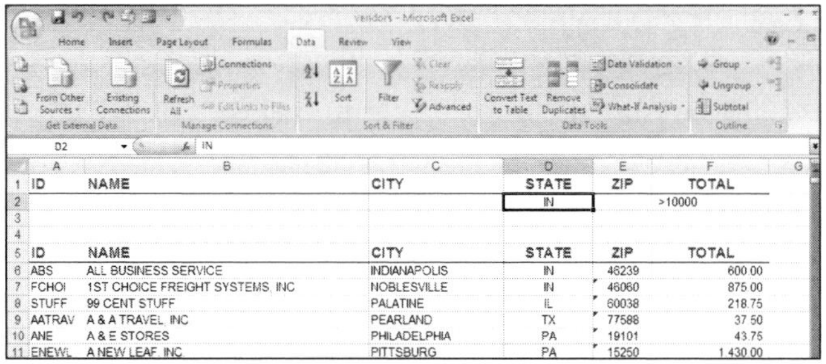

**Figure 14-17:** Enter the criteria range.

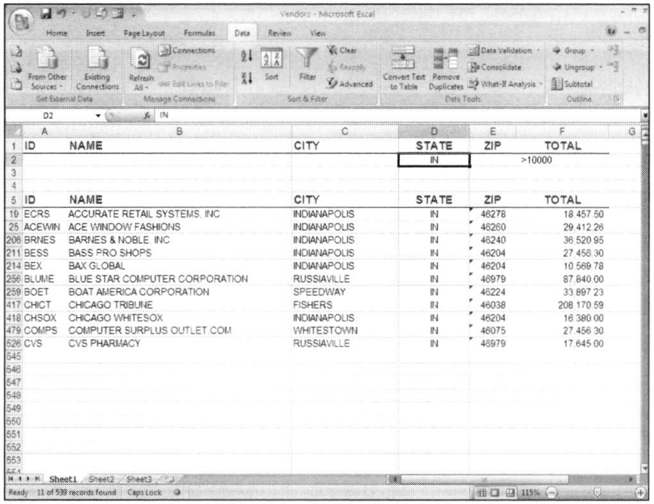

**Figure 14-18:** A filtered database.

 You cannot place filtered data on a different sheet from the original data, but you can copy and paste it to a different sheet.

# Creating PivotTables

**M**any people don't use PivotTables because they find them overwhelming. Yet, this powerful Excel tool enables you, in an instant, to see your spreadsheet data in a variety of different ways. PivotTable reports allow you to group information, along with varying levels of detail, by different criteria such as date or category. These reports also automatically subtotal the data on a separate worksheet, leaving your raw data untouched.

Furthermore, PivotTable calculations aren't limited to adding the numbers. You can use Count, Average, Maximum, Minimum, and a number of other statistical functions to help you view the overall picture of your data.

You can fill any of the four main PivotTable areas with data by a drag of the mouse, and you can display the data in a table format or in one of Excel's many chart formats.

In this chapter, you find out how you can, within a matter of seconds, generate and extract meaningful information from a large amount of data, thereby saving potentially dozens of hours of manual calculations.

# Chapter 15

## Get ready to . . .

# Create a PivotTable

1. Organize your data in a list, while keeping these points in mind:

   - Each column should contain only one type of data; for example, put dates in one column and values in another.

   - Make sure each column in the list has a heading label directly above the data. (See Figure 15-1 for an example.) PivotTables use the column headings as PivotTable fields.

   - Do not leave any blank rows between the data and the row headings and no blank columns within the data.

   - Avoid blank cells within the data. If you have duplicate data, use the Copy command to replicate it in the blank cells.

   - If you have more than one list on the same worksheet, make sure at least one blank column and one blank row separate them. Figure 15-2 illustrates a worksheet with multiple data tables. Although you can create multiple PivotTables in a workbook, you can work with only one table at a time when creating a PivotTable.

   - Remove any Excel-generated subtotals or grand totals in the data by choosing Data⇨Outline⇨Subtotal⇨Remove All.

   - Plan the questions that determine how you want your data analyzed. For example, if your data is sales information, perhaps you want to know your sales totals by region or a specific salesperson, or even deeper such as by both salesperson and by quarter.

**Figure 15-1:** A PivotTable data example.

**Figure 15-2:** Separate multiple data ranges with blank rows and columns.

2. Optionally, click any cell containing the data you want to analyze.

3. Choose Insert⇨Tables⇨PivotTable. The Create PivotTable dialog box appears.

4. Make a selection. Excel needs to know where your data will come from:

   • Microsoft Excel list or database: This choice creates the PivotTable from organized data in a Microsoft Excel worksheet.

   • External data source. This choice creates a PivotTable from data stored in a non-Excel database.

5. Verify that Excel correctly identified your data range, including the headings. If not, specify the correct area in the Table/Range box as shown in Figure 15-3.

If the data is in another worksheet in the same workbook or a different saved workbook, type the workbook and worksheet name like this: **[*workbookname*]***sheetname!range*.

6. Choose whether to add the PivotTable to a new worksheet in your workbook or to another existing worksheet. If you choose to add it to an existing worksheet, you must specify a cell location.

7. Click OK. Excel creates a new worksheet with a blank PivotTable along with PivotTable Field List, which contains each field from your data range (see Figure 15-4). PivotTables contain three primary elements:

   • **Rows:** The Rows area displays your data vertically, with one item per row.

   • **Columns:** The Columns area displays the data horizontally, with one item per column.

   • **Values:** Data Fields summarize numerical data.

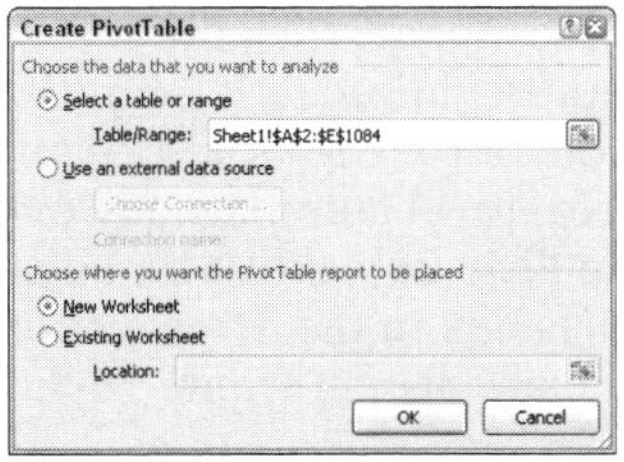

**Figure 15-3:** Specify the data you want to analyze.

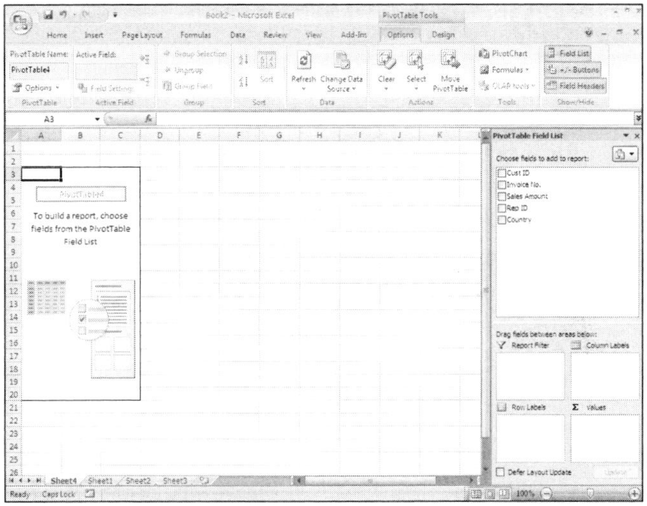

**Figure 15-4:** A blank PivotTable.

Excel also places two new PivotTable tabs on the Ribbon.

8. From the PivotTable Field List pane, click the check box next to the field you want categorized. For example, if you want to determine how much each salesperson sold, select the Rep ID field. Excel automatically places each unique item into the Pivot Table rows and displays the name in the Row Labels box in the Areas section located beneath the field name list. In Figure 15-5, Excel displays the name of each Sales Rep.

 If you want the categorized field displayed horizontally instead of vertically, drag the field to the Column Labels box of the Areas section.

9. From the PivotTable Field List pane, select the field, such as Sales Amount, you want summarized and perform one of the following actions. Excel instantly takes the data and adds the totals to create the summary PivotTable (see Figure 15-6).

   • Click the check box next to the field.

 The PivotTable Field List indicates fields used in the PivotTable with bold lettering. You don't have to use all the fields in the PivotTable, and you don't have to place fields in every area of the PivotTable.

   • Drag the field to the Values area in the Areas section.

 If you drag a field to an incorrect area, uncheck the field name check box or drag the field name out of the Areas section onto the Excel worksheet.

 To delete a PivotTable, choose PivotTable Tools Options⇨Actions⇨ Select⇨Entire PivotTable. Press the Delete key. Optionally, delete the entire worksheet.

To move a PivotTable to a different location, choose PivotTable Tools Options⇨Move PivotTable. In the resulting dialog box, specify or point to a new location for the current PivotTable.

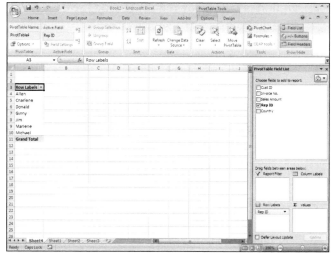

**Figure 15-5:** Placing a row field.

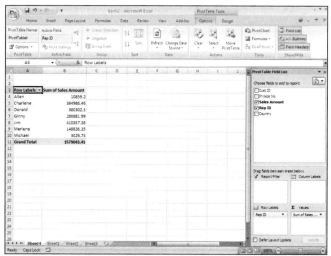

**Figure 15-6:** A completed PivotTable.

# Select and Manage PivotTable Data

1. On the PivotTable, click the down arrow in the Row Labels heading section. A list of individual items, such as sales rep names, appears. The items that appear depend on the values you used in your data.

2. Remove the check mark next to any item you don't want included in the PivotTable.

3. Click OK. In Figure 15-7, only data for two specifically selected sales reps appears in the PivotTable.

> To clear the filter, click the heading arrow and choose Clear Filter or check Select All.

4. Select any of the following methods to update the PivotTable with any changes made in the original data:

   - Choose PivotTable Tools Options⇨Data⇨Refresh.

   - Right-click anywhere on the PivotTable and choose Refresh from the shortcut menu.

   - Make the PivotTable automatically refresh whenever you reopen the file by choosing PivotTable Tools Options⇨PivotTable⇨Options. From the Data tab of the PivotTable Options dialog box, select Refresh Data When Opening File.

5. Double-click any data value to display the specific details that comprise the data. In Figure 15-8 you see the detail for Sales Rep Charlene displayed on a separate worksheet.

> You can safely delete the separate individual worksheet without affecting the PivotTable.

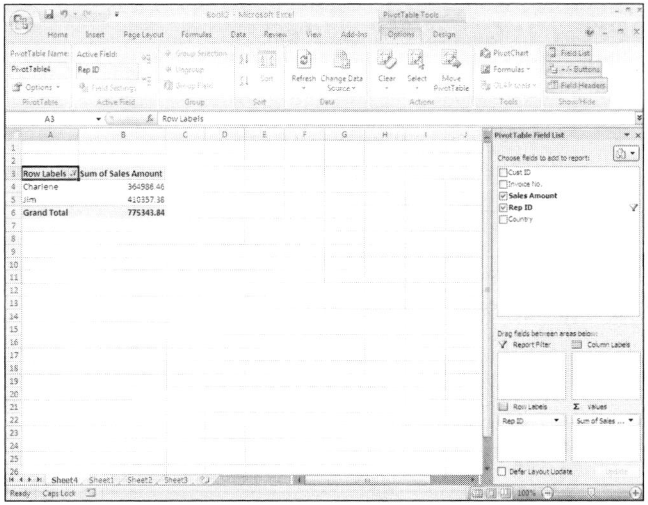

**Figure 15-7:** Filter data from a PivotTable.

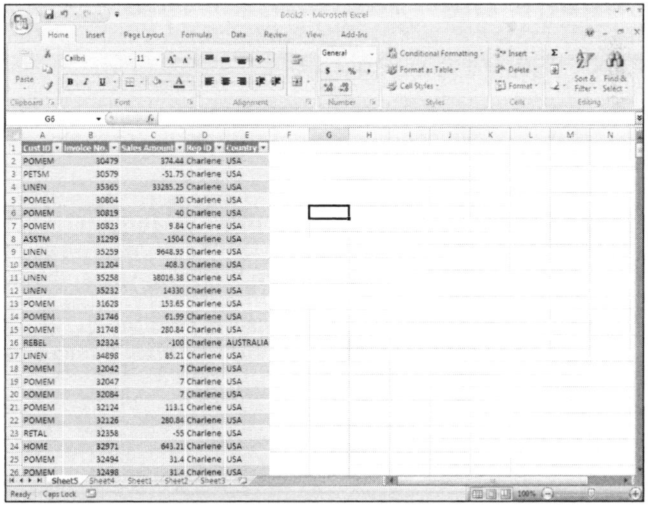

**Figure 15-8:** Examine the individual data from a PivotTable subtotal.

# Sort PivotTable Data

1. Click anywhere in the field you want to sort.

2. Choose PivotTable Tools ⇨Sort.

> Depending on the data type, the option may say Sort Smallest to Largest or Sort A to Z.

3. Click a Sort button. The PivotTable data sorts according to your choice. In Figure 15-9, the data is sorted by the Sum of Sales Amounts.

> Click the Sort button to display the Sort by box.

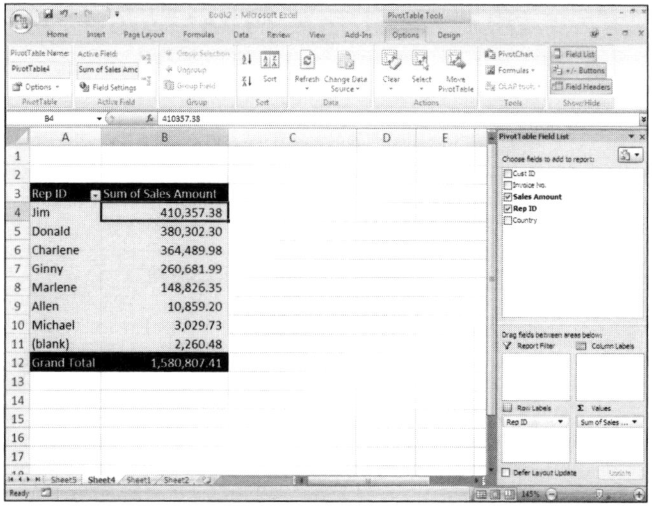

# Change the Calculation Type

1. Click anywhere in the subtotaled data field.

2. Choose PivotTable Tools Options⇨Active Field⇨Field Settings. The Value Field Settings dialog box, shown in Figure 15-10, appears.

3. From the Summarize By list, select the function you want to use. Choices include Sum, Count, Average, Max, Min, Product, CountNums, StdDev, StdDevp, Var, and Varp.

4. Click OK. Excel resummarizes the field based on the function you selected. The field title also changes to reflect the selected function.

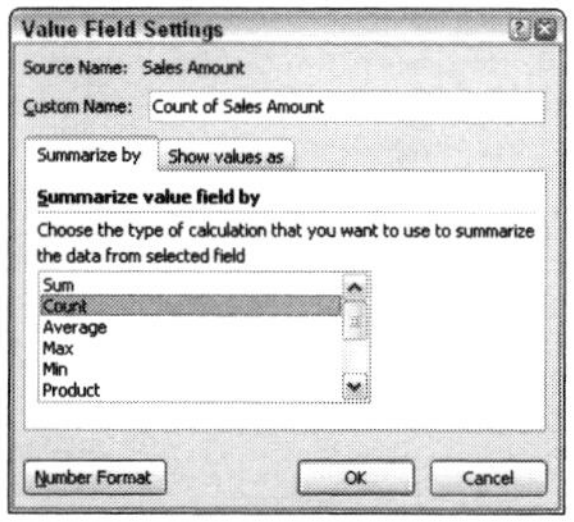

**Figure 15-9:** Sorting PivotTable data.

**Figure 15-10:** Select a different summarizing function.

> If you don't want to display grand totals at the bottom, choose PivotTable Tools Design⇨Layout⇨Grand Totals and choose On for Rows only.

# *Rename a PivotTable Field*

1. Click anywhere in the field data you want to rename.

2. Choose PivotTable Tools Options⇨Active Field⇨Field Settings. The Field Settings dialog box opens (see Figure 15-11).

    Optionally, click the field name in the PivotTable and begin typing a new name. Press Enter when you are finished.

3. In the Custom Name box, type the new field name.

4. Click OK. Both the PivotTable field and the Field List names change.

    You cannot rename a field the same as the original field name. For example, you cannot change Sum of Quantity to just Quantity. You can, however, add a space at the end of Quantity, which gives it a unique name.

# *Format PivotTable Values*

1. Select the PivotTable field you want to modify.

2. Choose PivotTable Tools Options⇨Active Field⇨Field Settings.

3. From the Field Settings dialog box, click the Number Format button.

4. From the Format Cells dialog box (see Figure 15-12), select the Number format you want.

5. If applicable, select the number of decimal places you want.

6. Click OK twice.

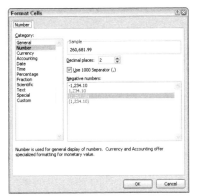

**Figure 15-11:** Rename a PivotTable field.

**Figure 15-12:** Setting value formats.

 To change the format of PivotTable text, select any text cells and format them from the Home tab. See Chapters 5 and 6.

# AutoFormat PivotTables

1. Choose PivotTable Tools Design⇨PivotTable Styles.

2. Click the More arrow. A gallery of PivotTable styles appears as shown in Figure 15-13.

3. Select a format. Excel provides over 85 different predefined PivotTable formats, or you can create your own format.

 To remove the formatting, Choose PivotTable Tools⇨Design⇨ PivotTable Styles⇨More⇨Clear.

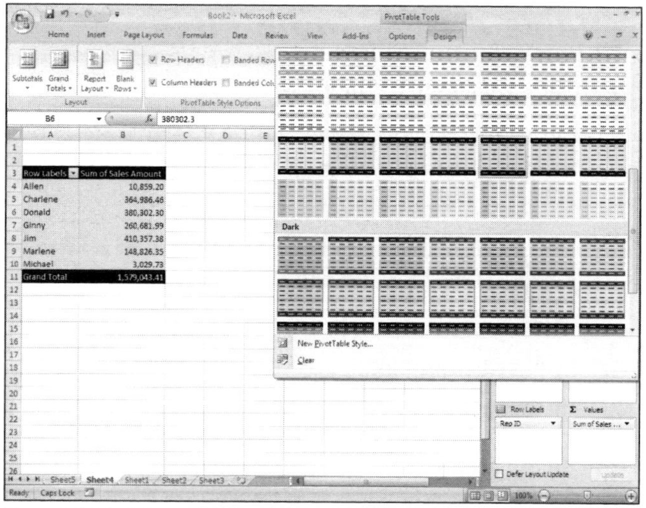

# Group Data Together

1. Create a PivotTable (see the "Create a PivotTable" section, earlier in this chapter).

2. Click in any cell of the field you want to group. A popular field to group is a date field.

3. Choose PivotTable Tools Options⇨Group⇨Group Field.

4. From the Grouping dialog box, select the grouping option you want to use. The options that appear depend on the type of data you are grouping.

5. Click OK. Figure 15-14 illustrates two PivotTable examples — one with the dates in detail and the other with the dates grouped by month.

 To ungroup categories and redisplay the entire list, click the PivotTable button and choose Group and Show Detail⇨Ungroup.

If you need to change the PivotTable data source, choose PivotTable Tools Options⇨Data⇨Change Data Source and specify different cells.

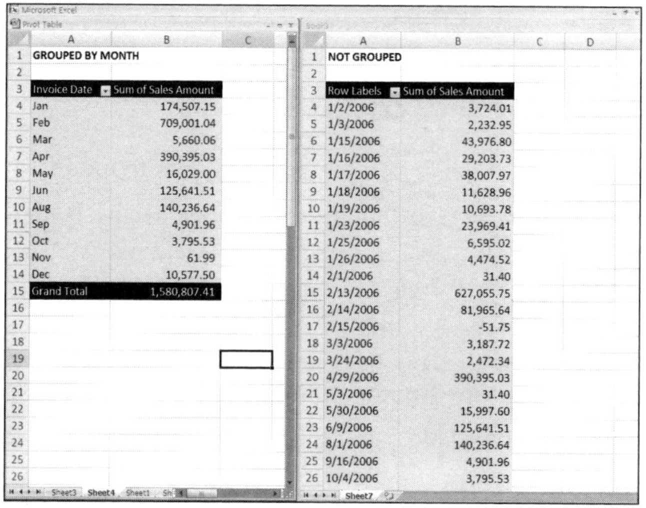

**Figure 15-13:** Select an AutoFormat from any of the many options.

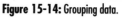

**Figure 15-14:** Grouping data.

# Generate Multilevel Totals

1. Create a PivotTable (see "Create a PivotTable" earlier in this chapter).

2. To create a second summary level, drag the next field you want to subtotal from the PivotTable Field List onto the desired PivotTable area, keeping these pointers in mind:

   - If you want to create a second category, such as by Country and then by Salesman, drag the field into the Row area. Figure 15-15 shows a PivotTable with two categories. The field closest to the data is called the inner row (in this example, Invoice Date). The other field is called an outer row (in this example, Salesperson). Excel displays data in the inner row under each of the outer row fields.

   - If you want to change the order of the inner and outer row fields, from the Area box, drag the field you want as the outer row to the top of the box.

   - If you want to total additional fields, drag the field into the Data area.

    You can add even more data fields to your PivotTable. PivotTable data fields are only limited by the amount of memory in your computer.

   - If you want to sum different fields or if you want to create two different total types (such as count and sum, or max and min), select a field you have already used. Currently used fields are listed in bold type. In Figure 15-16, the sales are both summarized and counted.

   - Click the minus sign to collapse a row heading such as a particular salesperson's name. Click the plus sign to expand the row again to see all the data.

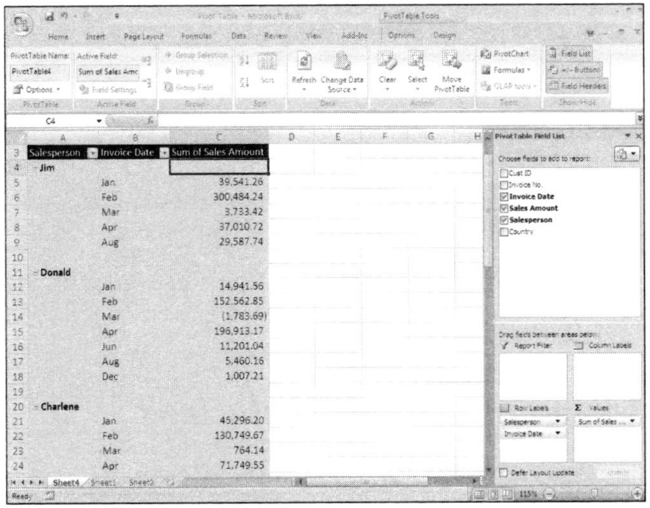

**Figure 15-15:** Multiple category fields.

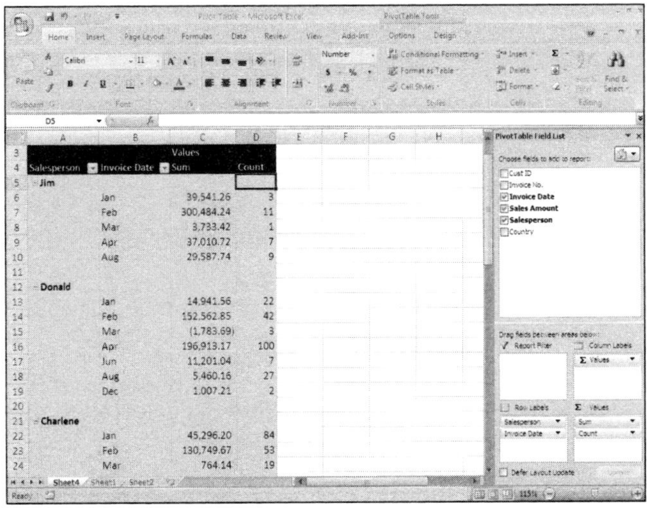

**Figure 15-16:** Multiple data fields.

# Calculate a Percent of Totals

1. Add a second totals field and display the two fields side by side. (See the earlier section, "Generate Multilevel Totals").

2. Select the second totals field and choose PivotTable Tools Options➪Active Field➪Field Settings.

3. Click the Show Values As tab and from the drop-down list, (see Figure 15-17); then choose % of Column. Click OK.

# Add Your Own Calculations

1. Choose PivotTable Tools Options➪Tools➪Formulas➪ Calculated Field.

2. In the Name text box, type a name for the formula.

3. In the Formula box, delete the =0 and create your own formula, following these tips:

   • Like other Excel formulas, it begins with an equal sign, but you use field names instead of cell references. You can't use cell references in a formula, but you can use static values.

   • Double-click any field name in the Fields box to add it to the formula.

   • Use the standard formula operators such as plus, minus, multiply, and divide (+, −, *, and /).

4. Click OK. Excel creates a new data column with the calculated value. Figure 15-18 shows a PivotTable with a calculated field next to the data field.

**Figure 15-17:** Create special calculations.

**Figure 15-18:** A customized formula calculation added to a PivotTable.

If you no longer want the calculated field on your PivotTable, drag the calculated field heading out of the Values Areas box.

# Create a PivotChart

1. Create a PivotTable (see the earlier section, "Create a PivotTable").

2. Click anywhere in the PivotTable. Choose Insert➪Charts and select a chart type. As you see in Figure 15-19, Excel automatically creates a chart from your PivotTable. All PivotTable data, except for the totals and subtotals, appear in the PivotChart.

 Changes to the PivotTable affect the PivotChart, and field changes to the PivotChart affect the PivotTable.

3. Format the chart (see Chapter 11) with the following exceptions:

   • You cannot move or resize the plot area.

   • You cannot add data to the PivotChart from outside the PivotTable.

   • PivotCharts cannot be Scatter, Bubble, or Stock types.

   • You can click the Axis Fields drop-down list to filter the row headings you want to use. See Figure 15-20.

 To delete the PivotChart, select the chart boundaries and press the Delete key.

 To convert the PivotTable to standard data that you can use to create a standard (non-PivotChart) chart, select the PivotTable report data that you want to use and choose Copy and Paste➪Paste Values commands to duplicate the data to a blank area of the workbook. You can then create a standard chart of your choosing.

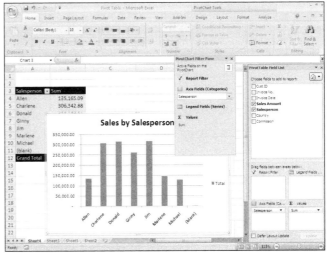

**Figure 15-19:** Create a Pivot Chart.

**Figure 15-20:** Display selected data using the PivotChart buttons.

# Building Simple Macros

*Y*ou can often save yourself time by automating tasks you perform frequently. The automation takes the form of an *Excel Macro*, which is a series of commands and functions grouped together as a single command. Macros are created in a special programming language called Visual Basic and can be run whenever you need to perform the task.

Although you can write your own very complex macros in the Visual Basic programming language, the easiest method for creating many macros is to use the Excel Macro Recorder. When you record a macro, Excel stores information about each step you take as you perform a series of commands. You then run the macro to repeat, or *play back*, the commands.

The macro recorder is very literal and records every action you complete. Therefore, planning your macro before you begin the recording process is very important so you don't record unnecessary steps.

Security is an important issue when working with macros. If you open worksheets containing macros from outside sources, these macros can be harmful to your computer. By default, Excel protects you from running macros, but if you're creating your own macros, you'll probably change these protective security settings.

In this chapter, you find out how to change your security settings, as well as how to record, run, and delete Excel macros.

## Get ready to . . .

# Display the Developer Tab

1.  Choose Office Button⇨Excel Options. The Excel Options dialog box appears.

2.  From the Popular section, check the option Show Developer Tab in the Ribbon.

3.  Click OK. The Developer tab appears, with Macro options. See Figure 16-1.

# Record a Macro

1.  Choose Developer⇨Code⇨Record Macro. The Record Macro dialog box, shown in Figure 16-2, appears.

2.  Type a name and optional description for the macro.

3.  From the Store Macro In drop-down list, select where you want to store the macro:

    *   **This Workbook:** Save the macro in only the current workbook file.

    *   **New Workbook:** Create macros that you can run in any new workbooks created during the current Excel session.

    *   **Personal Macro Workbook:** Choose this option if you want the macro to be available whenever you use Excel, regardless of which worksheet you are using.

4.  Click OK. The Record Macro option changes to Stop Recording.

5.  Perform the actions you want to record. Excel is recording your keystrokes as you type.

6.  Choose Developer⇨Code⇨Stop Recording.

You can also manage macros by choosing View⇨Macros⇨Macros.

The first character of the macro name must be a letter, and the name cannot contain spaces or cell references. Macro names are not case-sensitive.

Excel records your steps exactly — such as (Select cell C3) — but you can also record the steps relative to any current cell — such as (Go up one row and insert a blank line). To do so, choose Developer⇨Code⇨Use Relative References. You can turn the Relative Reference function on and off as often as you need to when recording the macro.

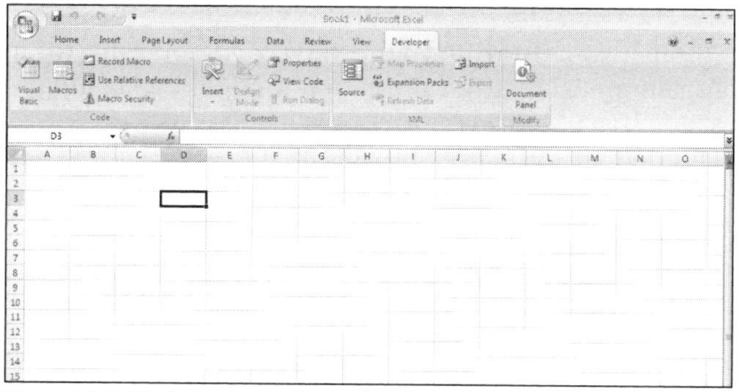

**Figure 16-1:** Displaying the Developer tab.

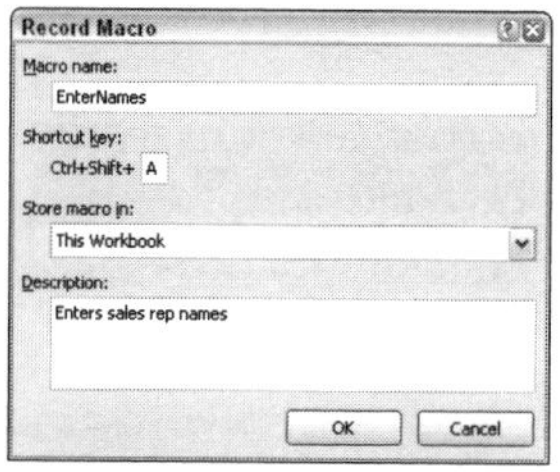

**Figure 16-2:** The Record Macro dialog box.

# Assign a Macro Keystroke

1. Choose Developer⇨Code⇨Record Macro.

2. In the Macro Name text box, type a name for the macro.

3. From the Store Macro drop-down list, select where you want to store the macro.

4. Optionally, in the description box, type a description of the macro.

5. Assign a keystroke combination (see Figure 16-3). If you select a shortcut key already used in Excel, the macro shortcut key overrides the Excel shortcut key while the workbook that contains the macro is open.

 If you enter a lowercase letter, Excel assigns it a CTRL+lowercase letter combination. If you type an uppercase letter, you must press CTRL+SHIFT+the letter to run the macro. The shortcut key cannot be a number or special character.

6. Click OK.

7. Perform the actions you want to record.

8. Click the Stop Recording button on the Stop Recording toolbar, or choose Tools⇨Macro⇨Stop Recording.

9. To execute the macro, press the shortcut key you assigned or choose the macro from Tools⇨Macro⇨Macros.

# Run a Macro

1. Choose Developer⇨Code⇨Macros. The Macro dialog box, shown in Figure 16-4, appears.

2. Select the macro you want to run.

3. Click Run. Excel executes the selected macro.

 It's a good idea to save your file before running a newly created macro. Excel cannot undo the steps taken by the macro.

 Optionally, press the shortcut key combination you assigned to the macro.

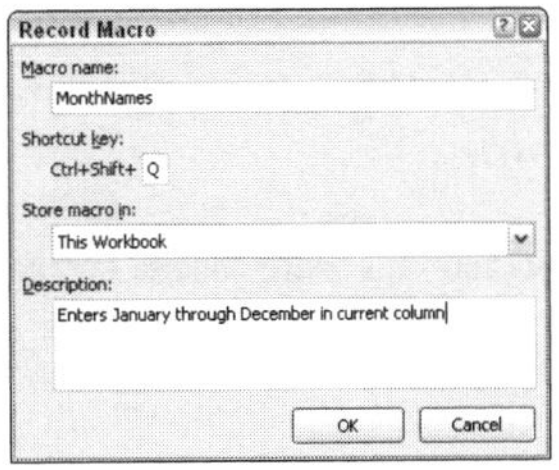

**Figure 16-3:** Assign a shortcut key to a macro.

**Figure 16-4:** Select a prerecorded macro.

# Save a Macro-Enabled Workbook

**1.** Choose Office Button➪Save As. The Save As dialog box appears.

**2.** Enter a name and select a location for your workbook.

**3.** Click the Save as Type drop-down arrow. A list of file types appears.

**4.** Choose Excel Macro-Enabled Workbook. Excel adds the .xlsm extension to the filename.

 If you neglect to save the workbook as a Macro-enabled workbook, you see the warning message (shown in Figure 16-5) telling you that the macro will not be retained.

# Open a Macro-Enabled Workbook

**1.** Open a workbook containing a macro. The workbook opens as usual but a Security Warning message appears below the ribbon.

**2.** Click Options. The Microsoft Office Security Options dialog box you see in Figure 16-6 appears.

**3.** Click Enable This Content only if you know where the macro originated.

**4.** Click OK. The dialog box closes, along with the Security Warning message.

**Figure 16-5:** The Macro warning message.

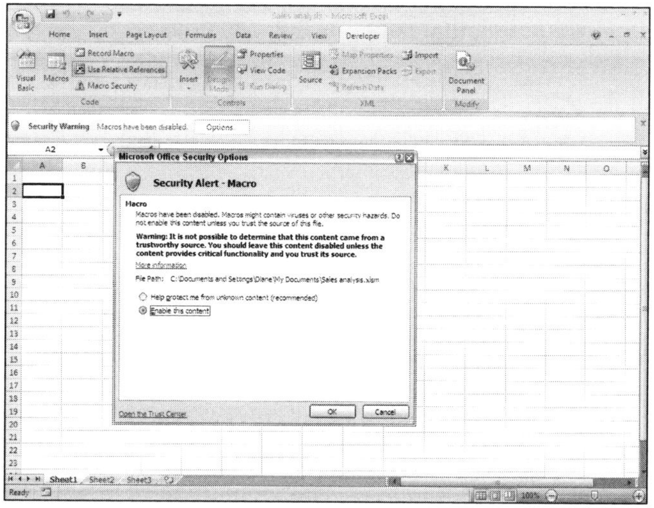

**Figure 16-6:** The Security Options dialog box.

# Check Macro Security Level

1. Choose Developer➪Code➪Macro Security. The Trust Center dialog box shown in Figure 16-7 appears.

2. Set a security level:

   • **Disable all macros without notification**: Allows you to run only macros that are stored in a trusted location. Click the Trusted Location section to manage these trusted locations. (See Figure 16-8). Also, since the macros are automatically disabled, this option disables security alerts.

   • **Disable all macros with notification**: Displays a security alert when a workbook with macros opens. You can then decide whether to enable the macros associated with the workbook. This is the Excel default setting.

   • **Disable all macros except digitally signed macros**: You can only run only those macros that are digitally signed.

    A digital signature is an electronic, encrypted, secure stamp of authentication obtained from a commercial certification authority. Excel's Visual Basic programming language contains a self-certifying digital signature tool, but because it doesn't come from a third party, Excel still considers it unauthenticated and displays a warning box before running self-certified macros.

   • **Enable all macros:** Allows macros to run without a notification. This can be helpful if you run a lot of macros, but be aware of the risk when using macros from unknown sources.

3. Click OK.

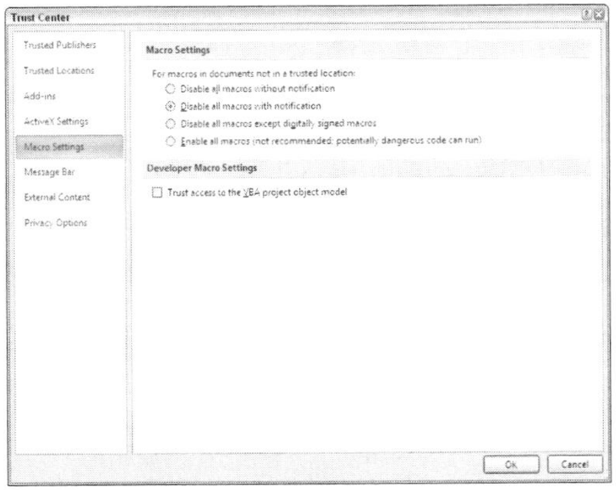

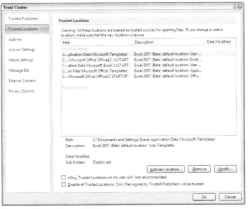

**Figure 16-7:** The Trust Center dialog box.

**Figure 16-8:** Trusted file locations.

## Add a Macro Button to the Quick Access Toolbar

1. Choose Office Button⇨Excel Options.

2. Click the Customize section

3. From the Choose command from drop-down list, select Macros.

4. Select the macro you want displayed on the Quick Access toolbar.

5. Click Add. An icon is added to the right panel.

6. Click the newly added macro command.

7. Click Modify. You see the Modify Button dialog box, shown in Figure 16-9.

8. Choose an icon to represent the macro.

9. Click OK.

10. Click OK to close the Excel options dialog box. Excel now displays a macro button in the Quick Access toolbar.

11. To run the macro, click the toolbar button.

## Delete a Macro

1. Open the workbook containing the macro you want to delete.

2. Choose Developer⇨Code⇨Macros. The Macro dialog box appears (see Figure 16-10).

3. From the Macro dialog box, select the name of the macro you want to delete.

4. Click Delete. A confirmation box appears.

5. Click Yes.

Deleting a macro does not remove the button you placed on the Quick Access toolbar. To delete a button from the Quick Access toolbar, right-click the macro icon and choose Remove from Quick Access Toolbar.

**Figure 16-9:** Change the look of an icon.

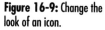

**Figure 16-10:** Select a macro to delete.

# Saving Time with Excel Tools

# Chapter 17

*T*his chapter is about stuff . . . Excel stuff. In the earlier chapters, I show how Excel has lots of power to make your computing life a little easier. This chapter contains a diverse group of Excel tools designed to speed up data entry and improve spreadsheet quality.

In this chapter you discover:

➡ How to add special characters such as the copyright symbol, the registered trademark, foreign characters, or smiley faces.

➡ Split data into multiple columns where you can break up data containing multiple words such as a first name and last name, or city, state, and zip code, into separate columns.

➡ Merge columns by using the Excel Concatenate function to combine data.

➡ Manage Excel's AutoCorrect feature to have Excel automatically correct many common misspelling or formatting issues.

➡ Work with SmartTags, those funny little indicators that often appear when you perform certain Excel functions or enter a particular type of Excel data.

➡ Check your workbook for spelling errors.

➡ Find just the right word with the thesaurus.

## Get ready to . . .

# Add Special Characters

1. Click the location where you want the symbol. Special characters can be in their own cells or amid other text or values.

2. Choose Insert➪Text➪Symbol. The Symbol dialog box appears (see Figure 17-1).

3. From the Symbols tab, click the symbol you want to use.

4. Click Insert. Excel inserts the symbol into the current cell. Click the Close button.

# Check Your Spelling

1. Choose Review➪Proofing➪Spelling. The Spelling dialog box opens, displaying the first potential error as you see in Figure 17-2.

2. Select one of the following options:

   • Choose a correction suggestion and then click Change. This changes just the current instance of the spelling mistake.

   • Choose Change All if you think you made the mistake more than once.

   • Choose Ignore Once or Ignore All if you don't want to correct the spelling item.

   • Choose Add to Dictionary to add a word, such as a product name or scientific term, to Excel's built-in dictionary, thus ensuring that word won't be flagged as an error in the future.

3. Continue with the next error until the spell-checking is complete and then click OK.

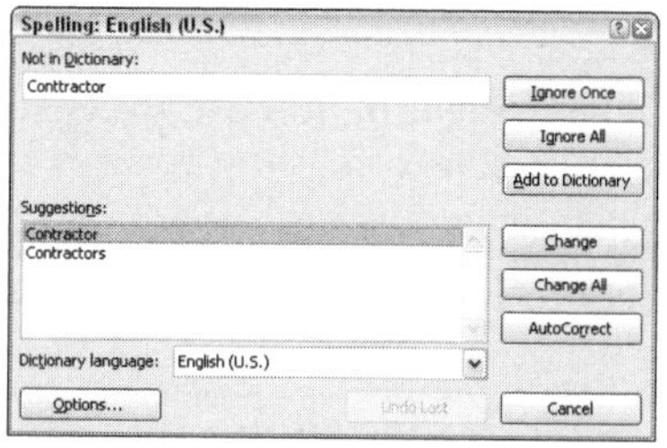

Different fonts display different symbols. If you don't see the symbol you want, select a different font from the Font drop-down list. For a large variety of unusual characters, look at the Wingdings fonts. Additional special characters are available on the Special Characters tab.

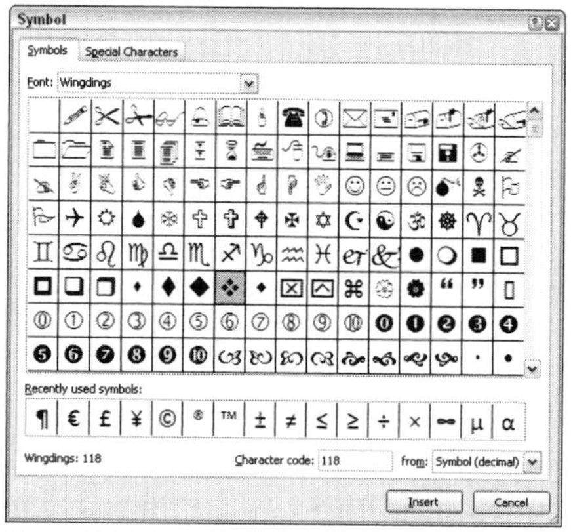

**Figure 17-1:** Insert symbols such as the copyright character into a cell.

**Figure 17-2:** Check your workbook for spelling errors.

# *Find Words with the Thesaurus*

1. Select the word you want to replace with another word.

2. Choose Review⇨Proofing⇨Thesaurus. The Research task pane opens with a list of suggestions.

3. Click the arrow next to the word that fits best as a replacement. A list of options appears. See Figure 17-3.

4. Choose Insert. Excel replaces the highlighted word with the new word.

# *Manage AutoCorrect*

1. Choose Office Button⇨Excel Options. The Excel Options dialog box appears.

2. From the Proofing section, choose AutoCorrect Options. The AutoCorrect dialog box opens.

3. Remove the check marks from any option you do not want Excel to automatically correct.

4. In the Replace box, type a common typing mistake. For example, if you frequently type *profitt* instead of *profit*, type **profitt** in the Replace box.

5. In the With text box, type the correct word as shown in Figure 17-4.

6. Click Add.

7. Click the AutoFormat As You Type tab.

8. Remove the check mark from any action you don't want Excel to automatically perform.

9. Click OK twice.

To remove any unwanted entry, select the entry and click the Delete button.

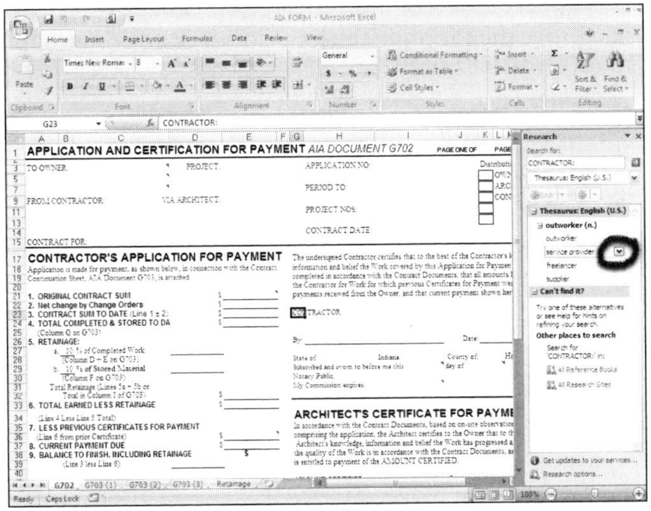

**Figure 17-3:** Find an elusive word with the thesaurus.

**Figure 17-4:** AutoCorrect Options.

# *Work with Smart Tags*

1. Choose Office Button⇨Excel Options. The Excel Options dialog box appears.

2. From the Proofing section, choose AutoCorrect Options. The AutoCorrect dialog box opens.

3. Click the Smart Tags tab (see Figure 17-5).

4. Check the Label Data With Smart Tags option.

5. Click OK twice.

6. From the worksheet, click a Smart Tag icon. Each Smart Tag type appears with a different icon appearance including:

   - **Paste:** This icon appears over pasted data (as shown in Figure 17-6), offering choices for pasting such as whether to include formatting, values, or both.

   - **AutoFill:** This icon appears after you enter data in a worksheet, offering tips on how to fill in the text or data.

   - **Insert:** This icon appears next to inserted cells, rows, or columns, offering a list of formatting options.

   - **AutoCorrect:** This icon is a small, blue box that appears near text that was automatically corrected, offering to undo an AutoCorrect action.

   - **Financial**: This icon appears over a cell with a U.S. stock symbol and offers options to check stock prices. Financial Smart Tags are indicated by a purple triangle in the lower-right corner of a worksheet cell.

   - **Error Checking:** This icon appears over potential formula errors in the same way as the Error-Checking feature. Error-Checking Smart Tags are indicated by a small green triangle in the upper-left corner of a worksheet cell.

 The availability of some Smart Tag options depends on other software installed on your computer.

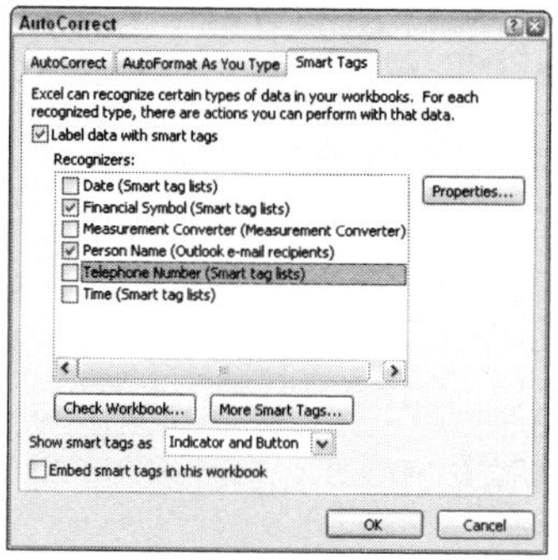

**Figure 17-5:** Enable additional Smart Tags.

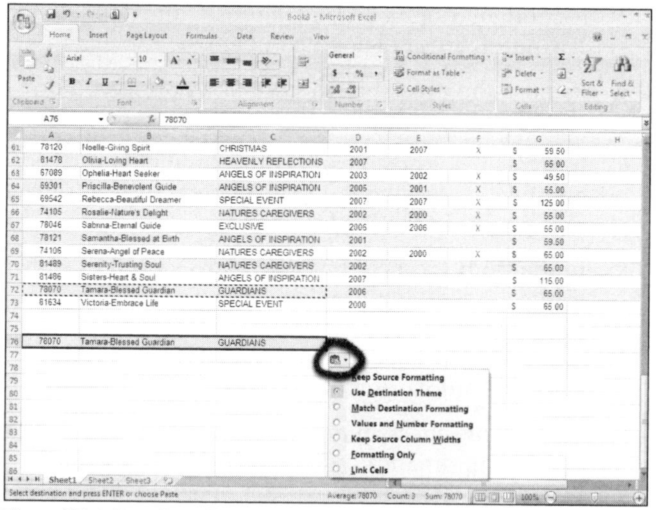

**Figure 17-6:** Paste Smart Tag options.

# *Split Data into Multiple Columns*

1. If necessary, insert blank columns to the left of the cells you want to convert into multiple columns. If you want your data in three columns, you must have two blank columns.

2. Select the cells you want to convert.

 You can't split empty cells, and you can't split merged cells. You must first unmerge the cells. See Chapter 5 for information about merged cells.

3. Choose Data⇨Data Tools⇨Text to Columns. The Convert Text to Columns Wizard appears.

4. Select the Original Data type that best suits your existing data. For example, if you're separating text that is variable in length such as a first name and last name, select Delimited. The Delimited data type works best if your data has a similar format. If all cells contain a specific number of characters, choose Fixed Width. See Figure 17-7.

 If your data type is delimited, be sure each section is separated by a common character such as a comma, period, apostrophe, or tab.

5. Click Next. The option you see next depends on which data type you selected in Step 4.

6. If you selected Fixed Width, click the ruler bar where you want the data to split. If you selected Delimited, enter the character you use to separate your text. In Figure 17-8, the text is separated by a comma.

7. Click Finish. Excel separates the selected cells into multiple columns.

8. Click OK.

 To split data into two lines in the same cell, press Alt + Enter at the point where you want to break the line.

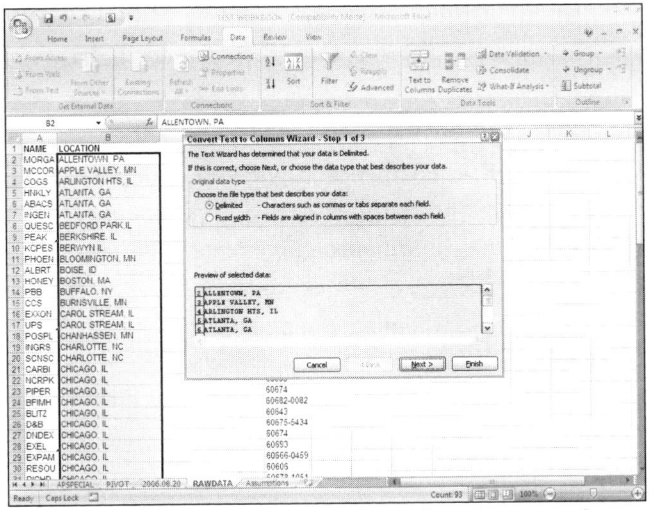

**Figure 17-7:** Convert text to multiple columns by specifying what separates the text sections.

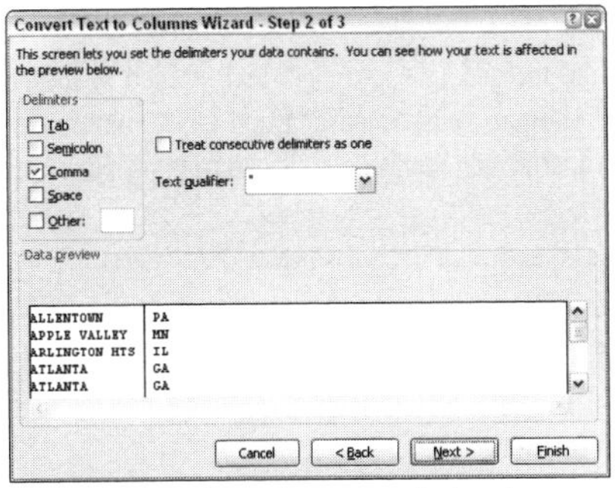

**Figure 17-8:** Splitting data into multiple columns.

# Merge Columns

1. Click in the cell where you want to put the merged data.

2. Choose Formulas➪Function Library➪Insert Function.

3. From the Or Select A Category drop-down list, choose Text.

4. Select Concatenate. (See Figure 17-9.)

5. Click OK. The Function Arguments dialog box appears.

6. Type the first cell address or click the cell you want to add to the combination. Excel enters the cell address in the Text1 box.

   Optionally, if you want to add specific text that's not in a cell address, type the text or punctuation (including any spaces) on any line. Excel places any spaces, punctuation, or text in quotation marks.

7. In the Text2 box, click the cell or type the text you want next. Each element must go on its own Text-box line. Figure 17-10 shows an example.

8. Click OK.

   To convert the merged cells into plain text, instead of formulas, select the merged cells, choose Edit➪Copy; next, choose Edit➪Paste Special; and finally, select Values from the Paste Special dialog box.

   Optionally, use the ampersand (&) between cell addresses to join text items. For example, =A1&B1 returns the same value as =CON-CATENATE(A1,B1). However, the cells you connect with the ampersand cannot be blank.

You can also use the CONCATENATE command along with a couple of other functions, to display only certain digits — for example, the last four digits of cell containing a credit card number. If cell C5 contains the credit card number, and you want cell D5 to display ****-****-1234, enter the following formula in cell D5. =CONCATENATE(REPT("****-",3), RIGHT(C5,4)). The REPT function repeats the "****-" text three times and combines that with the last four digits of the credit card number, which are derived from the RIGHT function.

**Figure 17-9:** Combining multiple columns into a single column.

**Figure 17-10:** Concatenating text columns.

# Part V
# Utilizing Excel with Other People and Applications

The 5th Wave      By Rich Tennant

At FEMA, employees often use Excel's custom format function to create formulas for disaster.

# Collaborating in Excel

# Chapter 18

Chances are, you have an Excel workbook that others need to access. You may copy the workbook to another disk and hand it to your coworkers, the others may access it directly from your computer, or you may even e-mail or post the file on the Internet. Excel provides several features aimed at helping people collaborate on a workbook. All users can add their own comments, track revisions as multiple people edit the workbook, and merge multiple copies of the workbook.

Comments are notes that you attach to cells, separate from other cell content. Using comments allows you or others reviewing a workbook to provide instruction, for example, noting how a complex formula works, entering thoughts, questions, and even specifications about the type of information you want the end user to enter into the cells. Adding a comment does not change the overall appearance of the worksheet. You can think of comments as sticky notes for an individual worksheet's cells.

When multiple people edit a workbook it can be difficult to determine which person made which changes. Revision tracking helps you determine who added changes to the file and what the changes were — including formatting changes and data additions or deletions. The tracking feature changes the color for each person's edits, making it easy to see who changed what in the workbook. When you review the workbook, you can choose to accept or reject the changes.

# Add Comments

**1.** Choose Review➪Comments➪New Comment. A yellow comment box with your name and a blinking cursor appears.

> With the comment box open, you can drag the lower-right corner of the comment box to make it larger.

**2.** Type your comment. Comments can be up to 32,767 characters in length.

**3.** Click a cell other than the commented cell. Excel accepts the comment and displays a triangle in the upper-right corner of the commented cell. See Figure 18-1.

> Point at the comment triangle to display the actual comment text.

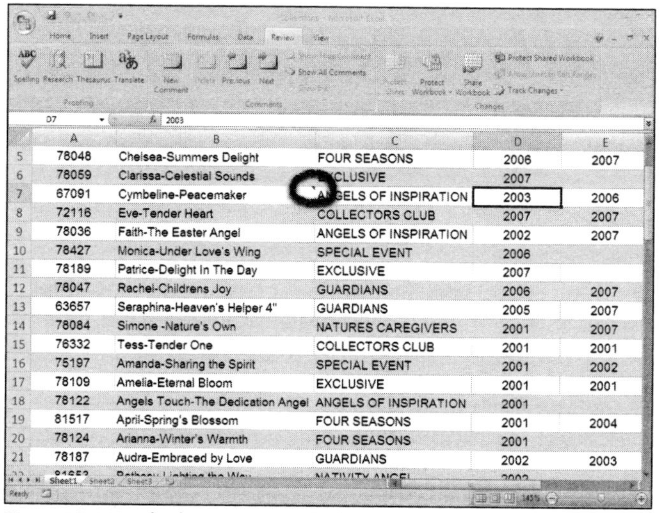

# Edit Comments

**1.** Select the cell with the comment you want to edit.

**2.** Review➪Comments➪ Edit Comment. The comment box reopens for editing as you see in Figure 18-2.

> To delete a comment, choose Review➪Comments➪Delete Comment.

**3.** Make any desired changes, and then click any other cell to close the comment box.

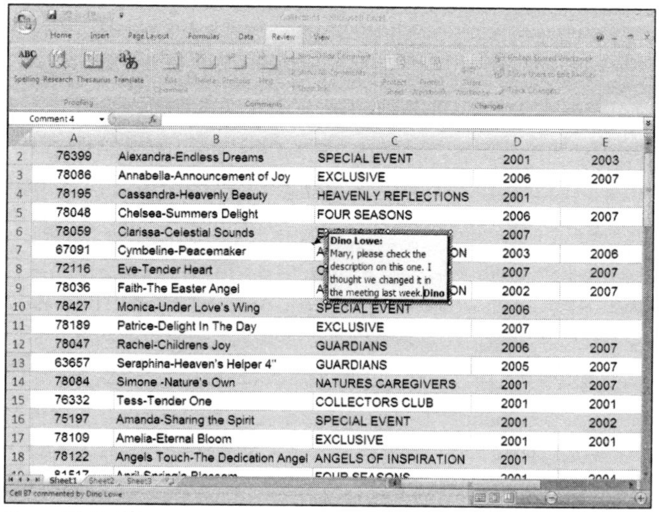

**Figure 18-1:** Excel indicates commented cells with a red triangle.

**Figure 18-2:** Edit a comment.

# *View Multiple Comments*

1. Click a cell with a comment and pause your mouse over the comment indicator. Excel displays the comment text; but as you move your mouse away from the comment indicator, the comment text hides.

2. Try the following options:

   - Choose Review➪Comments➪Next or choose Review➪Comments➪Previous. Excel opens and displays another comment.

   - Choose Review➪Comments➪Show/Hide Comment. Excel keeps the current comment displayed on the screen until you recheck this option.

   - Choose Review➪Comments➪Show All Comments. Excel displays all comment boxes on the current worksheet. (See Figure 18-3.) Click the Show All Comments option again to turn off the comment display.

# *Share a Workbook*

1. Choose Review➪Changes➪Share Workbook. The Share Workbook dialog box appears.

2. From the Editing tab shown in Figure 18-4, click Allow Changes by More Than One User at the Same Time.

3. Click OK. The Share Workbook dialog box closes, and if any changes have been made to the workbook, Excel prompts you to save the file.

4. Click OK. Excel resaves the workbook. Excel denotes a shared workbook with the word [Shared] in the title bar.

 Repeat the preceding steps and remove the check mark to unshare a workbook. Excel displays a confirmation box. Click Yes.

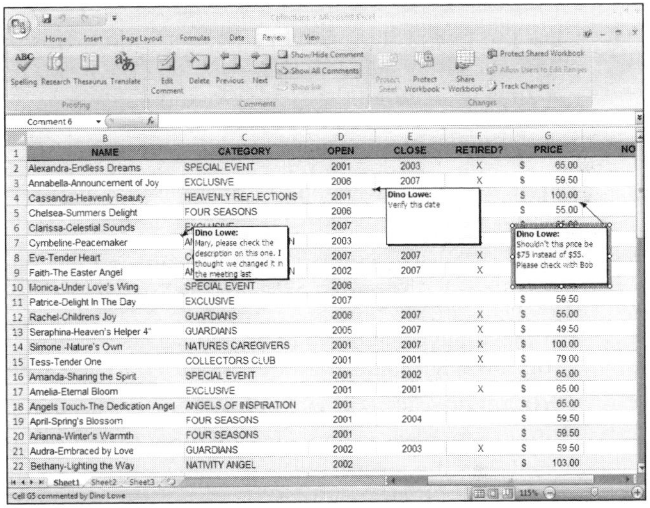

**Figure 18-3:** Viewing multiple comments.

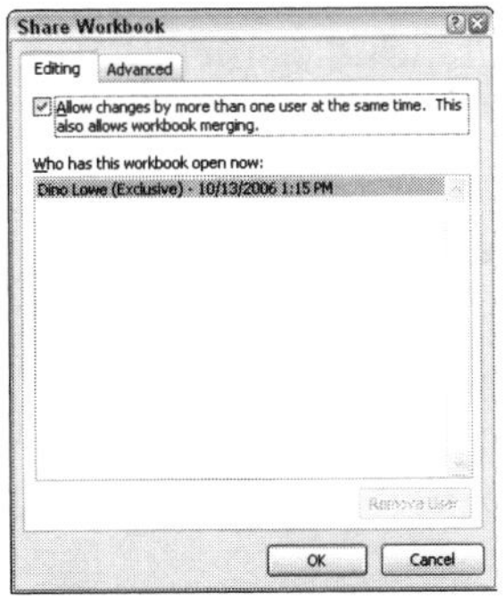

**Figure 18-4:** Allow more than one user to edit the workbook at the same time.

# Track Changes

1.  Choose Review➪Changes➪Track Changes. The Highlight Changes dialog box, shown in Figure 18-5, opens.

2.  Click the Track Changes While Editing option. This option automatically creates a shared workbook file if you have not already activated the Share Workbook feature.

3.  Select any desired options:

    *   **When**: Select the default of All Changes or choose Since I Last Saved, Not Yet Reviewed, or specify a date.

    *   **Who**: Choose from specific users currently using the workbook, Everyone, or Everyone But Me.

    *   **Where**: Specify a range in the workbook to track. If this option is left blank, Excel tracks the entire workbook.

    *   **Highlight Changes On Screen**: When selected, modified cells have a triangle in the upper-right cell corner. Rest the mouse over the triangle to review the change and who made it.

    *   **List Changes on a New Sheet**: When this is selected, Excel adds a special History worksheet in the workbook for viewing each edit including the detail, author, date, and time. See an example in Figure 18-6.

4.  Click OK. Excel activates its tracking feature and highlights any changes in the worksheet with a colored triangle in the upper-left corner of edited cells along with a colored border around the cell.

5.  Make a change in any cell.

To view details about a change and its author, pause the mouse pointer over a changed cell.

Each user who opens the workbook must activate revision tracking for his or her changes to be marked.

**Figure 18-5:** Track cell changes.

**Figure 18-6:** Change history.

# *Accept or Reject Changes*

1. Save the workbook. If you don't save the workbook, Excel prompts you to save it when you proceed to Step 2.

   Excel notes each user's revisions with a different color.

2. Choose Review⇨Changes⇨Track Changes⇨Accept/Reject Changes. The Select Changes to Accept or Reject dialog box appears.

3. Select which changes you want to review and then click OK. The Accept or Reject Changes dialog box, like the one shown in Figure 18-7, appears with the first change.

4. Choose one of the following actions:

   • **Accept**: Keeps the change and removes the revision marker. Excel then locates the next changed cell.

   • **Reject**: Returns the changed cell to its previous value and removes the revision marker. Excel then locates the next changed cell.

   • **Accept All**: Accepts all changes and removes the revision indicators.

   • **Reject All**: Returns all changed cells to their previous values and removes the revision indicators.

   • **Close**: Makes no changes and cancels the change review.

5. If a cell has conflicting changes from multiple users, Excel displays the dialog box shown in Figure 18-8. It displays the original cell value and the value added by each user. Select the cell value you want, and then choose Accept.

The dialog box on the right appears when you save a workbook with conflicts.

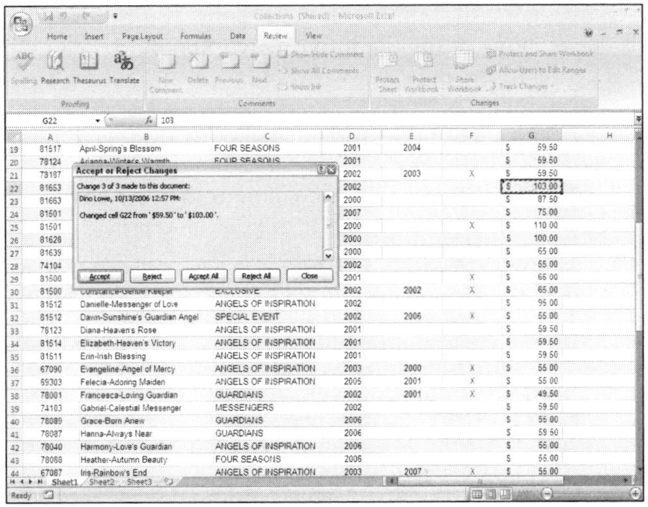

**Figure 18-7:** Select an action for the change.

**Figure 18-8:** Resolve conflicting changes.

# Merge Workbooks

You can merge shared workbooks to create a single final file incorporating every user's input. For example, if each user saves the same file with a different name, you can incorporate all the versions of the file into one workbook to include everyone's edits to the data.

1. From one shared workbook choose Office Button➪Save As and save a copy for each user.

2. Allow each user to make changes to her own workbook version.

3. Add the Compare and Merge Workbooks command to the Quick Access toolbar. See Chapter 1 for a refresher on adding tools to the Quick Access toolbar.

 The Compare and Merge Workbooks command is listed under the category Commands Not on the Ribbon.

4. Click Compare and Merge Workbooks. Excel may prompt you to save the workbook.

5. Click OK. The Select Files to Merge into Current Workbook dialog box, shown in Figure 18-9, opens.

6. Navigate to the folder containing the workbooks you want to merge.

7. Click the file names you want to merge.

8. Click OK. Excel merges all the workbooks into one. In Figure 18-10, Excel incorporates other users' data into the workbook and marks changes with revision mark indicators.

 To click multiple files, press and hold Ctrl key while clicking filenames.

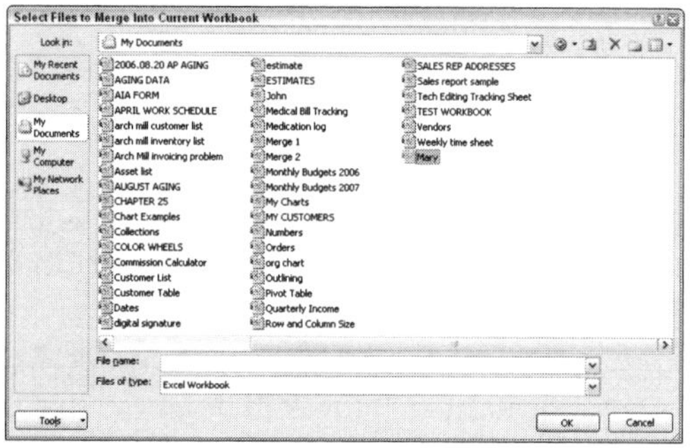

**Figure 18-9:** Locate files to merge.

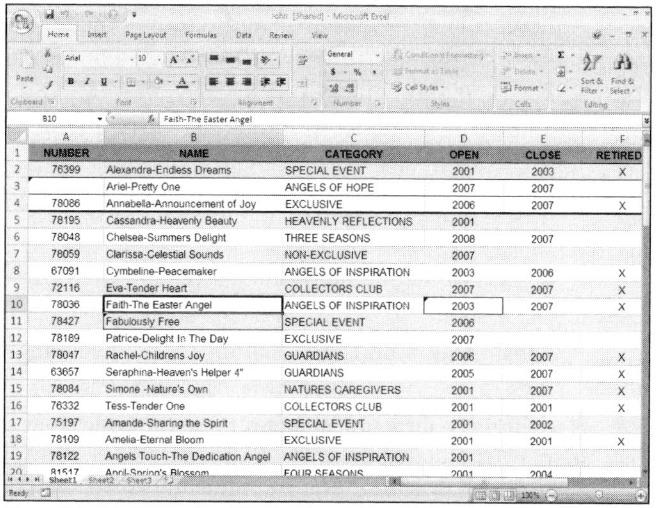

**Figure 18-10:** A merged workbook with revision markers.

# *Integrating Excel into Word*

# Chapter
# 19

*N*o single computer program does everything, and in reality, you don't want it to. You probably use multiple applications for different tasks such as playing solitaire, surfing the Internet, reading e-mail, and of course, working with Excel. If you use Excel, you probably use Microsoft Word to create memos, letters, and other such documents.

In this chapter, I show you how to integrate two major Microsoft Office applications: Word and Excel. You discover how you can create a worksheet in Excel and include it in the middle of a Word document.

If you create a table in Word and then conclude that you are better off working in Excel, you can copy the Word table into any Excel worksheet. You don't need to start completely over.

Take a look and see how easily these two powerful applications work together!

## Get ready to . . .

# Copy Excel Cells into Word

1. From the Excel worksheet, highlight the cells you want to copy into a Word document.

2. Choose Home⇨Clipboard ⇨Copy, or press Ctrl + C. The highlighted cells now have a marquee around them.

3. Open or create the Word document in which you want to place the Excel cells. Make sure the blinking cursor is at the location where you want the cells.

4. Choose Home⇨Clipboard⇨Paste, or press Ctrl + V. Excel pastes the cells into a Word table. Figure 19-1 shows both the Excel worksheet and the new Word table.

5. Modify the Word table using any of the following:

   • **Replace any cell value**: Highlight any existing text in a cell and type the replacement text.

   • **Delete a column or row**: Click in a cell of the column or row you want to delete and then choose Table Tools Layout⇨Rows & Columns⇨Delete⇨ Delete Columns (or Delete Rows).

   • **Insert rows or columns**: Click in a table cell where you want to insert the new row or column, and then choose Table Tools Layout⇨Rows & Columns. Next, select Insert Above, Insert Below, Insert Left, or Insert Row.

   • **Widen a column**: Click a cell in the column you want to widen and then choose Table Tools Layout⇨ Cell Size. Next, change the Width option spinner until the column is the width you want.

   • **Delete the table from the Word document**: Select the row above the table, the table itself, and the row below the table and then press the Delete key. (See Figure 19-2.)

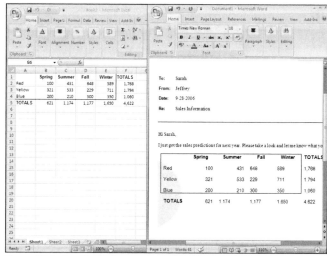

**Figure 19-1:** Copy Excel cells into a Word table.

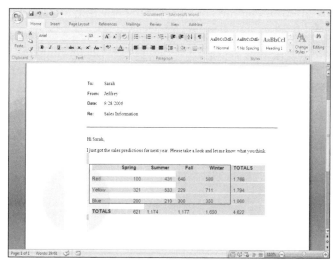

**Figure 19-2:** Remove the table from Word.

# Insert a Saved Excel Worksheet into Word

1. In a Word document, position the insertion point where you want the worksheet to appear.

2. Choose Insert➪Text➪Object➪Object. The Object dialog box opens.

3. From the Create From File tab, click the Browse button. The Browse dialog box opens.

4. Locate and double-click the Excel file you want to include in your Word document. (See Figure 19-3.) The Object dialog box reappears.

5. Click OK. The Excel workbook appears as a Word table. The cells in the Word table contain the same formatting as the Excel workbook.

# Edit an Inserted Worksheet

1. Click once in the Word table.

2. Perform one of the following actions:

   • Press Delete to delete the table.

   • Drag one of the handles to resize the table.

   • Double-click the table to edit the actual values. The Excel Ribbon appears, along with column headings, row numbers, and any formulas you created in Excel. (See Figure 19-4.)

3. Click outside of the table to deselect the table.

 Any changes you make are saved in Word only, not in the original Excel workbook.

 Even if your worksheet contains multiple sheets, only the top sheet with all the cells containing data appears. You cannot specify a particular range of cells. If you want an Excel chart, save the workbook with the chart sheet on top before inserting into Word.

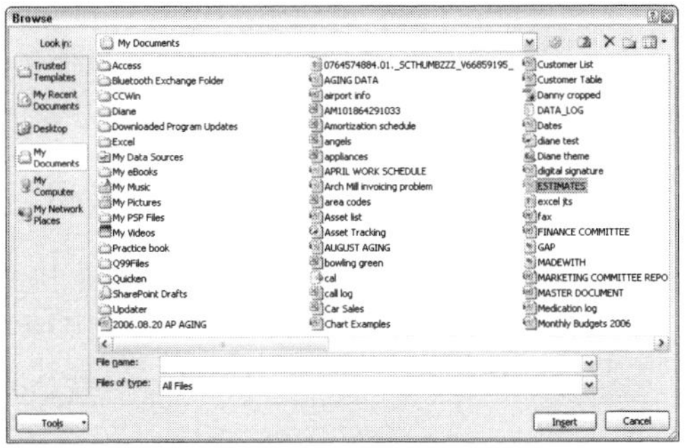

**Figure 19-3:** Insert a worksheet as an object.

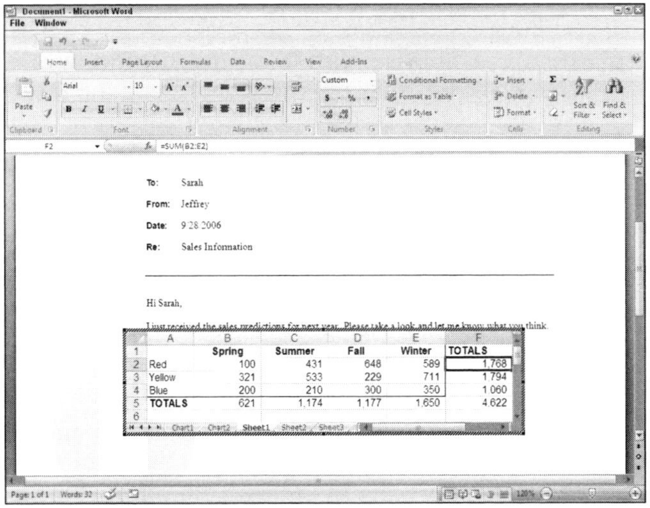

**Figure 19-4:** Edit cells, formulas, or formatting.

# *Embed an Excel Worksheet into Word*

**1.** Follow Steps 1 through 4 of the "Insert a Saved Excel Worksheet into Word" section.

**2.** Check the Link to File check box shown in Figure 19-5. With this option selected, any changes you make to the original Excel workbook are reflected in the Word document each time you open the Word document.

**3.** Click OK. The Excel workbook appears as a Word table.

 To resize the Word table, click once on the table that displays the eight sizing handles, and drag any handle until the table reaches the size you want.

 To delete the table, click once on the table and press the Delete key.

**4.** The Word table is linked to the original Excel worksheet. You can ensure that any changes made in the Excel workbook are reflected in the Word document by using any of the following methods:

- With the Word document already opened, right-click the Word table and choose Update Link.

- Double-click the Word table, which launches the Excel program and opens the linked workbook. If you make any changes in Excel; the Word table automatically updates.

- When you reopen the Word document, the dialog box shown in Figure 19-6 displays. It prompts you to update the Word document from the original Excel file. Click Yes.

 If you check Display as Icon, Word inserts an Excel icon into the document instead of displaying the workbook as a table. Double-clicking the icon opens the workbook in Excel; however, the Excel program must be installed on the PC that is trying to open the workbook.

**Figure 19-5:** Insert an Embedded worksheet into a Word document.

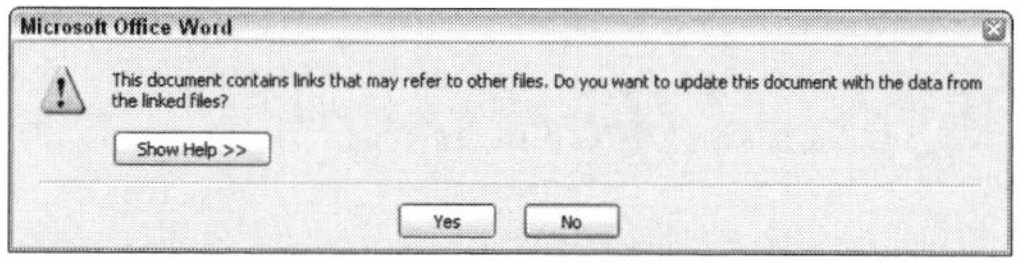

**Figure 19-6:** Updating the Excel-to-Word link.

# Copy a Word Table to Excel

1. In Microsoft Word, create a table by choosing Insert⇨Tables⇨Table.

2. Enter data in the Word table.

 Press Tab to move from cell to cell, or click the mouse in any individual cell.

3. Drag across the table to highlight the cells you want to copy as shown in Figure 19-7.

4. Choose Home⇨Clipboard⇨Copy, or press Ctrl+C.

 To move, instead of copy, the Word table to Excel, choose Home⇨Clipboard⇨Cut, or press Ctrl + X.

5. Open or create the Excel workbook in which you want to place the Word table.

6. Click the cell in which you want the table to begin.

7. Choose Home⇨Clipboard⇨Paste, or press Ctrl+V. The Excel worksheet displays the Word table. As shown in Figure 19-8, each cell in the Word table occupies one cell in the Excel worksheet.

 If the Word table cells have a border around them, the Excel cells also have a border around them.

 The Word table and the Excel worksheet are not linked. Any changes made to one will not change the other.

8. Format the cells as desired. See Chapter 5.

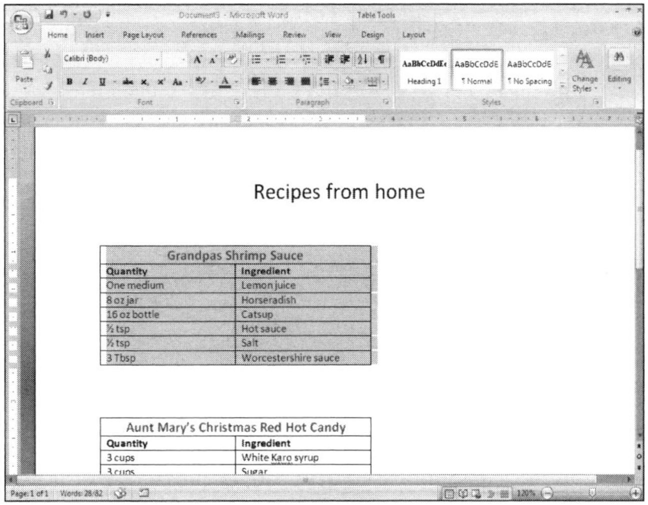

**Figure 19-7:** Highlight the table cells you want to take to Excel.

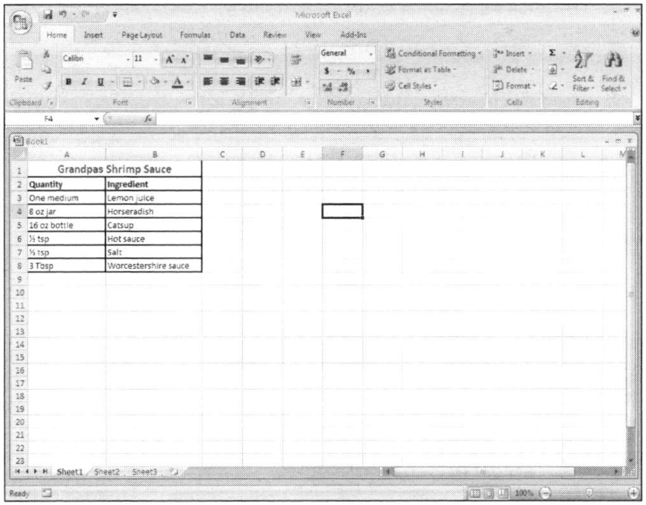

**Figure 19-8:** Copy a table from Word to Excel.

# Create a Word Mail Merge Form Letter Using an Excel List

1. Create and save an Excel worksheet with the data you want to merge in an Excel list. The Excel worksheet does not need to be open.

2. In Word, with a blank document on the screen, choose Mailings⇨Start Mail Merge⇨Step by Step Mail Merge Wizard. The Mail Merge task pane appears on the right side of your screen.

3. Select the Letters option. (See Figure 19-9.)

4. Click Next: Starting Document.

5. Choose whether to create the mail merge from the current Word document or from another existing Word document.

6. Click Next: Select Recipients.

7. Select the Use an Existing List option.

8. Click Browse. The Select Data Source dialog box appears.

9. Locate and double-click the Excel file containing your list. The Select Table dialog box opens as shown in Figure 19-10.

10. Select the range name, sheet name, or area containing data.

11. Click OK. A Mail Merge Recipients list containing your data appears.

12. Remove the check mark next to any record that you don't want to include and then click OK.

13. Click Next: Write your letter.

 The data will be easier for you to identify later if it has column headings (although they are not a requirement). If you are merging names, you might want to list the first name and last name in separate columns.

 If the first row of your list does not contain headers, remove the check mark from the First Row Of Data Contains Column Headers option.

 Optionally, Click Clear all to clear all the check marks or click Select All to check all the records. Click the arrow next to any heading to sort the data.

**Figure 19-9:** Select a mail merge document type.

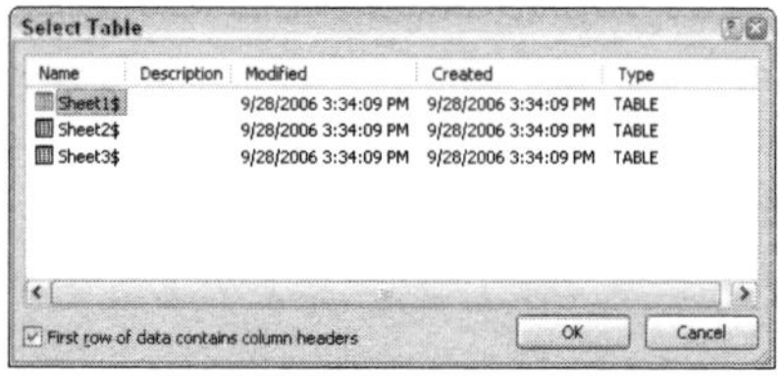

**Figure 19-10:** Select the data area you want to merge.

**14.** Type the form-letter document, leaving blanks where you want the variable (such as name, address, phone number, or product) information to appear. See Figure 19-11.

**15.** Click the insertion point at the first location where you want the variable information (such as the recipient name and address location).

**16.** From the task pane, select the desired option:

- **Address Block**: Displays the Insert Address Block dialog box from which you can select an address layout.

- **Greeting Line**: Displays the Greeting Line dialog box, which inserts a greeting of your choice along with the recipient's first name (if you have such a field in your database) followed by a comma or colon.

- **Electronic Postage**: Prints Electronic postage on your envelopes if you subscribe to an Electronic postage service such as Stamps.com.

- **Postal Bar Code**: Prompts you for the zip code field from your Excel list and then inserts a bar code matching the zip code field.

- **More Items**: Displays the Insert Merge Field dialog box (see Figure 19-12), which displays each field listed in your Excel list. Click the field you want to insert into Word and click the Insert button.

**17.** Click Next: Preview your letters. The document you created appears with the first data record from your Excel list.

**18.** Click Next: Complete the merge. You can now print your form letters.

 To edit a specific letter, click Edit individual letters. To make a change to the master document, click the Previous button until you get to Step 4 and then make any desired changes. Click Next again, until the merge is completed.

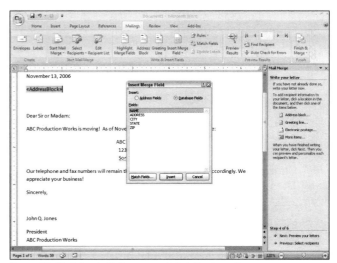

**Figure 19-11:** Create the base letter.

**Figure 19-12:** Select the fields you want included in the mail merge.

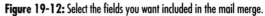

# Make Mailing Labels with Word & Excel

1. Create and save an Excel worksheet with the data you want to merge in an Excel list. The Excel worksheet does not need to be open.

2. In Word, with a blank document on the screen, choose Mailings⇨Start Mail Merge⇨Labels. The Label Options dialog box seen in Figure 19-13 appears.

3. Choose the label manufacturer and size you are using and then click OK. You see a blank document on the screen. Without the gridlines showing, however, it's difficult to see the individual labels.

4. Choose Table Tools Layout⇨Table⇨View Gridlines.

5. Choose Mailings⇨Start Mail Merge⇨Select Recipients⇨Use Existing List. The Select Data Source dialog box opens.

6. Locate and double-click the Excel file containing your list. The Select Table dialog box opens.

7. Select the range name, sheet name, or area containing data.

8. On the first label, choose Mailings⇨Write & Insert Fields⇨Address Block. The Insert Address Block dialog box appears.

9. Choose the address block format you want to use. Click OK.

10. Choose Mailings⇨Write & Insert Fields⇨Update Labels. The fields you inserted appear on each label.

11. Choose Mailings⇨Preview Results⇨Preview Results. You see the labels as they will print. See Figure 19-14.

12. Choose Mailings⇨Finish⇨Finish & Merge. You can then choose to edit the individual labels or print them.

 Optionally, choose Insert Merge Field and select the individual field you want to use.

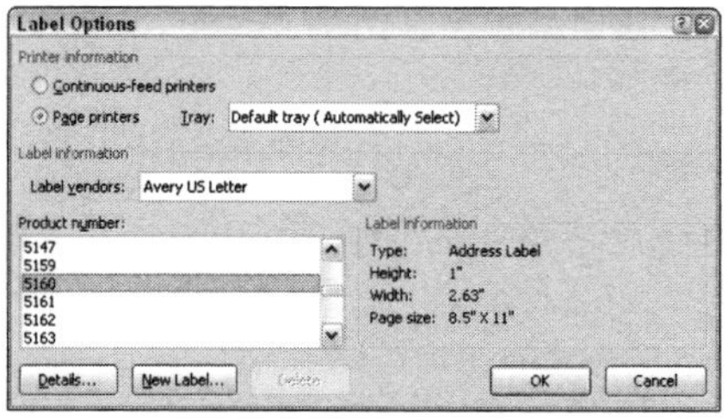

**Figure 19-13:** The Label Options dialog box.

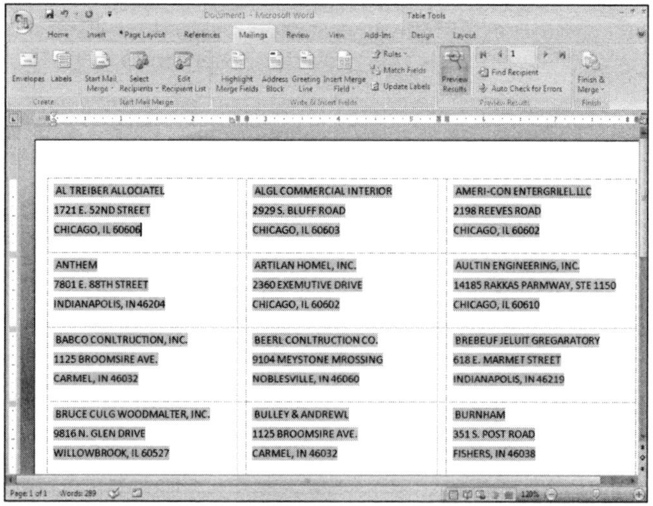

**Figure 19-14:** Preview the merged Excel list as Word labels.

# Blending Excel and PowerPoint

*O*ne of the most common ways to make others aware of your work is by giving a presentation. The Microsoft Office product PowerPoint is one of the most effective presentation products available in today's market. And since PowerPoint is part of the Microsoft Office suite, it's very easy to integrate information from other Office applications (in this example, Excel) into a PowerPoint presentation.

My mother always told me to do things right the first time. If you already spent the time and energy to create information in Excel, why should you have to re-create it in your PowerPoint presentation?

That's what this chapter is about. You learn how to take the powerful worksheet data or creative chart that you created in Excel and copy it to a PowerPoint slide. You can simply copy it once from Excel to PowerPoint, or you can create a link so that if the data in Excel changes, your PowerPoint presentation automatically reflects the changes. That's doing it right the first time . . .

## Get ready to . . .

## Copy Excel Cells into a PowerPoint Slide

1.  From the Excel worksheet, highlight the cells you want to copy into a PowerPoint slide and choose Home⇨Clipboard⇨Copy or press Ctrl+C. A marquee appears around the highlighted cells. (See Figure 20-1.)

2.  Open or create a PowerPoint presentation. Make sure you display the slide on which you want to paste the cells.

3.  Choose Home⇨Clipboard⇨Paste, or press Ctrl+V. Excel pastes the cells into a PowerPoint table.

4.  Modify the PowerPoint table using any of the following methods:

    *   Replace any cell value: Highlight any existing text in a cell and type the replacement text.

    *   Delete a row: Click in the row you want to delete, right-click, and choose Delete Rows. Optionally, drag across the row to highlight it first, and then right-click and select Delete Rows.

    *   Delete a column: Highlight the column you want to delete, right-click, and choose Delete Columns.

    *   Change a column width: Position the mouse at the invisible boundary line (as shown in Figure 20-2) to the right of any column and drag to the left or right.

    *   Resize the table: Position the mouse pointer over a table handle and drag to the desired size.

    *   Move the table: Position the mouse pointer over an edge, but not a handle, of the table boundary box and drag to the desired location.

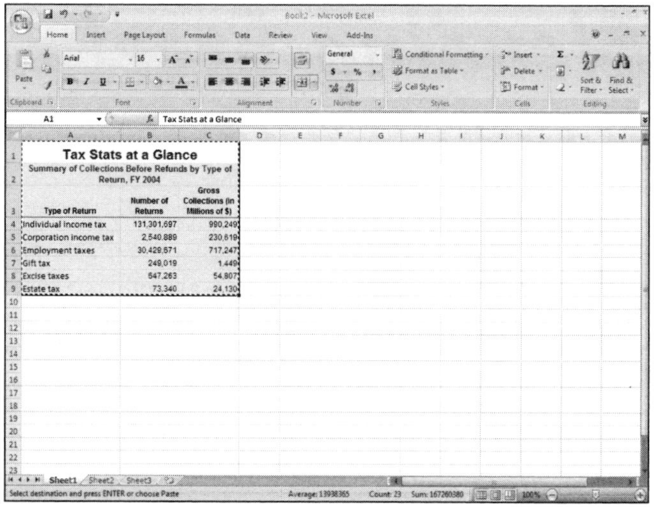

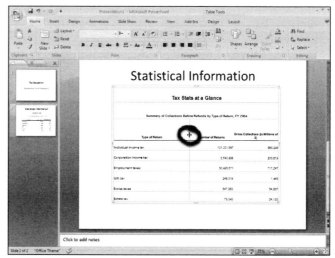

**Figure 20-1:** Use your favorite Copy and Paste commands to duplicate cells.

**Figure 20-2:** Make sure the cursor looks like this in order to resize the column widths.

# Drag an Excel Table into a PowerPoint Slide

1. Open both the PowerPoint presentation you want to use and the Excel workbook. Make sure to display the PowerPoint slide you want.

2. Resize and arrange the PowerPoint and Excel windows so that both are visible at the same time. Use either of the following methods:

   • Right-click a blank area of the Windows Task Bar and choose Tile Windows Vertically or Tile Windows Horizontally.

   • Click the Restore button in each window so they are no longer maximized and then drag the window borders to resize them. Drag the title bars to move them until both windows are the desired size and in the correct location.

3. Select the Excel data you want to copy.

4. Position the mouse around the outside border of the selected Excel data and drag the data from the Excel window until it is on the PowerPoint slide. As you drag the mouse, the pointer changes to a small box like the one you see in Figure 20-3.

5. Release the mouse button. The Excel data appears on the PowerPoint slide.

6. Maximize the PowerPoint window to restore it to full screen. You can then format, resize, or edit the data as desired. See Figure 20-4.

 To delete the table from the slide, click once to select the table object (the table object boundary has blue boundary edges) and then press the Delete key.

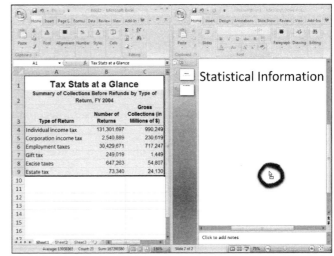

**Figure 20-3:** Use the drag-and-drop method to copy data from Excel to PowerPoint

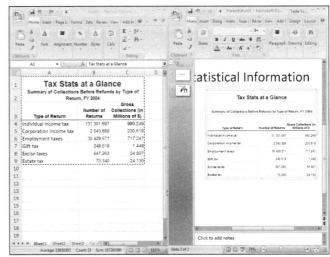

**Figure 20-4:** The Excel data in both Excel and PowerPoint.

# Insert a Saved Excel Worksheet or Chart onto a PowerPoint Slide

1. In a PowerPoint presentation, display the slide where you want the worksheet or chart to appear.

2. Choose Insert⇨Text⇨Object. The Insert Object dialog box opens.

3. Click the Create From File option. See Figure 20-5.

4. Click the Browse button. The Browse dialog box opens.

5. Locate and double-click the Excel file you want to include in your PowerPoint presentation. The Object dialog box reappears and the path and filename you selected appears in the File Name text box.

6. Click OK. As you see in Figure 20-6, the Excel workbook or chart appears on the current PowerPoint slide.

7. Modify the PowerPoint table or chart using any of the steps from the section, "Copy Excel Cells into a PowerPoint Slide," or by using any of the following:

   - Click once on the PowerPoint object. Eight selection handles appear around the table. Drag one of the handles to resize the object.

   - Double-click the table or chart to edit the actual values. The Excel Ribbon appears along with row numbers. The worksheet includes any formulas you created in Excel.

8. Click the slide background to return to PowerPoint and deselect the object.

Before proceeding, if you want to copy a chart onto the slide, make sure to save the Excel workbook with the chart sheet as the top sheet. If your workbook contains multiple worksheets, only the top sheet appears in the PowerPoint slide.

**Figure 20-5:** Inserting data from a previously saved Excel workbook.

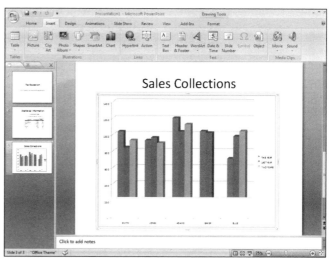

**Figure 20-6:** An Excel chart inserted into a PowerPoint slide.

# *Link an Excel Worksheet to a PowerPoint Slide*

1. Open the desired Excel file. When creating a link, the originating Excel file must be a previously saved file.

2. Select the portion of the file you want to duplicate in PowerPoint.

3. Choose Home⇨Clipboard⇨Copy, or press Ctrl+C.

4. Display the PowerPoint slide on which you want to create the link and then choose Home⇨Clipboard⇨Paste (arrow)⇨Paste Special, which displays the Paste Special dialog box shown in Figure 20-7.

5. Choose the Paste Link option. With this option selected, any changes you make to the original workbook reflect in the PowerPoint slide each time you open the PowerPoint presentation.

6. Click OK. The pasted and linked object appears on the PowerPoint Slide.

7. The PowerPoint table is linked to the original Excel worksheet. You can cause any changes made in the Excel workbook to be reflected in the PowerPoint presentation by using any of the following methods:

   - With the PowerPoint presentation already opened, right-click the PowerPoint table and choose Update Links. (See Figure 20-8.)

   - Double-click the PowerPoint table to launch the Excel program and open the linked workbook. Make any changes in Excel, and the PowerPoint table automatically updates.

   - When you reopen the PowerPoint presentation, a dialog box displays, prompting you to update PowerPoint from the original Excel file. Click Yes to update PowerPoint.

 If you check Display As Icon, instead of displaying the linked object as a table or chart, PowerPoint inserts an Excel icon onto the slide. Double-clicking the icon opens the workbook in Excel; however, the Excel program must be installed on the PC trying to open the workbook.

**Figure 20-7:** The PowerPoint Paste Special dialog box.

**Figure 20-8:** Updating the PowerPoint slide object.

# Using Excel with Access

*Y*ou can share data between Access and Excel in many ways. You can copy data from an open worksheet and paste it into an Access datasheet, import a worksheet into an Access database, or simply load an Access datasheet into Excel using the Analyze It with Excel command.

This chapter shows you how you exchange data between Access and Excel through one of several processes:

➡ Importing, which creates a copy of an Excel spreadsheet in Access format.

➡ Linking, which connects an Access table to an Excel worksheet so that you can view and edit the data in both the original program and in the Access file. Linking is useful when Excel data must be shared between Excel and Access users.

➡ Exporting, which allows you analyze your Access data in Excel format.

Entire books are written about using Access, so this chapter assumes you already know about general database terms, such as records, fields, tables, queries, and primary keys. I also assume you know the basics of creating and using an Access database.

# Chapter

# 21

## Get ready to . . .

# Import Data from Excel to an Access Table

1. Prepare your Excel worksheet data before importing into Access:

   - If you don't want to import the entire worksheet, create a named range in the Excel workbook that contains the cells you want to import. (See Chapter 2.)

   - Make sure the cells are in tabular format. If the worksheet contains merged cells, the contents of the cell are placed in the field that corresponds to the leftmost column, and the other fields are left blank.

   - If the Excel spreadsheet has a cell containing more 255 characters, Access truncates the data to 255 characters.

2. If you don't already have an Access database created, from the Access Getting Started screen, click Blank Database. If you already have an Access database, open the database and skip Step 3.

3. Enter a name and click Create. (See Figure 21-1.)

4. Choose External Data⇨Import⇨Excel. The Get External Data — Excel Spreadsheet dialog box appears.

5. Click the Browse button to locate and select the Excel file from which you want to import data. The file name appears in the File Name text box. (See Figure 21-2.)

6. Specify if you want the data in an existing table or a new table. If you want it in an existing table, you select the table name.

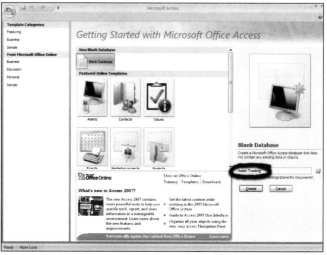

**Figure 21-1:** Create a new database for importing Excel data.

**Figure 21-2:** Select the Excel file you want to import.

If you select an existing table, Access appends the data to the table. Make the sure the number of columns in the worksheet or named range matches the number of fields in the table. The name, date type, and position of each column must also match those of the corresponding field in the Access table.

7. Click OK. The Import Spreadsheet Wizard appears.

8. Select the worksheet you want to import or a specific named range. (See Figure 21-3.) If the workbook has no named ranges and only one worksheet, you do not see this screen.

9. Click Next.

10. Specify if the first row of your worksheet contains column headings. Access creates field names from the column headings.

11. Click Next.

12. Assign field names to each column by clicking the desired column and typing a name in the Field Name text box. (See Figure 21-4.)

 If a column name violates the field naming rules in Access, Access assigns a valid name to the field.

13. Assign field types to each column.

14. Choose Yes or No if you want the field indexed.

 Optionally, click on a column you don't want to include and click the Do Not Import Field (Skip) option. You can skip columns during the import, but you can't skip rows.

15. Click Next.

16. Select an option regarding the primary index key. You can let Access create one for you, select your own primary key, or choose not have a primary key.

17. Click Next.

18. If you are creating a new table, enter a name.

19. Click Finish. Access imports the data and prompts you to save the import settings for future imports.

 You can import only one worksheet or named range at a time during an import operation.

 If any errors incur during the import, Access creates an error log table in the database and displays the name of the table in a message. It's a good idea to open the error log table and review the errors.

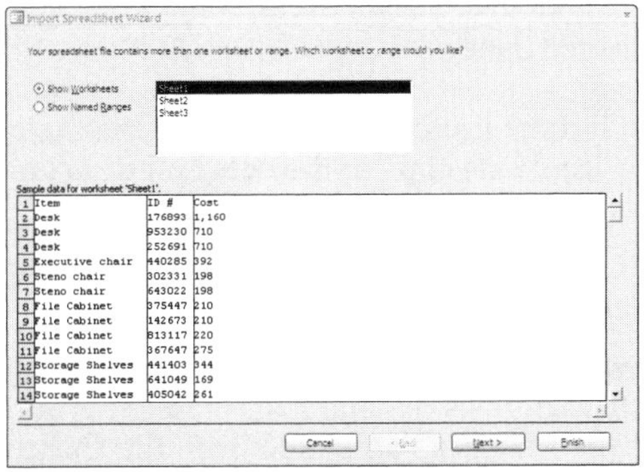

**Figure 21-3:** Choose the area you want to import.

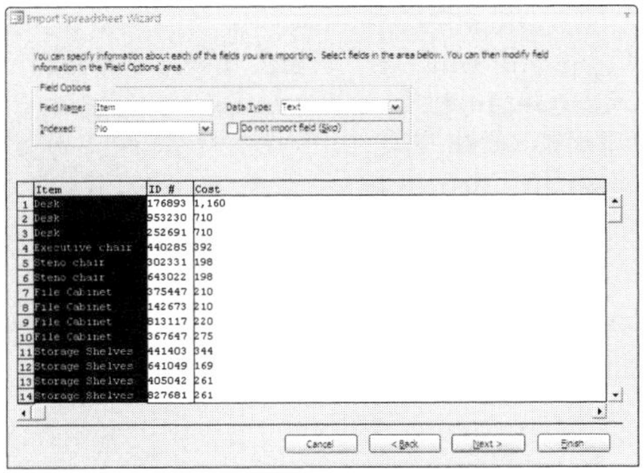

**Figure 21-4:** Assign field names for the Access table.

**20.** Click the Close button. A new table appears in Access, as you see in Figure 21-5.

 To import multiple worksheets or named ranges, repeat the import process for each worksheet or range.

**21.** Double-click the Access table and review the imported data. (See Figure 21-6.) Keep in mind the following facts about imported data:

- **Imported data:** Importing a worksheet into Access creates a duplicate copy of the data and does not make any changes to the source Excel file.

- **Graphical elements:** Access does not import graphical elements, such as logos, charts, and pictures.

- **Data type:** Access determines the data type based on the first 25 rows of data. If any values beyond the 25th row are not compatible with the chosen data type, Access ignores those values and does not import them.

- **Calculated values:** Access imports only the results of a calculated cell, not the formula itself. For example, if cell D13 contains the formula B13*C13, which results in a value of 100, only the value of 100 goes into Access, not the B13*C13. To update the formulas, you can link the Excel worksheet to Access. See the next section.

- **Hyperlinks:** Access imports cells containing hyperlinks as text fields.

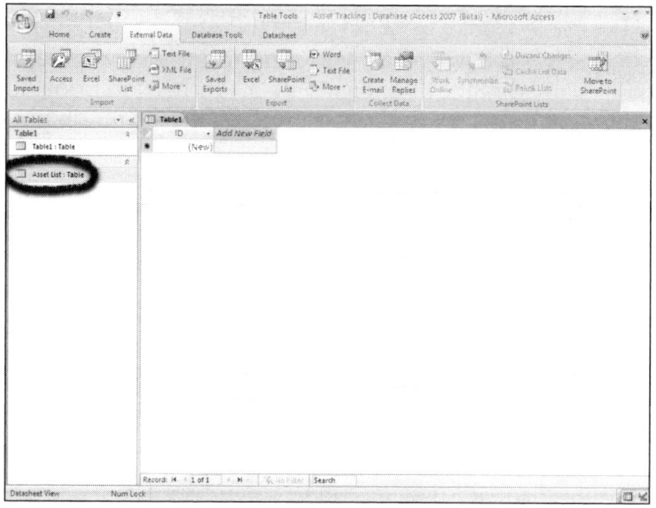

**Figure 21-5:** A new Access table created from Excel data.

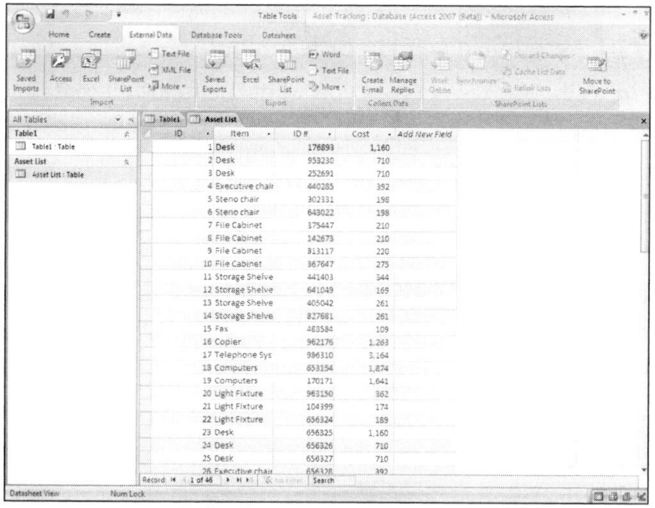

**Figure 21-6:** Review the data for import inaccuracies.

# *Link an Excel Worksheet to an Access Database*

1. Begin by referring to Steps 1 through 5 of the previous section.

2. Choose Link to the Data Source by Creating a Linked Table.

3. Click OK. The Link Spreadsheet Wizard opens.

4. Select which worksheet you want to import or a specific named range. If the workbook has no named ranges and only one worksheet, you do not see this screen.

5. Click Next.

 You can link only one worksheet or named range at a time. To link multiple worksheets or named ranges, repeat the link operation.

6. As you see in Figure 21-7, specify if the first row of your worksheet contains column headings. If so, Access creates field names from the first row. If not, Access assumes the first row is a record.

7. Click Next.

8. Enter a name for the table.

9. Click Finish. A completion message box like the one you see in Figure 21-8 appears.

10. Click OK.

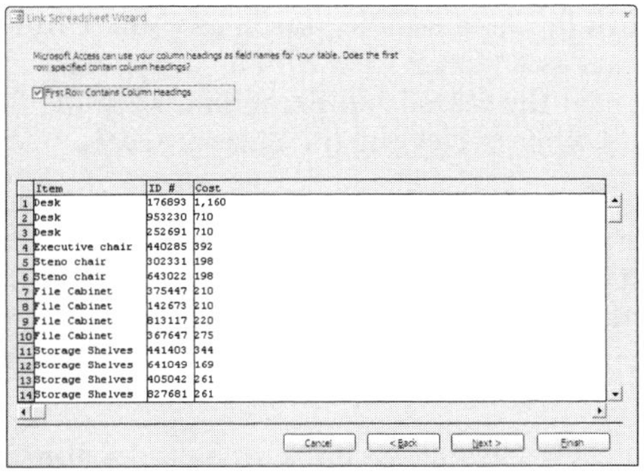

**Figure 21-7:** Indicate whether the first row contains column headings.

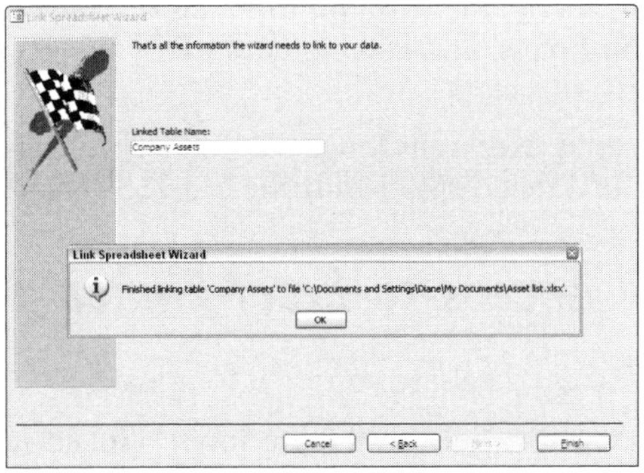

**Figure 21-8:** Creating a linked Excel table in Access.

**11.** Double-click the Access table which, as you see in Figure 21-9, appears as an Excel icon with an arrow next to it, indicating that the table is an Excel link. Keep the following in mind when reviewing the data in Access:

- When you create a link, Access creates a new table but the data is actually stored in the source worksheet, not in the database table. Any changes you make to the data in the Access table updates the source Excel file. Any change you make in the Excel file, Access automatically reflects in the linked Access table.

- Graphics, such as logos, charts, or pictures stored in the Excel worksheet, are not visible in Access.

- You cannot change the field data type or size.

- The source cells that contain formulas display only as results in Access, and you cannot modify the values in Access.

- Access stores Excel cells longer than 255 characters in a memo field that displays only the first 255 characters.

# Update an Access-to-Excel-Linked Table

**1.** Open the Access database you want to update.

**2.** Choose Database Tools➪Database Tools➪Linked Table Manager. The Linked Table Manager dialog box, shown in Figure 21-10, appears.

**3.** Click the check box next to the table you want to manually update and click OK.

**4.** A confirmation message appears indicating the linked tables were successfully updated. Click OK.

**5.** Click Close to close the Linked Table Manager.

 If you delete the table from Access, you are only deleting the link, not the actual Excel worksheet.

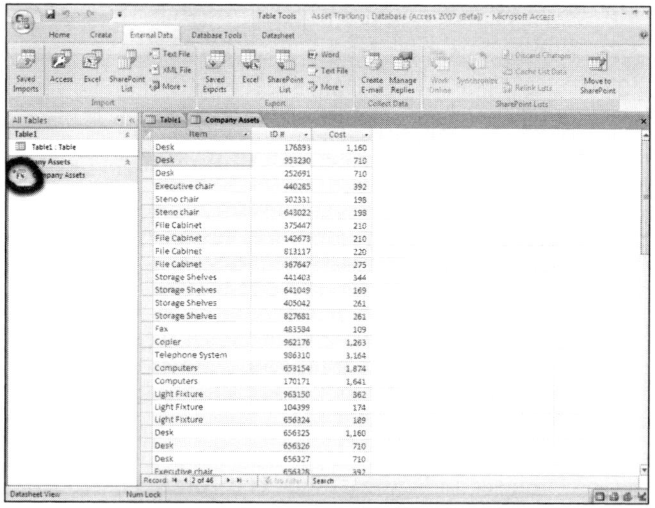

**Figure 21-9:** An Excel-linked icon in an Access database.

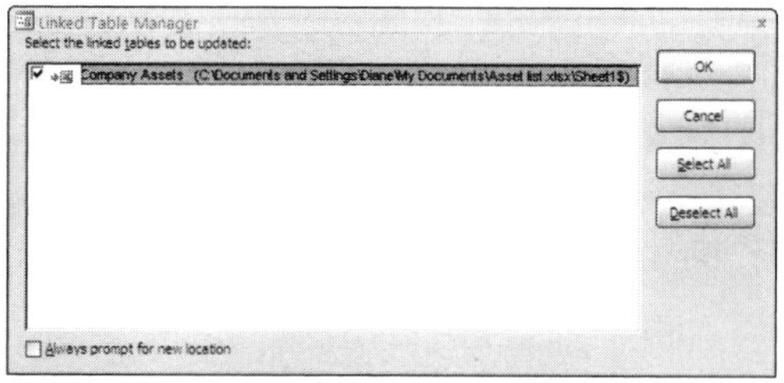

**Figure 21-10:** Manually updating an Access to Excel link.

# *Export Access Data to Excel*

1.  Open the Access database and select the database object that you want to export. The following table illustrates what Access exports, depending on the object and the view you have open when performing the export:

     You can only export an Access table, query, form, or a report. You cannot export data access pages, macros, or modules.

## Access-to-Excel Export Options

| Object | View | What Exports |
|---|---|---|
| Tables, Queries, or Forms | Database window | Everything, unless you preselect an area before exporting. |
| Form | Form view | All fields and records, even if the fields aren't included in the view. |
| Report | Database window, Print Preview, or Layout Preview | All data Group Header and Detail text boxes, and any text box in a Group Footer that has a Sum function. Access uses Excel's outline feature. |

2.  Choose External Data⇨Export⇨Excel. The Export — Excel Spreadsheet dialog box shown in Figure 21-11 appears.

3.  In the File Name box, enter a name for the file. By default, Access suggests the Access object name.

4.  Click the File Format drop-down list and make a different selection if you do not want to use the Excel 2007 format.

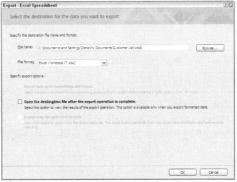

**Figure 21-11:** The Export to dialog box.

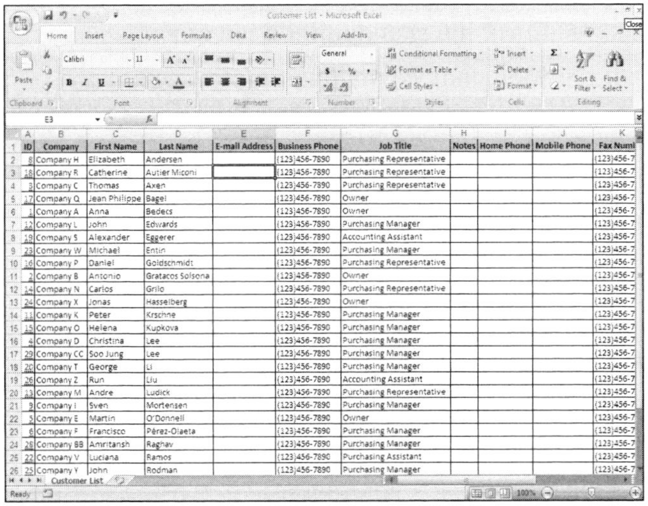

**Figure 21-12:** Data exported to Excel from Access.

5. Optionally, check Open The Destination File After The Export Operation Is Complete.

6. Click OK. Access exports the data and prompts you to save the export settings for future imports.

7. Click the Close button.

8. If you did not prompt Access to automatically open the Excel worksheet, open it yourself and review the exported data. (See Figure 21-12.) Note that the following actions occur during the export:

   - Graphic items such as images do not export.

   - Only calculation results export, not the calculation itself.

   - Check boxes on forms do not export.

   - Subreports export, but subforms do not.

   - Date values earlier than Jan 1, 1900, do not export and are replaced with a Null value.

# Part V
# Practical Applications for Excel

The 5th Wave — By Rich Tennant

"I started running 'what if' scenarios on my spreadsheet, like, 'What if I were sick of this dirtwad job and funneled some of the company's money into an off-shore account?'"

# Designing an Organization Chart

*Y*our office is changing rapidly. The staff appears to grow by leaps and bounds, and you see quite a few new faces around. When that happens, it's often difficult to remember who's who and their job titles.

You've been assigned the task of creating an organization chart to illustrate the reporting relationships in your company. Creating quality organization charts can be challenging, especially if you're not a professional designer. You'll be happy to learn that Excel 2007 includes more than 120 different SmartArt graphics, each with its own purpose, including some for creating hierarchy graphics such as an organization chart. In general, SmartArt graphics provide visual information you can use to quickly and easily communicate a message.

SmartArt graphics are most effective when the number of shapes and the amount of text are limited. Larger amounts of text can distract from the visual appeal of your SmartArt graphic and make it harder to convey your message visually.

This chapter takes you through the steps of creating a designer-quality organization chart using the Excel SmartArt graphic function. Go ahead . . . ask for a raise.

# Create a Basic Organization Chart

1. Choose Insert➪Illustrations➪SmartArt. The Choose A SmartArt Graphic dialog box, shown in Figure 22-1, appears.

2. In the category list on the left, click Hierarchy.

3. Click the first option, Organization Chart, and then click OK. On the current worksheet, Excel creates a basic organization chart with five graphic placeholders (one manager, one assistant, and three subordinates).

 To delete the organization chart, click the blue border surrounding the graphic and press the Delete key.

# Use the Text Pane

1. Choose SmartArt Tools Design➪Create Graphic➪Text Pane. Excel displays a Text pane to the left of your organization chart.

2. Type your organization's top management name and/or position.

3. Press the down arrow key. The insertion point moves to the Assistant position. (See Figure 22-2.)

4. Type the assistant's name and then press the down arrow key. If you don't need an assistant level, leave the line blank. You'll see shortly how to delete unwanted positions.

5. Type any subordinate names. If you need more lines when you get to the bottom of the list, press the Enter key. New shapes are automatically added to the graphic.

 As you add content in the Text pane, the SmartArt graphic automatically updates.

 To indent the new shape, press Tab from within the Text pane. To delete an indent, press Shift+Tab.

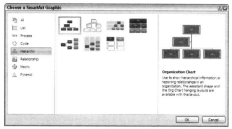

**Figure 22-1:** Select a SmartArt Graphic to create an organization chart.

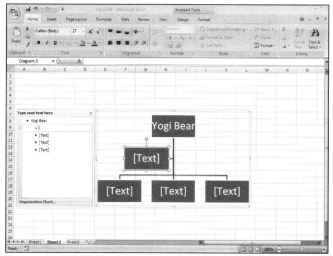

**Figure 22-2:** Entering text in the Text pane.

# Manage the Text Pane

1. Manage the Text pane using any of the following actions:

   - **Close:** Close the Text pane by clicking the Close button or by choosing SmartArt Tools Design⇨Create Graphic⇨Text Pane.

   - **Move:** Move the Text pane by dragging the top of the pane. See Figure 22-3.

    Text pane moves and resizes are temporary, and only remain until you close the text pane or close Office. When you redisplay the text pane, it appears in its default size and positioned at the side of the SmartArt graphic.

   - **Resize:** Resize the Text pane by pointing to any edge of the Text pane and then, when the pointer changes to a double-headed arrow, drag the border to resize.

    Format text either by selecting the text in the shape or by selecting it in the Text pane and choosing options from the Home tab.

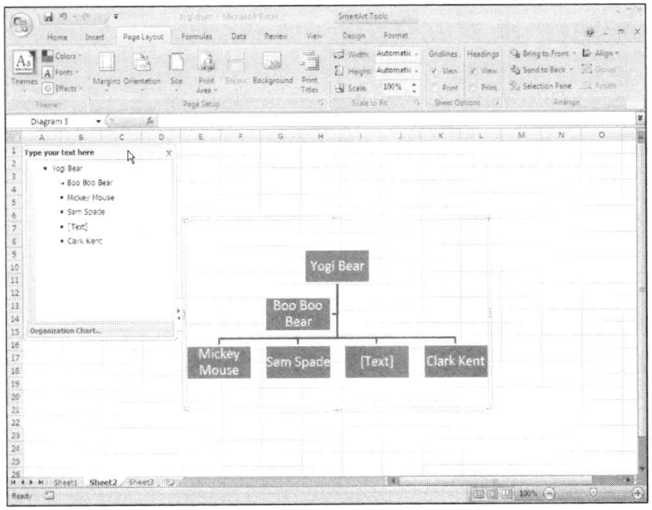

# Edit Text Using Placeholders

1. Click inside a graphic box. If there is no text in the box, the placeholder words [Text] disappear and you see a blinking cursor.

    Placeholder text is not printed.

2. Type the text you want. The text size decreases as you type more text. (See Figure 22-4.)

3. Click anywhere outside of the graphic box.

4. Repeat for each graphic box you use.

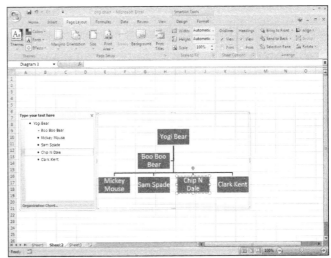

**Figure 22-3:** Move the Text pane out of your way.

**Figure 22-4:** Edit text in a specific box.

# Delete a Position

1. Choose one of the following options:

   - From the Text pane, highlight the unwanted position and press the Delete key. (See Figure 22-5.)

   - Click the unwanted shape placeholder box border and press the Delete key.

# Add a Position

1. Click the shape that is located closest to where you want to add the new position.

2. Choose SmartArt Tools Design⇨Create Graphic group and click the arrow under Add Shape.

3. From the list you see in Figure 22-6, choose one of the following options:

   - **Add Shape After**: Inserts a shape at the same level as the selected shape but following it.

   - **Add Shape Before**: Inserts a shape at the same level as the selected shape but before it.

   - **Add Shape Above**: Inserts a shape one level above the selected shape.

   - **Add Shape Below**: Inserts a shape one level below the selected shape. The new shape is added after the other shapes at the same level.

   - **Add Assistant**: Adds an assistant shape above the other shapes at the same level in the SmartArt graphic.

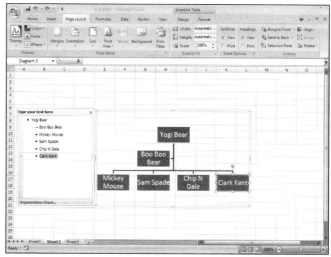

**Figure 22-5:** Deleting an unwanted shape from the organization chart.

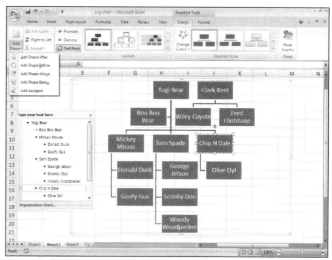

**Figure 22-6:** Choose a position for the new shape.

# Switch Layouts

1. Choose SmartArt Tools Design⇨Layouts.

2. Click More to display a gallery of organization chart layouts.

3. Pause your mouse over any selection to see how your chart looks in a particular layout. (See Figure 22-7.)

4. Click the layout you want to use.

# Modify Hanging Style

1. Select the top shape in your organization chart. Changing the hanging layout affects the layout of all shapes below the selected shape.

2. Choose Under SmartArt Tools Design⇨Create Graphic⇨Layout. A list of options appears.

3. Choose one of the following options:

   - Standard: Centers all the shapes below the selected shape. This is the default option.

   - Both: Centers the selected shape above the shapes below it and arranges the shapes below it horizontally with two shapes in each row. Figure 22-8 shows our organization chart with this option.

   - Left Hanging: Arranges the selected shape to the right of the shapes below it and left-aligns the shapes below it vertically.

   - Right Hanging: Arranges the selected shape to the left of the shapes below it and right-aligns the shapes below it vertically.

 Click SmartArt Tools Design⇨Reset⇨Reset Graphic to quickly change the chart to the default-style settings.

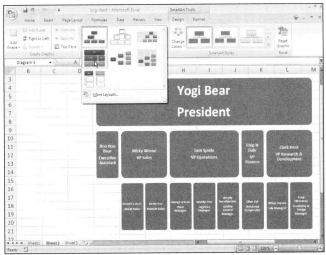

**Figure 22-7:** Pick a design to complement your organization chart.

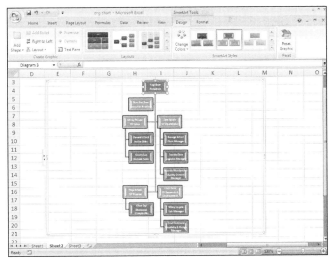

**Figure 22-8:** Changing the way the organization chart hangs down.

# Change the Color Scheme and Style

1. Choose SmartArt Tools Design➪SmartArt Styles➪ Change Colors. A gallery of color options appears.

2. Select the color combination you want to use.

3. Choose SmartArt Tools Design➪SmartArtStyles.

4. Click More to display a gallery of styles.

5. Pause your mouse over any selection to see a description of the selection and review how your chart looks in a particular style. Some choices are more subtle than others. Several are three-dimensional, and some even include special features such as soft or glowing edges. (See Figure 22-9.)

6. Select the choice best suited for your organization chart.

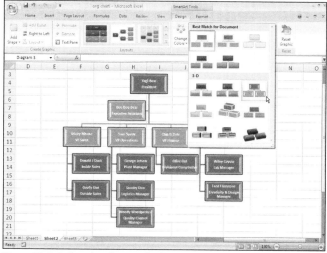

**Figure 22-9:** Pick a color scheme and style.

# Change a Shapes Style

1. Select a shape box you want to change. Usually this is the top-level box or an assistant box.

2. Choose SmartArt Tools Format➪Shapes➪Change Shape. A gallery of shapes appears.

3. Select the shape you want to use. The selected shape box changes to the new style as you see in Figure 22-10.

4. Optionally, with the shape box still selected, choose SmartArt Tools Format➪Shapes➪Larger. The selected shape grows in size.

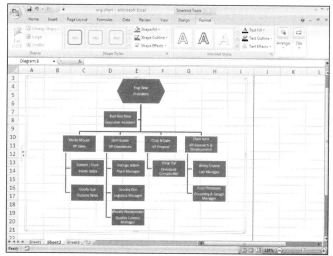

**Figure 22-10:** Emphasize a position by changing the shape box.

# Modify Other Shape Attributes

1. Select the shape boxes you want to change.

    If you want to change the frame surrounding the organization chart instead of the individual shapes, don't select any individual shapes.

2. Choose SmartArt Tools Format➪Shapes➪Shape Fill. A list of choices appears.

3. Select a fill option. Figure 22-11 illustrates using a picture to fill the shape.

    Using a picture as a fill can make the text hard to read.

4. Choose SmartArt Tools Format➪Shapes➪Shape Outline.

5. Select an option for the line outlining the shape. Choose Weight to select a heavier border line style or choose Dashes to select a different border style.

6. Choose SmartArt Tools Format➪Shapes➪Shape Effects. A list of options appears.

7. Select a special effect. Most options offer an additional fly-out with secondary options.

# Change Chart Direction

1. Choose SmartArt Tools Design➪Create Graphic➪Right to Left. Excel reverses the flow of your organization chart as you see in Figure 22-12.

2. Choose SmartArt Tools Design➪Create Graphic➪ Left to Right. Excel changes the flow to the default.

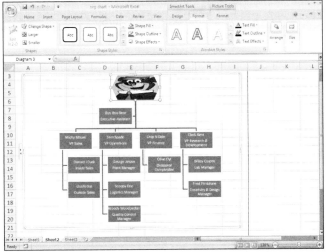

**Figure 22-11:** Use a picture to further define the organization chart shape.

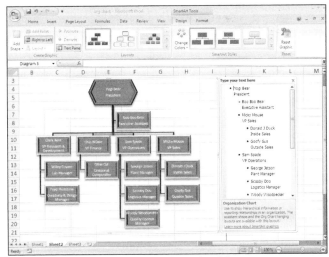

**Figure 22-12:** Changing the position flow from right to left.

# Creating a Commission Calculator

*S*uppose you're a business owner, and you pay your salespeople a sliding commission rate based on their total sales for a specified period, such as a month. First, you need a sheet of paper to list each salesperson's sales. Then, at the end of the period, you have to subtotal each person's sales. Finally, you have to figure out which commission percentage to give each person based on that subtotal.

A Commission Calculator worksheet, designed using basic Excel features, along with several Excel functions (SUMIF, COUNTIF, and nested IF statements) can do everything for you except enter the individual sales. Excel saves you precious time and reduces the chance for human error. To set up a worksheet, you perform the following tasks:

➡ Enter basic headings.

➡ Create a sliding commission rate table.

➡ Define the data input area where you track the individual sales.

➡ Design the calculation area where Excel calculates the totals and commission.

➡ Enhance the worksheet appearance so it's easier to read.

➡ Protect and save the worksheet as a template.

## Enter Headings

1. In cell A1, type **Commission Calculator**.

2. In cell A2, type **For the month of:**.

3. In cells A3, B3, C3, and D3, type the following column headings: **Sales Person**, **# of Sales**, **Total Sales Amount**, and **Commission Amount**.

4. Move down the correct number of rows to accommodate all your salespeople's names (plus add a couple of extra rows), and in column A of the row, type **Totals**.

5. Beginning with cell A4 and moving down the column, type the names of your salespeople.

6. Move down three more rows and type the following column headings: **Sale Date**, **Transaction Number**, **Sales Person**, **Sale Amount**. Your worksheet should look like the one shown in Figure 23-1.

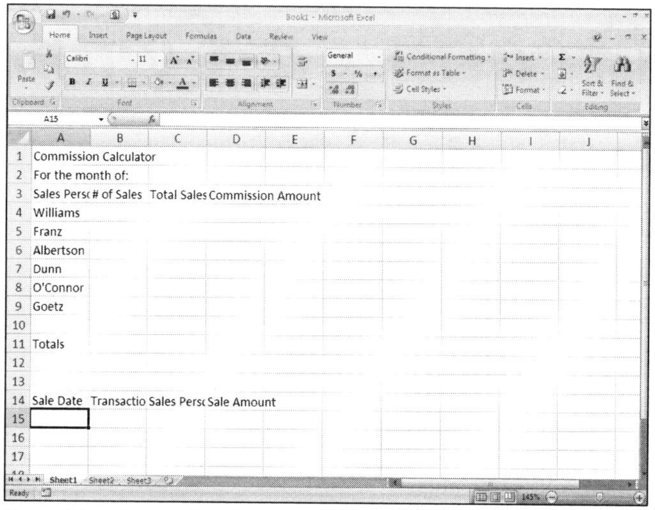

## Create the Commission Table

1. In an unused area of the worksheet, enter your commission breakdown.

2. In the cells next to the breakdown, enter the commission percentage.

3. Add any desired headings to further identify the table.

4. Format the sales dollar values as currency and the commissions as percentages (see Figure 23-2).

5. Select the commission table and choose Formulas⇨ Defined Names⇨Define Name⇨Define Name. The New Name dialog box appears.

6. Type **CommissionTable** or another name for the table. Click OK.

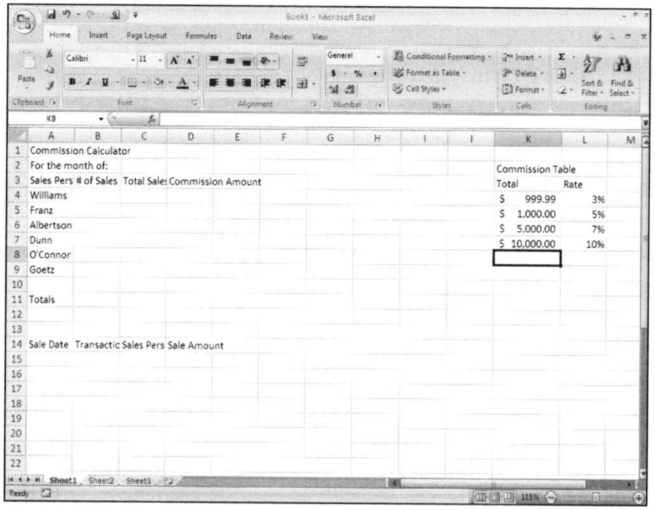

**Figure 23-1:** Enter headings for a commission worksheet.

**Figure 23-2:** Create a commission table.

# Define the Sales Data Input Area

1. At the bottom of the worksheet where you will enter the individual sales, select the cells in the Salesperson column. In Figure 23-3, I selected cells C15 through C114, which gives room for 100 sales entries.

2. Choose Formulas⇨Defined Names⇨Define Name⇨ Define Name. The New Name dialog box appears.

3. Type **SalesRep** for the range name; then click OK.

4. In the same worksheet section, select the cells you will use in the Sales Amount column. Be sure to include the same number of cells you included in Step 1.

5. Choose Formulas⇨Defined Names⇨Define Name⇨Define Name. The New Name dialog box appears.

6. Type **SalesAmt** for the range name; then click OK.

 To verify the formulas you create in the next several sections, enter some sample data in the sales data input area.

# Total Sales with the SUMIF Function

1. In cell C4, enter the following formula and then press the Enter key: **=SUMIF(SalesRep,A4,SalesAmt)**. If you entered sample data in the sales data input area, you see the total sales for the salesperson.

2. Copy the formula in C4 to the end of your salesperson list (see Figure 23-4). Chapter 3 shows how to copy formulas.

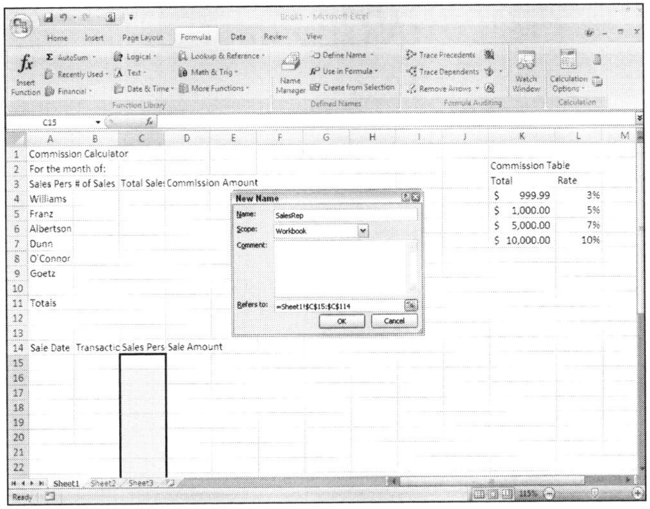

**Figure 23-3:** Define the salesperson data input area.

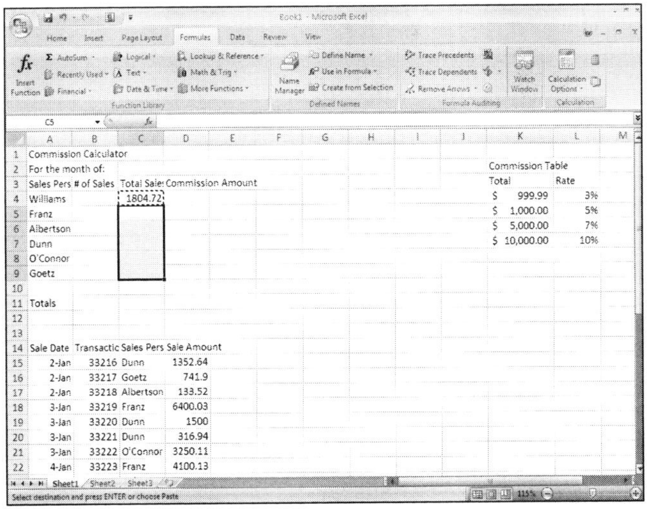

**Figure 23-4:** Copy the formula down the rows.

## Use the COUNTIF Function to Count Sales

1. In cell B4, enter the formula **=COUNTIF(SalesRep,A4)** and then press the Enter key. If you entered sample data in the sales data input area, you see the total number of sales for the salesperson.

2. Select cell B4 and choose Home⇨Clipboard⇨Copy. A marquee appears around cell B4.

3. Highlight cells B5 through the end of your salesperson list.

4. Choose Home⇨Clipboard⇨Paste. Excel duplicates the formulas to include all the salespeople. (See Figure 23-5.)

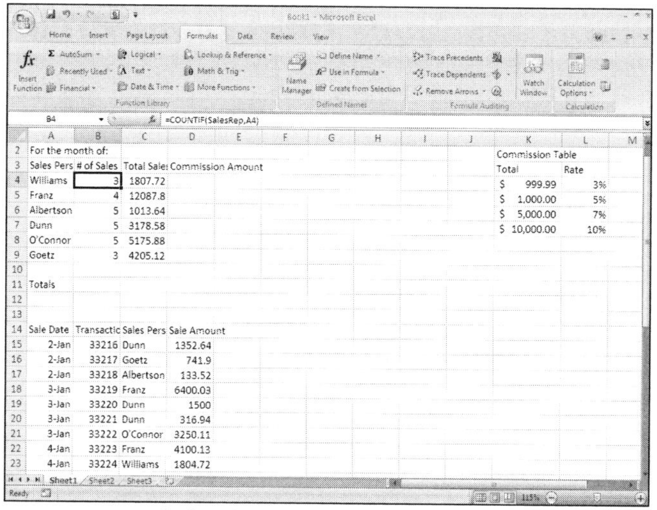

## Calculate Commission with a Nested IF Statement

1. In cell D4, enter the beginning function and the first parameter to check the total sales for the salesperson against the commission table. Type **=IF(C4<$K$5** and a comma.

2. Enter the first True result. Type **C4*$L$4** and a comma.

3. Enter the first False result that begins another IF statement. Type **IF(C4<$K$6** and a comma (see Figure 23-6).

 Be sure to place the dollar signs in front of the cell references to make them an absolute reference to a specific cell.

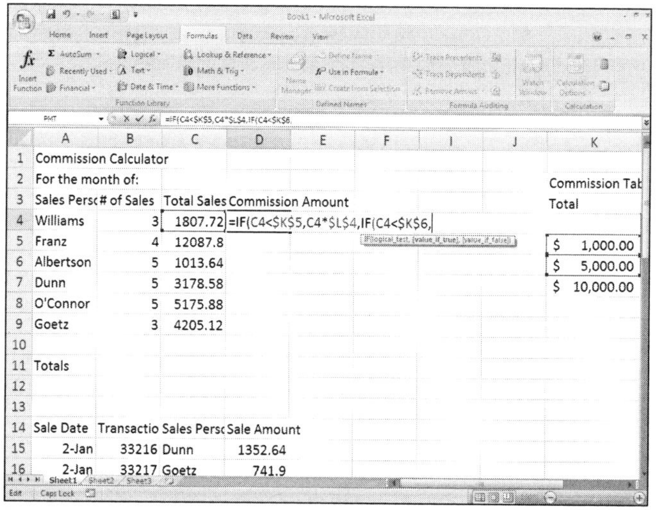

**Figure 23-5:** Copy the formula throughout the rows.

**Figure 23-6:** Beginning a nested IF statement.

4. Enter the next True result. Type **C4\*$L$5** and a comma.

5. Enter the next False result that again begins another IF statement. Type **IF(C4<$K$7** and a comma.

6. Enter the third True result, if applicable. Type **C4\*$L$6** and a comma.

7. Enter the third False result, which in my example is the last level to check. Type **C4\*$L$7**.

8. Type three closing parentheses, enough to match the number of opening parentheses and press Enter. Figure 23-7 illustrates the final formula and its results.

9. Copy the formula to the other rows.

 The Excel IF function evaluates a condition you specify and returns one value if the statement is TRUE and another value if it evaluates to FALSE. In this example, if the sales are less than the first commission level, making the first condition TRUE, it calculates the sales multiplied by the first-level commission percentage. If the statement is not TRUE, then Excel checks if the sales are less than a second commission level, and if so, it multiplies the sales times that commission level percentage. The nesting continues until Excel checks all commission levels, resulting in a commission amount.

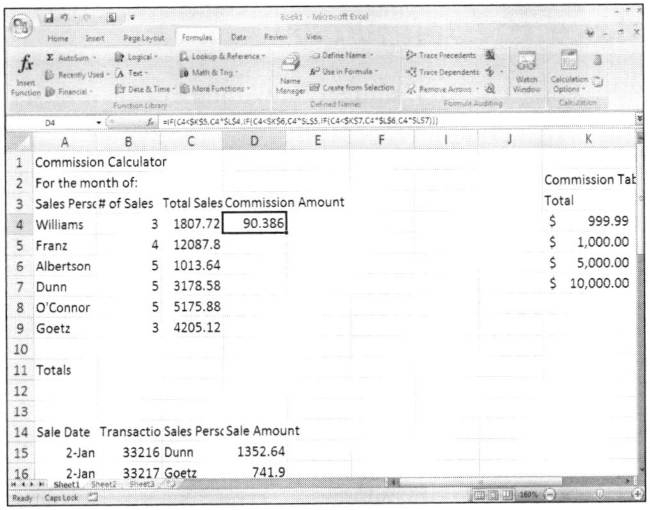

# Create Totals

1. In cell B11, or the cell below your last sales rep, create a SUM function to total the cells above it. In Figure 23-8, the formula =SUM(B4:B10) totals the sales orders.

2. Select the formula in cell B11. Choose Home⇨Clipboard⇨Copy, or press Ctrl + C.

3. Select the cells C11 and D11 and choose Home⇨Clipboard⇨Paste, or press Ctrl+V. Excel duplicates the formulas, which total the sales and commissions, respectively.

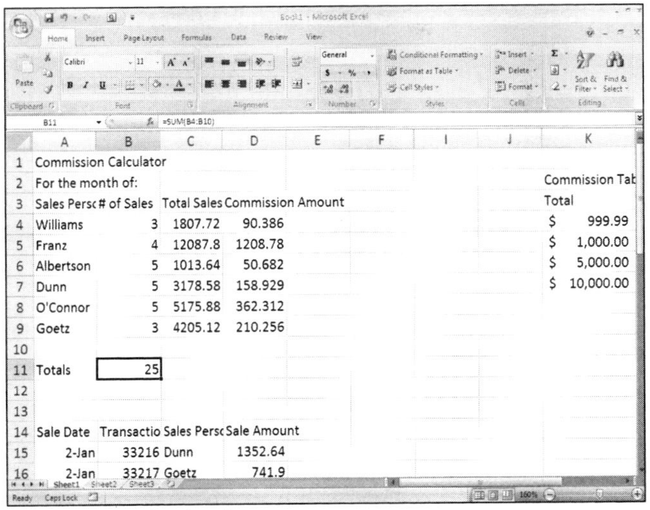

**Figure 23-7:** A completed nested IF statement.

**Figure 23-8:** Totaling the sales items.

# Make It Look Nicer

1. Apply currency number formatting to cells with currency. See Chapter 5.

2. Widen columns to allow all cell data to appear. See Chapter 5.

3. Enlarge the font size of the headings. See Chapter 5.

4. Merge and Center cells A2 and B2. See Chapter 5.

5. Merge and center cells C2 and D2.

6. Apply a table style. Choose Home⇨Format as Table and pick a style as shown in Figure 23-9. See Chapter 5.

7. Choose Office Button⇨Excel Options.

8. From the Advanced section, scroll down to the area called Display Options for this worksheet and remove the check mark from the Show a Zero in Cells That Have a Zero Value option. Click OK.

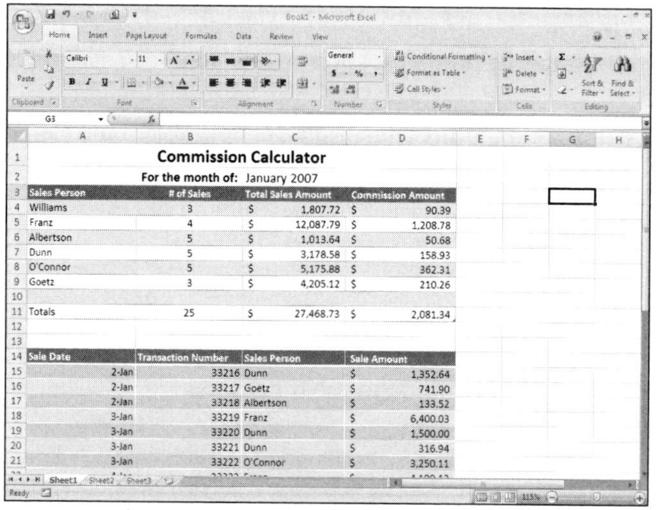

**Figure 23-9:** Alternate row shading makes a spreadsheet easier to read.

# Protect Your Work

1. Select the cells in which you will enter the entry month and the sales data. In my sample spreadsheet, cells C2 and A15 through D114 are the only cells in which I want to enter variable data.

2. Choose Home⇨Cells⇨Format⇨Lock Cells which unlocks the selected cells. See Figure 23-10.

3. Choose Home⇨Cells⇨Format⇨ Protect Sheet.

4. Click OK.

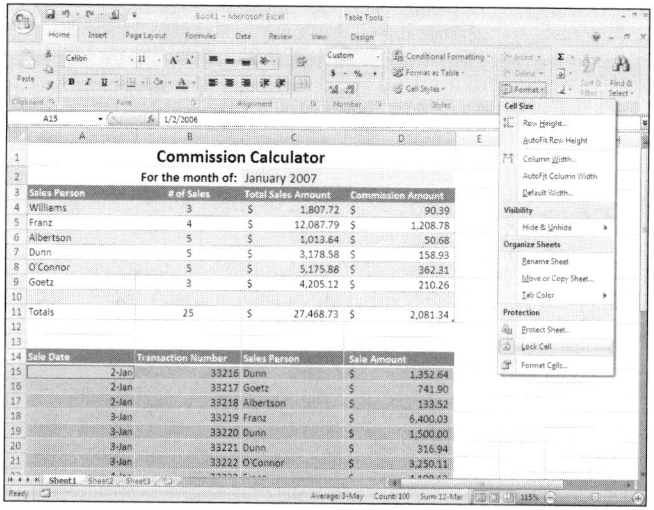

**Figure 23-10:** Unlock only the cells in which you want users to enter data.

# Tracking Medical Expenses

# Chapter

## 24

W ith today's high cost of medical care, very few of us can be without medical insurance. In fact, many of us have two insurance companies — perhaps Medicare and a supplemental insurance, or insurance through your employer and your spouse's employer.

Tracking medical costs is very important, especially when filing your annual tax return. In this project, you create an Excel spreadsheet that efficiently tracks your expenses, generating totals and even sorting out prescriptions from the rest of the medical-expense totals. See at a glance the total of your medical expenses, how much is paid by your insurance companies, and — most important — how much you have to pay out-of-pocket.

To accomplish this task, you use a number of Excel features, including data validation, duplication of worksheets, creating totals from other worksheets, and a few Excel mathematical functions.

I hope your health is good, and you won't need to use this worksheet a lot! But if you must . . . you'll be glad it's here.

## Get ready to . . .

# Enter Text Headings

1. In cell A1, enter a heading for the worksheet, such as **2005 Medical Bill Tracker**.

2. In cells B4 and B5, type **Total Billed** and **Total Paid by Insurance**, respectively. In cells D4 and D5, type **Total Paid Out-of-Pocket** and **Total Due**, respectively.

3. In cell D7, type **Totals**. In cells A8 through K8, type the following: **Bill Date, Provider, Rx?, Description of Services, Total Amount Billed, Insurance #1 Paid, Insurance #2 Paid, Write Off, Paid Out-of-Pocket, Check Number,** and **Amount Due**. Your worksheet should look similar to the one shown in Figure 24-1.

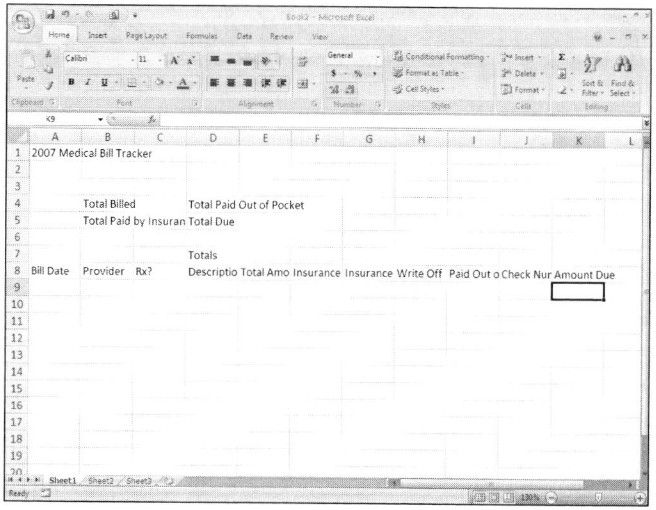

# Create Totaling Formulas

1. In cell E7, enter a formula to calculate the entire Total Amount Billed column, which begins at cell E9 and runs through at least row 50. Your formula should read **=SUM(E9:E50)**. You can make the formula longer or shorter depending on how many items you might list in a year.

2. Select cell E7 again, and then grab the AutoFill handle and drag across to cell K7. This duplicates the formula from F7 through K7. (See Figure 24-2.)

3. Select cell J7 and press the Delete key to delete the formula.

4. In cell C4, which references the total amount billed as shown in cell E7, type **=E7**. In cell C5, type **=F7+G7**, which adds the insurance payments.

5. In cell E4, type **=I7** to reference the total out-of-pocket expenses. In cell E5, type **=K7** to reference the total still due.

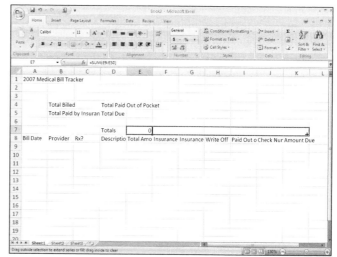

**Figure 24-1:** Enter headings for a medical-expense tracking worksheet.

**Figure 24-2:** Use AutoFill to easily duplicate a formula.

# Calculate the Amount Due

1.  Create a formula in cell K9 by typing =E9-SUM(F9:I9). This formula subtracts the total payments made from the total amount billed.

2.  Select cell K9.

3.  Press Ctrl+C or choose Home⇨Clipboard⇨Copy. A marquee appears around the copied cell.

4.  Click and drag the mouse from cell K10 down through the end of the calculation area. Use the same number of rows as you did in Step 1 of the section "Create Totaling Formulas."

5.  Press Ctrl+V or choose Home⇨Clipboard⇨Paste. Excel copies the formula down the worksheet. Figure 24-3 shows a value of 0 in each pasted cell.

# Specify Data Validation

1.  In two adjacent worksheet cells, preferably in an unseen worksheet area, type the words **Yes and No**.

2.  Select cells C9 through C50, or whichever row you use as your last worksheet row.

3.  Choose Data⇨Data Tools⇨Data Validation.

4.  From the Allow drop-down list, choose List.

5.  Click the spreadsheet icon in the Source box. The Data Validation dialog box temporarily collapses.

6.  Highlight cells Q1 and Q2 (or whichever cells you used in Steps 1 and 2) and then press the Enter key. The Data Validation dialog box reappears, as shown in Figure 24-4.

7.  Click OK. When you click cell C9 or lower, notice that a drop-down arrow appears with the Yes or No choices.

Notice in Step 1, the compound formula is created with a standard reference and an Excel function.

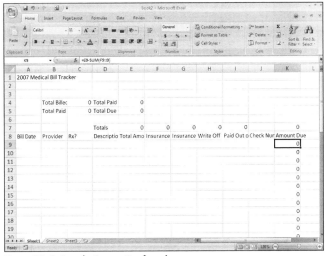

**Figure 24-3:** Copy the Amount Due formula.

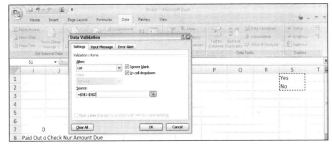

**Figure 24-4:** Setting a Yes or No validation answer for the Rx column.

## Format the Worksheet

1. Highlight worksheet cells you want to format.

2. Apply any desired formatting such as applying currency or number formatting, widening columns, bolding headings, and applying borders. (See Chapters 5 and 6.) Figure 24-5 illustrates a formatting example.

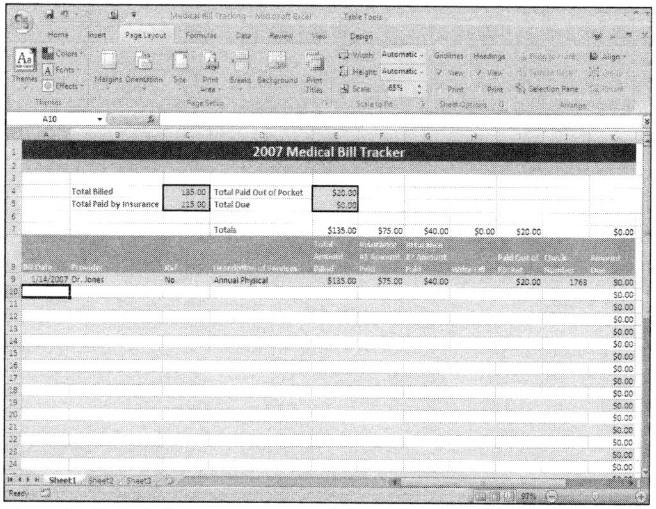

## Determine Print Settings

1. Choose Page Layout⇨Page Setup⇨Orientation⇨ Landscape.

2. Choose Page Layout⇨Scale to Fit⇨Width⇨1 page.

3. Choose Page Layout⇨Scale to Fit⇨Height⇨1 page.

 Depending on the number of rows in your sheet, you may want make the settings more than one page tall.

4. Choose Page Layout⇨Page Setup⇨Margins⇨Narrow.

5. Choose View⇨Page Layout View.

6. Click into the Header area.

7. Choose Header & Footer Tools Design⇨Header & Footer⇨ Footer⇨Page 1 of ? (See Figure 24-6.)

8. Choose View⇨Normal. Highlight cells A1:K50 (or however many rows you anticipate using).

9. Choose Page Layout⇨Page Setup⇨Print Area⇨Set Print Area.

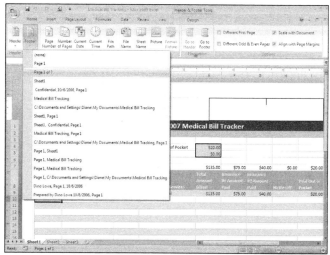

**Figure 24-5:** Apply formatting to your worksheet to make it easier to read.

**Figure 24-6:** Create a page footer.

## Add Protection from Accidental Changes

1. Select cells A1 and A2.

2. Choose Home⇨Cells⇨Format⇨Lock Cells to unlock the selected cells.

3. Select cells A9 through J50 (the data entry area).

4. Choose Home⇨Cells⇨Format⇨Lock Cells to unlock the selected cells.

5. Choose Home⇨Cells⇨Format⇨ Protect Sheet. (See Figure 24-7.)

6. Click OK. The worksheet is now protected against accidental changes.

## Duplicate the Worksheet for Other Family Members

1. In cell A2, type the patients' name. For this example, I entered **Catherine Smith**.

2. Right-click the Sheet1 tab. A shortcut menu appears.

3. Choose Rename. The Sheet1 name is highlighted.

4. Type the patients' name. I renamed the worksheet **Catherine**.

5. Press the Enter key. Excel renames the worksheet.

6. Right-click the newly renamed tab and choose Move or Copy.

7. Click the Create a Copy option. (See Figure 24-8.)

8. Click OK. Excel adds an identical sheet marked as Catherine (2) or whatever you named the tab in Step 4.

9. Right-click the new worksheet tab and rename it using the second patient's name.

10. In the second patient worksheet, click cell A2 and enter the second patient's name.

 If you need to unprotect the sheet to make changes, choose Home⇨Cells⇨Format⇨Unprotect Sheet.

**Figure 24-7:** Protect your worksheet from accidental changes.

**Figure 24-8:** Duplicate the worksheet for each family member.

# Create a Totals Worksheet

1. Rename the tab of Sheet2 (or any blank worksheet in the workbook). Use the new name Totals.

2. From one of the patient worksheets, copy cells A1 and A2 to cells A1 and A2 on the Totals worksheet.

3. From one of the patient worksheets, copy cells E8 through I8 to cells E8 through I8 on the Totals worksheet.

4. Widen the columns as needed to see the text.

5. In cell A2, type the word **Totals**.

6. In cell C8, type the words **Patient Name**.

7. In cell D8, type the word **Service**. (See Figure 24-9.)

8. In cells C9 and C10, type the first patient's name.

9. In cell D9, type **Rx**.

10. In cell D10, type **Other**.

11. In cell D11, type **Totals**. (See Figure 24-10.)

12. In cells E9 through I11, type the formulas in the following table, substituting Catherine for the first patient worksheet tab name.

 These formulas look at column C on the patient worksheet to determine if the expense is a prescription. They then add the values.

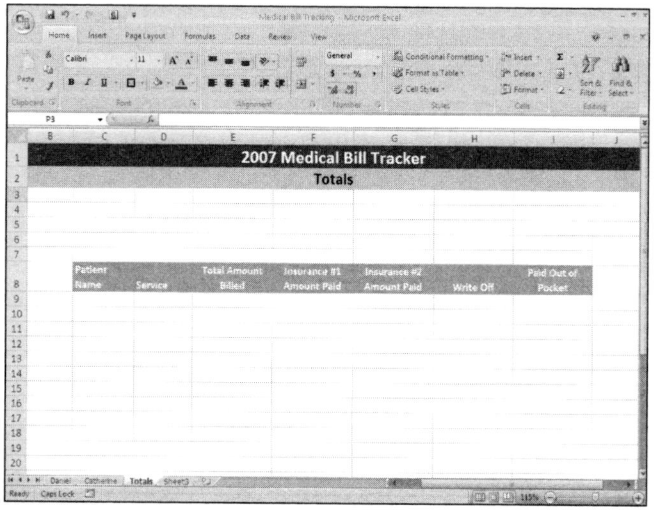

**Figure 24-9:** Entering headings on the Totals worksheet.

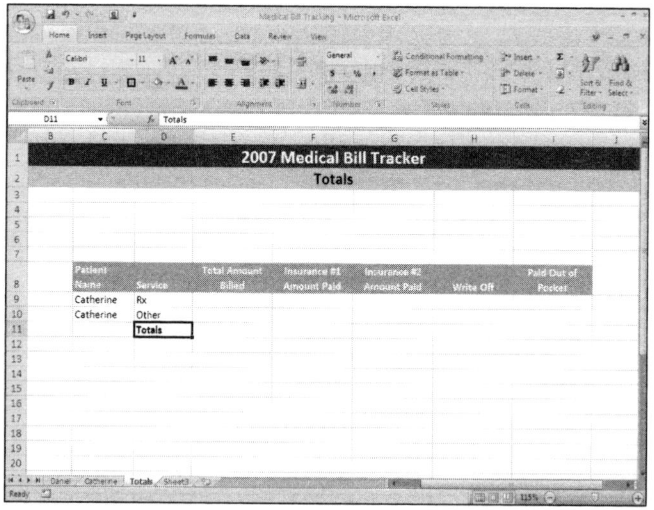

**Figure 24-10:** Preparing the Totals worksheet.

## Formulas in Cells E9 through I11

| In Cell | Type |
|---------|------|
| E9 | =SUMIF(Catherine!C:C,"Yes",Catherine!E:E) |
| E10 | =SUMIF(Catherine!C:C,"No",Catherine!E:E) |
| E11 | =SUM(E9:E10) |
| F9 | =SUMIF(Catherine!C:C,"Yes",Catherine!F:F) |
| F10 | =SUMIF(Catherine!C:C,"No",Catherine!F:F) |
| F11 | =SUM(F9:F10) |
| G9 | =SUMIF(Catherine!C:C,"Yes",Catherine!G:G) |
| G10 | =SUMIF(Catherine!C:C,"No",Catherine!G:G) |
| G11 | =SUM(G9:G10) |
| H9 | =SUMIF(Catherine!C:C,"Yes",Catherine!H:H) |
| H10 | =SUMIF(Catherine!C:C,"No",Catherine!H:H) |
| H11 | =SUM(H9:H10) |
| I9 | =SUMIF(Catherine!C:C,"Yes",Catherine!I:I) |
| I10 | =SUMIF(Catherine!C:C,"No",Catherine!I:I) |
| I11 | =SUM(I9:I10) |

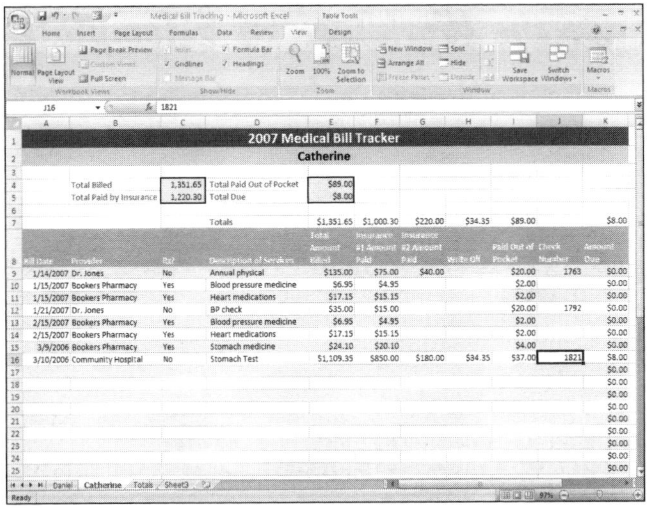

**Figure 24-11:** The Medical Bill Tracker worksheet with sample data.

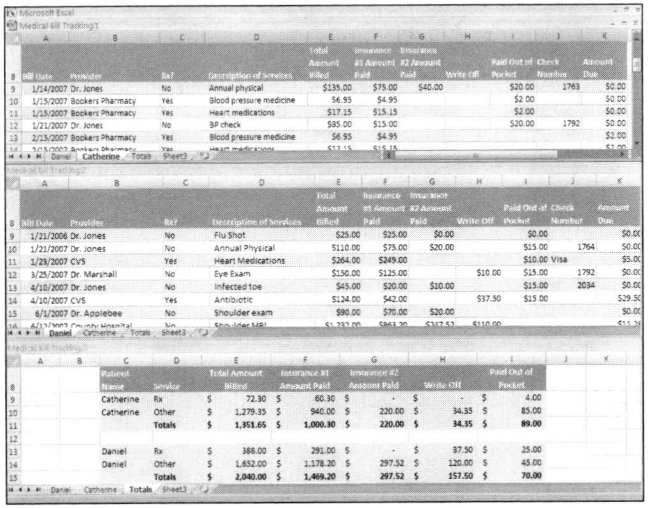

**Figure 24-12:** The Medical Bill Tracker worksheet showing totals.

13. Repeat Steps 8 through 12 for each patient. Figure 24-11 illustrates data entered into the Catherine worksheet and Figure 24-12 shows how the totals are reflected in the Totals worksheet.

14. Choose Home⇨Cells⇨Format⇨Lock Cells to unlock the selected cells. Choose Home⇨Cells⇨Format⇨Protect Sheet.

15. Click OK. The worksheet is now protected against accidental changes.

# Save the Workbook as a Template

1. Delete any data in the patient worksheets.

2. Choose Office Button⇨Save As. The Save As dialog box appears, as shown in Figure 24-13.

3. Enter a name for the template.

4. From the Save as Type drop-down list, choose Excel Template.

5. Click Save.

6. Close the template.

**Figure 24-13:** Save the workbook as a template.

# Open a New Medical Bill Tracking Workbook

1. Choose Office Button⇨New. The New Workbook dialog box opens.

2. Click My Templates. The New dialog box opens.

3. Choose Medical Bill Tracking, as shown in Figure 24-14.

4. Click OK. You can now safely enter data into a blank Medical Bill Tracker without the risk of modifying the original template and its formulas.

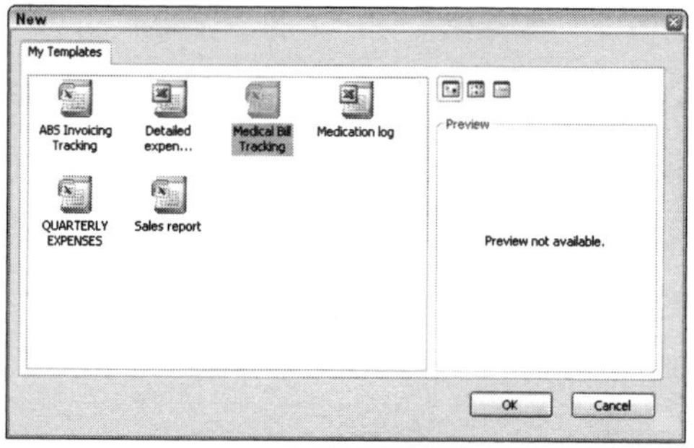

**Figure 24-14:** Create a new workbook from the template.

# Planning for Your Financial Future

**Y**our life is taking shape right in front of you. You and your spouse want to buy a house, raise a family, and enjoy life happily ever after. Your personal future depends a lot on your financial future. Fortunately, Excel has several functions you can use to plan for the future you want.

First, to maintain realistic expectations, you need to determine how much house you can afford to buy. But before you can buy the dream house, you know you must pay off some credit card debt. Also, from your own experience, you know that college is expensive, and the costs are bound to get much higher by the time the kids are ready. Finally come your golden years. You dream of the house on the beach or traveling to exotic places.

How are you ever going to save enough for that? This chapter shows you how to:

➠ Determine how much payments will run on that cute little ranch house down the street. Excel has a PMT function to help with that.

➠ Plan to pay off a credit card balance using the NPER function, which requires three key pieces of information: the interest rate, the current payment amount, and the credit card balance.

➠ Determine how much you need to save each month to reach a college-fund or retirement goal. Again, utilize Excel's PMT function.

## Get ready to . . .

# Plan to Purchase a House

1. In cell A1, type **OUR DREAM HOUSE**.

2. In cells A3 through A8, type **House Price, Down Payment, Loan Amount, Interest Rate, Loan Term,** and **Monthly Payment.**

3. In cell B3, enter the house price.

4. In cell B4, enter the down payment amount you plan on making.

5. In cell B5, enter the formula **=B3-B4**. This gives the amount you will finance.

6. In cell B6, enter the interest rate. Enter and format this amount as a percentage.

7. In cell B7, enter the loan term. Usually for a house, this value is in years. (See Figure 25-1.)

8. In cell B8, enter a PMT function to calculate the monthly payment. The PMT function has three required arguments (=PMT(RATE, NETPER, PV), so you enter **=PMT(B6/12,B7*12,B5).** (See Figure 25-2.)

   - RATE, which is the annual interest rate. You entered the Interest Rate in cell B6. To get a monthly rate, you divide this argument by 12.

   - NETPER is the term of the loan, which you entered in cell B7. Because this value is in years and you want monthly payments, you multiply this argument by 12.

   - PV represents the present value, which is the amount you will finance, not including interest. You calculated this amount in cell B5.

9. Apply any desired formatting to the cells.

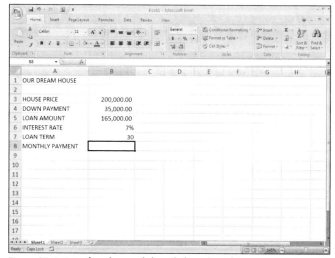

**Figure 25-1:** Enter the values needed to calculate a home loan payment.

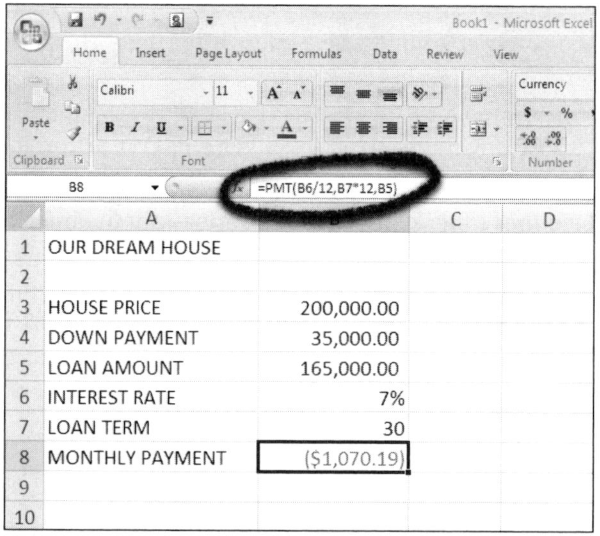

**Figure 25-2:** Using the Excel PMT function.

# Prepare To Pay Off a Credit Card Balance

1. In cell D1, type **PAY OFF CREDIT CARD**.

2. In cells D3, D4 and D5, type **Monthly percentage rate, Current payments, Credit card balance,** and **Months until paid off**, respectively.

3. In cell E3, create a formula to enter the *monthly* percentage rate you are paying on a credit card. For example, if you are paying a 21% annual interest, you enter **=21%/12**, or the 21% annual rate divided by 12 months, which displays a value of .0175 (1.75%). (See Figure 25-3.)

    For ease in understanding the cell contents, format the cells using the following steps as you enter the data.

4. In cell E4, enter your current payment amount preceded by a minus sign. Enter **–150** if you are making $150 payments every month against the credit card balance.

5. In cell E5, enter the remaining balance on the credit card. Like the payments, this must be entered as a negative value such as **–3700**.

6. Create a NPER formula to calculate how many months it will take to pay off the credit card. The formula should read **=NPER(E3,E4,E5)**. As you see in Figure 25-4, the resulting answer shows how many months it will take to pay off the credit card balance. The NPER function has three required arguments:

   - Interest rate, which is usually given annually. You divide it by 12 to obtain a monthly rate.

   - Payment amount, which you enter as a negative amount.

   - Present value, which is the amount of the loan not including interest.

See how much earlier you can pay the credit card off by entering a higher payment amount in cell B4.

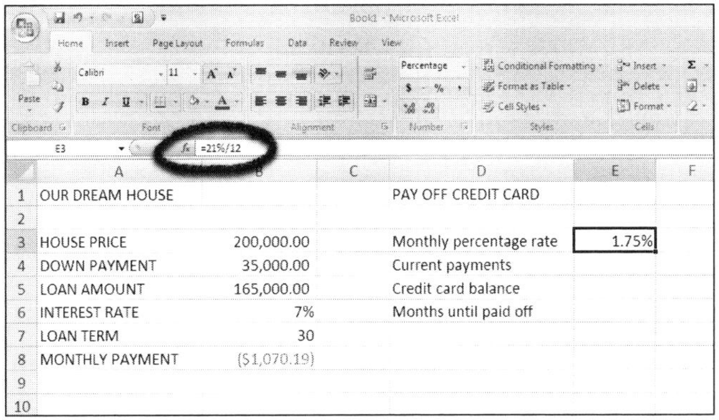

**Figure 25-3:** Enter the annual interest rate divided by 12.

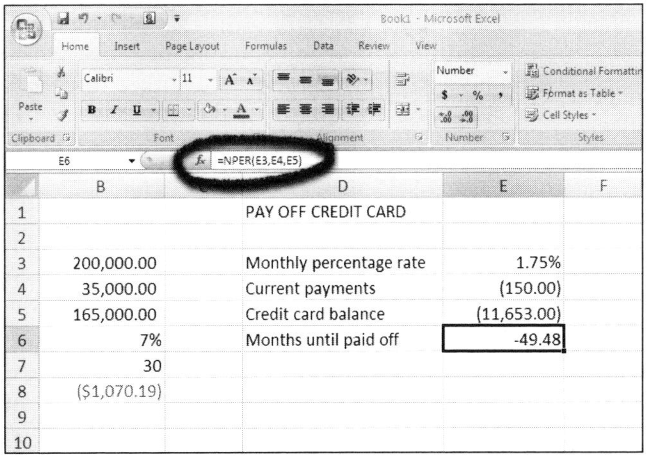

**Figure 25-4:** Using the Excel NPER function.

# Save for College or Retirement

1. In cell A12, type **OUR SAVINGS GOALS.**

2. In cell A14, type **Savings Goal Amount.**

3. In cell A15, type **Interest Rate.**

4. In cell A16, type **Years to Goal.**

5. In cell A17, type **Current Savings.**

6. In cell A18, type **Monthly Amount to Save.** (See Figure 25-5.)

7. In cell B14, enter the savings goal amount.

8. In cell B15, enter the annual interest rate.

9. In cell B16, enter the number of years you have until you need the money for college or retirement.

10. In cell B17, enter the amount you already have saved toward the goal.

11. In cell B18, create a PMT formula that includes the interest rate, term, and amount. You also need to add one of the optional arguments; the future value argument. This time, the PMT formula format is =PMT(interest rate, term, current value, future value) so you should enter **=PMT(B15/12, B16*12,B17,B14).** The PMT function actually has two optional arguments which are

   - Future Value, which is the balance of the loan after all payments have been made. You do not need to enter a future value unless the value at the end is not equal to zero. In this example, the end goal is your savings goal.

   - Payment Type one or zero, which indicates whether the payment occurs at the beginning of the month (1) or the end of the month (0).

12. Format the cells as desired. Figure 25-6 displays an example.

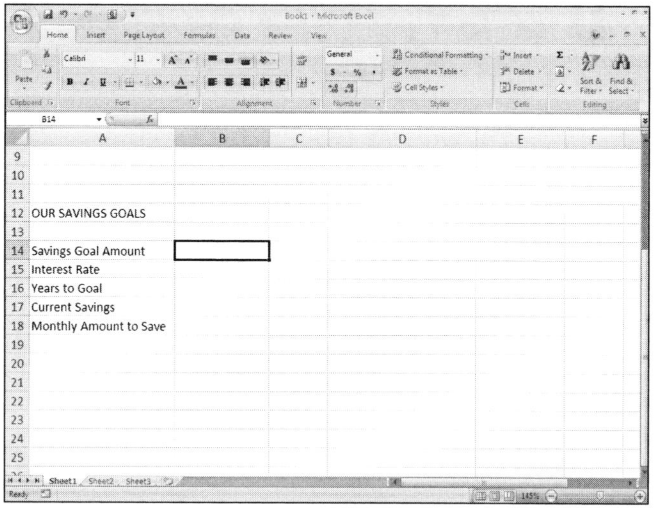

**Figure 25-5:** See how to reach your savings goals by using following the Excel function.

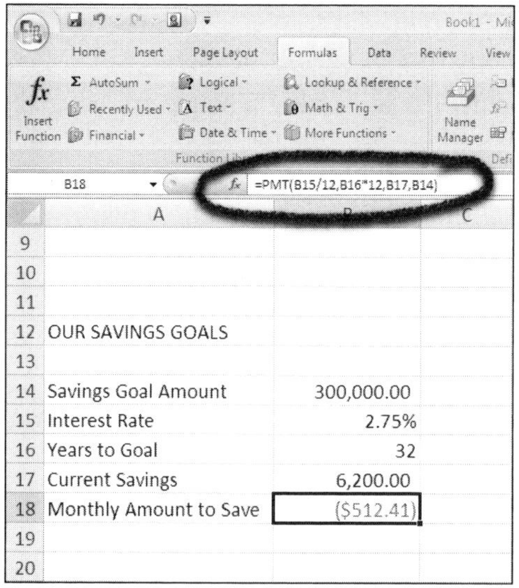

**Figure 25-6:** Format the worksheet so you can easily review the numbers.

# Index